The
Reference Shelf®

Immigration

The Reference Shelf
Volume 88 • Number 2
H.W. Wilson
A Division of EBSCO Information Services

Published by
GREY HOUSE PUBLISHING
Amenia, New York
2016

The Reference Shelf

The books in this series contain reprints of articles, excerpts from books, addresses on current issues, and studies of social trends in the United States and other countries. There are six separately bound numbers in each volume, all of which are usually published in the same calendar year. Numbers one through five are each devoted to a single subject, providing background information and discussion from various points of view and concluding with an index and comprehensive bibliography that lists books, pamphlets, and articles on the subject. The final number of each volume is a collection of recent speeches. Books in the series may be purchased individually or on subscription.

Publisher's Cataloging-In-Publication Data
(Prepared by The Donohue Group, Inc.)

Names: H.W. Wilson Company.
Title: Immigration / [compiled by] H. W. Wilson, a division of EBSCO Information Services.
Other Titles: Reference shelf ; v. 88, no. 2.
Description: [First edition]. | Amenia, New York : Grey House Publishing, 2016. | The reference shelf ; volume 88, number 2 | Includes bibliographical references and index.
Identifiers: ISBN 978-1-68217-064-9 (v. 88, no. 2) |
    ISBN 978-1-68217-062-5 (volume set)
Subjects: LCSH: United States--Emigration and immigration--Sources. | Emigration and immigration law--United States--Sources. | Immigrants--United States--Social conditions--Sources. | Illegal aliens--United States--Sources.
Classification: LCC JV6465 .I46 2016 | DDC 325.73--dc23

Contents

3

Popular Conceptions, Stereotypes, and Biases

4

Education, Culture, and Families

5

Global and Domestic Economies

Preface

Immigration in an Immigrants' Nation

The Statue of Liberty, a gift from the government of France in 1886, was intended to serve as a symbol of France and the United States' shared dedication to the principles of republican government and collective rejection of oligarchy and monarchy. In 1903, a plaque, inscribed with the poem 'The New Colossus' by Emma Lazarus, was mounted on the statue. The text of the poem, and the statue itself, became emblematic of America's role as an immigrant nation [1]:

> "Give me your tired, your poor,
> Your huddled masses yearning to breathe free,
> The wretched refuse of your teeming shore.
> Send these, the homeless, tempest-tost to me,
> I lift my lamp beside the golden door!"

Millions of European immigrants flooded into America's cities from the 1880s to the 1940s, fueling the industrial revolution that transformed the nation into one of the world's great powers. During this time, America's role as a refuge for the world's downtrodden and politically persecuted became part of a coalescing sense of patriotism and American identity. However, throughout this entire period immigration was also typically a complex, controversial issue, and immigration policy and public opinion on the issue were deeply influenced by racism, xenophobia, and fear. For as much as many Americans embraced the nation's role as a home for political asylees and took patriotic pride in the nation's cultural diversity, immigrants have also been consistently targeted and maligned as potentially dangerous, economically detrimental, and culturally destructive. With each generation, there have been some who favor isolationism, retaining America's economic and social bounty for those born in the nation, rather than spreading the benefits of American citizenship among new generations of immigrants. Reconciling the nation's ideological role with the financial and social burden of immigration is the underlying challenge behind the immigration debate, and it is a struggle that has been part of the nation's history since the beginning.

The Boundaries of Identity

Before the first colonists arrived in the United States, indigenous societies had already occupied most of North America for millennia. Native Americans who occupied what is now the American southwest migrated back and forth between fertile grazing and agricultural areas that now cross national borders. The establishment of the current U.S. territory was a violent process that involved the violent persecution of millions of Native Americans. Some historians have referred to the American expansion and treatment of the Native American people as an act of genocide. Regardless of how American citizens choose to view and depict the morality and ethics of the nation's violent foundation, gradually a new national identity was formed. Over the nation's 200-year history, U.S. citizens and politicians in each generation have been asked to continually reexamine the nation's role in the broader global community, and immigration is one of the key issues in this larger national evolutionary process. United States immigration policy affects millions around the world, in addition to those who are already citizens of the nation, and also plays a major role in the nation's future, determining how the United States will change, socially, culturally, and economically over the next decade, century, and millennium.

Attitudes about immigration differ according to political ideology, but also between American cities, towns, and states, each of which has its own regional relationship with immigration that plays a role in shaping immigration policy. Towns and cities close to the Mexican border, for instance, often have a perspective on Latin American immigration that differs from rest of the nation.

Ethnic and racial diversity also plays a key role in determining public opinion on the issue, as more diverse communities tend to embrace immigration to a greater degree than more cultural homogenous states and communities. At the far end of the liberal spectrum, there are some who support open immigration policies, and some who have argued that the right to immigrate to find work and support one's family should be globally recognized as a basic human right. At the extreme conservative side of the spectrum, there are those who favor a near complete ban on all immigration, believing that states and nations should look to preserve resources for the benefit of native-born populations in an increasingly competitive global environment.

Who Are Immigrants?

Currently, the United States attracts nearly 20 percent of all immigrants in the world. As of 2013, there were 41.3 million immigrants in the United States, constituting 13 percent of the population.[2] The United States has an estimated 11 to 14 million unauthorized migrants, approximately 30–40 percent of whom entered the nation legally but then stayed beyond the permitted timeframe. Approximately half of illegal immigrants migrated into the United States from Mexico or Central America.[3]

Facts and statistics on immigration fail to capture the complex issues that motivate both legal and unauthorized migration. Since the 1960s, American immigration policy has favored the immigration of individuals with higher education, and especially with advanced training in the STEM fields (science, technology, engineering, and mathematics). The 1965 Immigration and Nationality Act focused on immigration as a way to address the needs of the nation, attracting skilled workers, students, and professional migrants believed to be of the greatest benefit to American society.[4] Approximately 28 percent of American immigrants come from Mexico, due largely to the shared U.S./Mexico border. A variety of intersecting factors, including the influence of NAFTA and other trade agreements that primarily benefit U.S. corporations at the expense of agricultural workers in Mexico, have helped to create and maintain an economic crisis in Mexico in which approximately 53 percent of the population lives in poverty. Economic turmoil also leads to increased crime and gang violence, and together these factors have continued to motivate immigration into the United States for more than 200 years.[5]

On the whole, 20 percent of immigrants live below the poverty line and many have reduced income due to supporting family still living in their native nations. Most immigrants arriving in the United States in the twenty-first century come from Asia (including India) or Africa. Despite large numbers of immigrants from Latin America, Asians are the fastest growing ethnic group in the United States, and China is the leading nation for new immigrants as of 2013. Approximately 47 percent of immigrants living in the United States are naturalized citizens. In 2013, 48 percent of immigrants identified as white and 79 percent of the U.S. population, whether foreign or native-born, speak English as their primary language at home. In general, immigrants are more likely to have advanced degrees and doctorate degrees than native-born citizens and are also more likely to be entrepreneurs.

What is the Immigrant Problem?

The immigration debate can be divided into several interrelated issues. First, there are differing opinions about how many legal immigrants the United States should welcome each year for employment, education, or any other reason. Attitudes are heavily influenced by racism and ethnic prejudice. Fewer white Americans object to European immigration, for instance, than object to Latin American, African, or Asian immigration. Second, there is the debate over how to cope with the millions who migrate illegally in the United States each year or who overstay their permission to remain. This is the most controversial facet of the modern immigration debate. Finally, there is the issue of refugees and political asylees and what role the United States should play, if any, in extending aid and support to those suffering in international political turmoil.

A 2015 Gallup Poll report indicated that more than 67 percent of Americans are dissatisfied with U.S. immigration policy. Between 77 and 87 percent believe that unauthorized immigrants should be allowed to become citizens, as long as they pay taxes, learn English, and submit to criminal background checks. Further, 63 percent of Americans classify immigration as a "good thing" overall, even as many object to unauthorized immigration or believe that current policies require reform.[6] However, 77 percent also believe that America needs to do more to protect the nation's borders. Pew Research polls provide similar results, indicating that a majority of Americans believe that immigration strengthens society. Among groups that most opposed immigration were the "steadfast Republican conservatives," though more than 64 percent of fiscal conservatives approved of immigration. Approval of legal migration and of extending aid to political refugees is far higher than support for economic migration, though fewer Americans approve of granting asylum to individuals coming from Islamic nations or nations where terrorism is a major concern.[7]

Even among those who consider immigration a major problem, there is little consensus about *why* it is a problem and what should be done about it. On the issue of unauthorized migration, some feel unauthorized migrants steal jobs and depress wages for native-born workers, or may pose a threat in terms of crime and/or terrorism and so favor efforts to control borders and to deport illegal migrants. Others argue, from a human rights or labor rights perspective, that unauthorized migration is a human rights issue and favor policies that will help to ease pressure for migration and to prevent unauthorized migrants from being exploited.

While there are economic, political, social, and national security arguments on both sides of the debate, immigration cannot be reduced to practical, economic, or administrative concerns. Migration is a difficult process, whether one migrates with legal permission or chooses the dangerous path of unauthorized entry, and few immigrants make this decision lightly. Immigrants travel to find new opportunities and to protect or care for their families, and so the decision to accept or reject immigrants is always also an ethical, moral decision. Limiting immigration and/or deporting immigrants often means sending individuals back to nations where they face severe economic hardship and may also face violence from gangs, military dictatorships, or terrorist extremists. Yet some worry that simply accepting all immigrants as citizens will reduce resources available for native-born citizens. While there is no consensus on how to deal with immigration, it is generally believed that the current U.S. system in insufficient. America is an immigrant nation and, on some level, handling the immigration issue reflects how the nation has changed since its inception, while also providing an important framework for the nation's future evolution.

Micah L. Issitt

Notes

1. Roberts, "How a Sonnet Made a Statue the 'Mother of Exiles'."
2. Brown, "Key Takeaways on U.S. Immigration: Past, Present, and Future."
3. Zong and Batalova, "Frequently Requested Statistics on Immigrants and Immigration in the United States."
4. Gjelten, "The Immigration Act that Inadvertently Changed America."
5. Robbins, "Wave of Illegal Immigrants Gains Speed After NAFTA."
6. Newport, "American Public Opinion and Immigration."
7. "Beyond Red vs. Blue: The Political Typology," *Pew Research*.

1
Politics, the Law, and Immigration Reform

Official White House Photo by Lawrence Jackson

On July 16, 2013, in the Blue Room of the White House, President Barack Obama conducts a round of "Live from the White House" interviews with Spanish-language television anchors regarding immigration reform. Norma Garcia, KXTX Telemundo, Fort Worth, Texas, interviews the President.

Politics and Reform in an Immigrant Nation

American immigration policy is inextricably linked to the evolution of American cultural identity. The earliest immigration laws were designed to maintain the racial and cultural composition of the nation's population, while later laws abolished racially-based immigration criteria in favor of attracting individuals with skills, training, and expertise seen as useful to America's growing industrial society. During the so-called "golden age" of immigration, which some historians argue began in the 1830s and lasted for upwards of a century, the United States developed a global reputation as a nation that welcomed refugees and asylees and this became part of the nation's philosophical identity. In the 2010s, fear of terrorism, the effects of unauthorized immigration on the U.S. economy, and the nation's long-established role as a haven for social/political refugees are among the primary issues in the debate over immigration law and reform.

Eras of Immigration Policy

The 1790 Naturalization Act, one of the first U.S. immigration laws, limited citizenship to "free white persons" of "good moral character," who had lived in the nation for two years. While America adopted a host of additional naturalization laws, immigration remained fundamentally open from the founding of the nation until the twentieth century.[1] Between 1830 and 1924, more than 35 million immigrants came to the United States from Europe, an era sometimes called the "golden age" of immigration, or the "Century of Immigration." The massive wave of immigration was driven by the industrial revolution and the need to attract laborers to fill American factories and contribute to the nation's infrastructure. During this time, various laws were passed attempting to prevent the immigration of unwanted or unsavory individuals. Among these restrictions were laws banning anarchists, prostitutes, political radicals, alcoholics, stowaways, vagrants, illiterates, former convicts, and individuals with contagious diseases. In the 1880s, politicians alarmed by the rapid growth of Asian immigration, and fearing the loss of white cultural hegemony, began restricting Chinese immigration directly.[2] This was the beginning of a long series of racial immigration policies now generally seen by historians as racist and prejudicial.

America's century of immigration ended with World War I, as the resulting economic turmoil motivated a wave of new immigration restrictions based on a quota system that placed a numerical limit on the number of immigrants from each nation or region. Until the 1920s, America was ideologically committed to an open immigration policy with regard to Europeans, a philosophy enshrined in American ideology.[3] In his now famous "Letters from an American Farmer," French immigrant J. Hector St. John de Crèvecœur called America a "land of opportunity," in which the hegemony of the aristocratic system had finally ended. This idealized depiction of America, as a place where hard work translated directly into prosperity, became central to America's patriotic identity.[4] In practice, however, America remained a hostile, exploitative environment for non-Anglo immigrants and poor immigrants who lacked the resources to purchase their way into the American dream.

The era of European immigration tapered after World War II, though the U.S. absorbed a large number of refugees fleeing Europe after the war. The national quota system, long criticized as racially biased, began to lose favor in the early 1940s and by the 1950s, it was clear that a new system was needed. It was during this time that politicians like John F. Kennedy proposed radical shifts in immigration policy, based on the idea that the nation should seek to attract skilled workers, academics, and other persons of cultural value, regardless of national or racial origin. President Kennedy's book, *A Nation of Immigrants*, published posthumously in 1964, was an argument for comprehensive immigration reform. Kennedy argued that every U.S. citizen, with the exception of indigenous Americans, were either immigrants or the children of immigrants and that immigration had been a positive force in American history, enriching and empowering the nation by creating a cultural environment that fostered creativity, innovation, and advancement.

The landmark 1965 Immigration and Nationality Act created the now familiar laws that favor immigration to unite and preserve families and gives preference to immigrants with certain skills or types of training. While the 1965 laws were intended to liberalize immigration, ending the racially-biased quota system, the 1965 provisions also restricted temporary immigration from Latin America and this led to a massive explosion in unauthorized migration from Mexico and, to a lesser extent, Central America. Gradually, unauthorized migration became the top priority in immigration reform. The 1986 Immigration Reform and Control Act provided a legal avenue to citizenship for millions of unauthorized immigrants but also sought to strengthen control of the nation's Mexican border.[5] Despite efforts, unauthorized migration continued unabated into the 1990s. Latin American migration follows economic patterns increasing as jobs in the U.S. become more available and decreasing during times of U.S. economic turmoil.

Immigration in the Modern World

The new era in American immigration began with the September 11, 2001 terrorist attacks on the United States. Of the terrorists identified as having taken part in the attacks, all were legal temporary residents of the United States, and several were unauthorized immigrants, as their permission to remain in the nation had lapsed. In December of 2005, Congress passed the Border Protection, Anti-Terrorism, and Illegal Immigration Control Act, a Republican-sponsored bill seeking to assuage American fear of terrorism through immigration reform, while simultaneously addressing ongoing debates about the effect of Mexican immigration on the U.S. labor market. Emboldened with a resurgence of xenophobia and national security-related fears, the 2000s and 2010s have seen one of the strongest grassroots anti-immigrant movements in American history. The modern immigration debate is fueled by misinformation and ideological jargon as much as by legitimate concerns about the economic strain of unauthorized immigration. In the 2010s, the immigration debate has become highly polarized. While there is a large lobby pushing for immigration reform out of concern for the millions of migrants facing economic hardship and violence in the native nations, there is another lobby seeking to create new, stronger restrictions on immigration, out of the belief that America's jobs and resources should be preserved for native-born citizens and that isolationism will help to keep the nation safe from future terrorist threats.

Since mid-2015, for instance, there has been an upwelling of anti-Syrian immigration sentiment, due to the widely-publicized activities of radical Islamist groups like ISIS/ISIL/IS in Syria. Despite the fact that Islamic radicals constitute an extremely small percentage of the Middle Eastern or Islamic population as a whole, in 2015, the House of Representatives passed a bill that would place new restrictions on the admission of Syrian and Iraqi refugees, requiring Department of Homeland Security and Justice Department investigations before individuals from these nations would be allowed into the United States. President Obama argued against the house bill, saying that such restrictions hamper the nation's ability to offer aid to refugees seeking to escape one of the most violent regimes in the world. In speeches, President Obama compared the Syrian refugees of the 2010s to the Jewish refugees of World War II and urged the nation, and the nation's legislators, not to allow their political policies to be dictated by fear.[6]

The Present and Future of Immigration Reform

A deeply divided government was unable to agree on comprehensive immigration reform in the 2010s. In 2013, a group of four Republican and four Democratic senators (called the Gang of Eight in the media) proposed a comprehensive immigration reform bill in the Senate. The bill called for a path to citizenship for immigrants currently waiting for permanent status and millions currently living as undocumented migrants, as well as a more robust employment verification system, additional potential for agricultural workers to obtain temporary visas, and a fast-track system for permanent residence for immigrants with advanced science, technology, engineering, or mathematics backgrounds. Though the bill passed in the Senate, the Republican-controlled House of Representatives has (as of February 2016) refused to bring the bill to the floor.[7]

Frustrated by a lack of progress on the issue, in November of 2014 President Obama announced a program that would allow approximately 5 million undocumented migrants (45% of the estimated undocumented population at the time) to legally work in the United States on a temporary basis. The action was similar to a 1990 deferred action program enacted under George H.W. Bush. However, while former President Bush's executive action was allowed to proceed, Obama's program met with legal challenges, beginning in the federal courts of Pennsylvania where Judge Arthur J. Schwab ruled that the executive action was unconstitutional. As of February 2016, the United States Supreme Court has agreed to review the case, and the ultimate fate of the executive order therefore remains in question.[8]

Passionate, ideological debates over immigration are not a new feature in American politics. Immigration has been a contentious issue since the first wave of European migrants, who started a long process of displacing or otherwise removing the land's indigenous inhabitants, first began thinking of themselves as American. Since the moment these immigrants formed a new American society, there have been those working to monitor and control the potentially harmful influx of foreign elements and those committed to the perspective that immigration and the willing, purposeful embrace of cultural diversity, is and should remain a cornerstone of America's philosophical and political system. The conflict between those who fear immigration and those who welcome it continues to play a role in American politics, in which the contemporary issues can be seen as a recurrence and continuation of a very old debate.

Micah L. Issitt

Notes

1. Cohn, "How U.S. Immigration Laws and Rules Have Changed Through History."
2. "Chinese Exclusion Act," *Harvard University.*
3. Lehtinen, " 'America Would Lose Its Soul: The Immigration Restriction Debate, 1920–1924."
4. Taylor, "The American Beginning."
5. "History of U.S. Immigration Laws."
6. Foley, "Obama Responds to Anti-Immigrant Sentiment In Moving Speech to New Citizens."
7. Gomez and Davis, " 'Gang of Eight' Immigration Bill Clears Senate Hurdle."
8. Ford, "A Ruling Against the Obama Administration on Immigration."

Immigration Reform: Corporate Demands Trump Human Rights

By Michelle Chen
New Labor Forum, December 14, 2013

Immigration reform has been the year's most feared, least effective, most popular, and most hated legislative discussion in Washington. You might say that "comprehensive immigration reform"—the awkward legislative compromise that emerged last summer as Senate Bill 744 and now languishes in the gridlocked House—was dead on arrival because of its attempt to straddle so many competing, often conflicting interests, pushing for a panoply of reforms that would either open or harden the country's porous borders.

While the Republican-dominated House of Representatives wrestles with issues of war, budget deficits, and Obamacare, the chaos of Capitol Hill may well smother any chances of passing reform legislation this year. Despite its narrow chances of passage, however, the bill provides a crucial window for understanding the current alignment of powerful stakeholders advocating immigration reform.

Senate Bill 744 has drawn a melting pot of supporters who blur ideological lines. Earlier this year, the framework proposed by the so-called "Gang of Eight," a bipartisan cluster of leading Senate reformers, drew broad support from labor organizations, including the AFL-CIO, civil rights groups like the ACLU and NAACP, and business lobbyists such as the U.S. Chamber of Commerce—groups who usually stick to their own political orbits and, in the case of labor and employers, whose interests often collide.[1]

The Senate bill establishes clear preferences regarding the type of immigrant the United States should accept within its borders: the upward striving student with an impeccable record, the computer programmer recruited from Mumbai to Silicon Valley. And behind these elite migrants stand laborers in high demand, like the farmworkers who fuel our agricultural system. Under the reform plan sketched out by the Senate, these aspiring Americans would be incorporated into the workforce as long as they are deemed beneficial to the economy. Tens of thousands of immigrant workers would also be admitted through a convoluted scorecard system, allotting "points" based on economic and professional merits.

But others—the immigrants of lesser "merit"—would not make the cut. As the Senate proposal wended through the House in August, a group of undocumented carwash workers in Arizona were swept up in an Immigration and Customs

Enforcement (ICE) raid, despite Obama's promises to ease up on deportations of migrants deemed to pose no risk to public safety.[2]

Around the same time of the Phoenix raids, members of a group of 150 Jamaican migrant workers in Florida—all of whom had come on official H-2B work visas—went on strike. Backed by the National Guestworker Alliance, they accused their employer of hiring them out as housecleaners for luxury hotels, then stiffing them on their wages and threatening to get them deported in retaliation for protesting their treatment.[3]

Immigration reform could, in theory, help both of these groups of workers—those with work visas and those without papers. There is certainly momentum for reform coming from the growing Latino electorate, as well as mainstream liberals and pro-business conservatives.

But in the current political climate—polarized by race, class, and ideology—Washington's approach to reform is not about the rights of the hotel guestworker or the *carwashero*. It is about squeezing as much profit from their labor as possible, at the lowest cost to government. The politics of reform center on gaining more votes among the Latino electorate, and ensuring that specific industries, from Silicon Valley to carnival fairgrounds, have a guaranteed stream of labor-ready workers. And an extra perk is that the costs of "earning" that citizenship are borne largely by migrants themselves, extracting the heaviest possible toll at the gates of the American Dream.

Importing Workers

The Senate plan takes a two-pronged approach to controlling migration: it would simultaneously "legalize" a considerable portion of the current undocumented population and control the "future flow"—new migrants arriving to pursue jobs or reunification with their families—with various work-authorization policies.

A key plank for bringing in fresh migrant labor is a visa program, the W-Visa, that would admit "low-skill" blue-collar workers through a quota-based system. Unlike other work-based visas, the W-Visa technically offers more workplace and settlement rights, such as the ability to switch employers and a limited path to permanent settlement and eventually citizenship.[4]

In a nod to the technology industry lobby, lawmakers also seek a dramatic expansion of H-1B visas for "high-skill" workers, such as computer programmers. This measure purports to address a burgeoning demand for professionals in the science, technology, engineering, and mathematics (STEM) fields (and a supposed shortage of qualified U.S. workers).

The agricultural guestworker program would be restructured and expanded—a gift to farm owners and their lobbyists who pushed for more seasonal laborers. The reformed program, known as the "Blue Card," would give workers greater flexibility to change jobs or become legal permanent residents, rather than the current policy of keeping workers on temporary contract, tethered to a single grower.

Yearly immigration quotas would be established by a special commission of "stakeholders" led by appointed labor, government, and industry representatives. Immigration targets would be based on assessments of economic conditions and labor market "demands." Starting with a baseline of twenty thousand visas in 2015, up to two hundred thousand permits could be issued annually, according to news reports.

One of the most controversial aspects of the proposal is a merit-based "point system" that would evaluate prospective migrants. As a "scorecard" for allocating 120,000 to 250,000 visas each year, the criteria would likely prioritize economic "qualities," such as professional credentials, academic degrees, civic involvement, or in some cases the job availability in their occupational field. Although Britain and Canada have implemented point systems in their immigration policies, the United States has never tried to systematize its allocation of visas using a merit-based scorecard, in part because of controversy over how to weigh and prioritize the criteria.[5]

The scorecard starkly maps the profit motives driving immigration reform. Although other factors, like the migrant's family ties in the United States, might be considered in awarding points, employers' interests are served above all—not the social needs and aspirations of the would-be migrant, much less broader questions of economic justice.[6]

Tonally, the mainstream immigration debate reflects a neoliberal attitude toward social policy as an arm of economic growth. Only after market demands are sated do lawmakers contemplate the humanitarian and social aspects of reform—such as ensuring the cohesion of immigrant communities through family reunification, or offsetting the exploitation of migrant labor with strong labor protections.

Legalizing and Criminalizing

To the extent that the humanitarian issues of reform enter the debate, the proposals for "legalizing" undocumented workers attempt to answer the question of what the government should do with people who are living in the United States, contributing mightily to the economy, firmly settled, yet are denied basic legal rights and forced to live in day-to-day terror of deportation. The legalization process would prioritize the sympathetic "good immigrant." Dreamers—a term referring to young people who came to the United States as children and now seek citizenship, along with in-demand farmworkers and tech workers—are set to be "fast tracked" on the path to legalization, with a somewhat shorter timetable than the decade-plus that other migrants can expect. This provision would build on an earlier administrative directive issued by President Obama that expressly halted deportations for young people meeting the background requirements.

Other undocumented immigrants—namely, the millions of workers doing regular jobs—have been a "harder sell." So in exchange for a relatively broad program of legalizing the undocumented, conservative lawmakers demanded concessions aimed at tightening immigration strictures while opening a limited path to legal status (not so much for ethical reasons but as a practical alternative to the impossible task of deporting some 11.7 million people).

Republican lawmakers festooned the Senate bill with harsh enforcement provisions—such as sharply increased penalties for unauthorized border crossings—that would all but ensure that millions of dollars go toward the prosecution of undocumented immigrants, and by extension, massive investment in for-profit detention facilities. The bill sets an arbitrary goal of almost completely reducing unauthorized entry as a "trigger" to be reached before the legalization provisions kick in.

Immigrant rights activists point out the upside-down logic of the Republicans' insistence on prioritizing the enforcement boost as a condition of legalization—if people had a legal way of working in the country, fewer people would seek to migrate outside the law. But of course, there are political and economic rewards to be reaped from expanded "border enforcement" just as there are profits to be extracted from the workers that manage to filter in, lawfully or otherwise.[7]

Enforcement would extend into private workplaces, too. The Senate bill establishes a national tracking system for work authorization known as "E-verify," which would screen all workers to ensure they had proper documentation for employment. Civil rights groups worry that workers will be subject to privacy violations and technological identification errors, making it even easier for employers to discriminate against Latino workers based on suspected "unlawful" status.

> **Only after market demands are sated do lawmakers contemplate the humanitarian and social aspects of reform.**

The criminalization measures might become more vicious in the House, which (as of September 2013) has not yet issued its own version of a comprehensive bill. As of this writing, several Republican legislators have expressly rejected the idea of citizenship for the undocumented, though Republicans favor an expansion of guest-worker visas to grow the low-wage, low-rights migrant labor force. That is, if they do not scuttle the reform efforts altogether, they will only accept the most marginal, business-friendly "liberalization" of immigration policy, perhaps through a series of "piecemeal" measures as opposed to a comprehensive bill.[8]

The Citizenship Gauntlet

For the estimated 11.7 million undocumented immigrants currently in the United States, the Senate plan offers Registered Provisional Immigrant (RPI) status as a stepping stone toward obtaining a green card and eventually citizenship. But qualifying for RPI is a daunting multiple-step process, involving a $500 fine, background checks, paying back taxes (supposedly owed from past earnings), and roughly a decade of probationary status. During that time, they would have to demonstrate "continuous employment." Then, becoming a legal permanent resident would require, according to the Center for American Progress, paying an additional $1,000 fine and application fees, passing additional background checks, and by showing that he or she has either worked throughout their time in RPI status, or can demonstrate resources equal to 125 percent of the federal poverty line.

Attaining citizenship would take another three years of waiting.[9]

The "continuous employment" provision is based on a false assumption that immigrants need an added incentive to work. In fact, many advocates point out that the one thing that would keep workers from working is the dismal labor market and slumped economy.

In fact, with so many Americans now struggling at the brink of poverty and facing chronically high unemployment, it is clear that a large swath of the citizen population would probably struggle to maintain a steady job for a decade. That lawmakers demand this of undocumented immigrants seems even more delusional, with immigrant workers facing additional linguistic barriers, lack of access to health care and public benefits (even immigrants with green cards face a five-year bar from many federal welfare programs), and discrimination and segregation in the low-wage economy.

In an analysis of the Senate legislation, the Center for Human Rights argues that the "continuous employment" rule would "perpetuate and possibly increase opportunities for unscrupulous employers to violate health and safety, anti-discrimination, and wage and hour laws over the next ten to twenty years."

Overall, the proposed RPI criteria could potentially screen out millions of undocumented immigrants over the next several years. While roughly two million would qualify for RPI status under the less stringent requirements for farmworkers and dreamers, the Center for Human Rights estimates that of those undocumented immigrants remaining, "it is likely that approximately four to five million mostly low-income immigrants" will be turned away.[10]

A statement of opposition to the Senate bill, signed by various civil rights and Latino community organizations and issued by the advocacy network Presente.org, points out, "Even those 'fortunate enough' to meet the requirements to gain RPI status are at high risk to become indentured servants locked into overly burdensome continuous employment and income obligations for at least ten—and perhaps fifteen or more—years."[11]

As the Senate bill wended through Congress in early August, 2013, *National Journal* writer Fawn Johnson observed,

> No rational person would design a process so complicated and so convoluted that it is virtually guaranteed to produce frustration, abuse, and unintended consequences. But, then again, that's not the point. The main imperative of immigration legislation isn't that it will work. It's that it will pass.[12]

Unwelcome Guests

"Comprehensive" immigration reform involves not just legalization and regulation of migrants but establishing a coherent system of rights and protections, at least in theory. Guestworker programs, or temporary labor visa schemes, have a long history rife with examples of labor abuse. Wage theft and forced labor, which typically beset undocumented workers, are also shockingly widespread in the guestworker labor force. In recent years, scandals have erupted over the exploitation of temporary visa-based workers linked to the supply chains of brand-name corporations like Hershey's, McDonald's, and Walmart. They often work in the dregs of the contract labor economy; perhaps the best-known program is the seasonal farmworker system that funnels migrants in each year to harvest crops on industrial farms. But migrant guestworkers are also a major source of labor in industrial sectors, including construction and factory work, as well as temporary service jobs like ride operators or servers at tourist sites and traveling carnivals. Although the State and Labor Departments have sought to tighten regulations and oversight of employers who use visa workers, results have been piecemeal, and advocates have long pushed for an overhaul of the system.

To protect workers from retaliation for coming forward with reports of wage theft and other abuses, the Senate bill includes whistleblower protections to shield undocumented workers from deportation under ICE for undertaking a complaint process against an abusive employer.

Undocumented workers who suffered labor violations could also have more access to humanitarian-based relief through special visas for victims of trafficking and other crimes. To address corruption and abuse in the labor recruiting industry, which acts as a broker for migrant workers on behalf of many U.S. firms, the bill would institute new safeguards against abuses and discrimination by these recruitment agencies.

Nonetheless, the bill essentially still maintains a guestworker system that keeps migrants relegated to a "second-tier" labor force. The H-2B guestworker visa—the program that brought the Jamaican hotel cleaners to Florida—will remain in place. And unlike the new W-Visa workers, H-2B guestworkers could not change employers, so they would still be more vulnerable to abuse and coercion.

The fundamental problem is not how workers are categorized. It is that the basic structure of the labor force keeps immigrants disenfranchised politically and marginalized both legally and socially. The marginalization of immigrants is a political, legal, and cultural project—one that documentation alone cannot fix. As long as they lack equal rights, they are intrinsically more exposed to labor violations. It is both a cause and a symptom of this vulnerability that migrant labor clusters in sectors like construction and domestic work—replete with low wages, brutal conditions, and little career mobility, along with high rates of occupational injury.

Those issues are compounded by language barriers, institutional racism, and the attendant climate of fear in the immigrant workforce. Many undocumented and even documented workers fear further exposing themselves to legal trouble or abuse by complaining publicly about mistreatment at work, seeking medical care for an injury on a worksite, or even driving to work on a police-patrolled highway.

Immigration's Impact on "American" Workers

Many immigration restrictionists argue that tighter immigration limits would "protect" U.S. workers from perceived unfair competition from immigrants who are willing—or, rather, forced—to work for less. Yet mainstream reform advocates insist that more authorized immigrant workers will yield jobs and growth.

In fact, while immigration does disrupt labor markets in some ways, various studies link more open, legal channels for immigration with economic growth. The Senate proposal would, according to the Congressional Budget Office, yield "net fiscal gains" of roughly $1 trillion over twenty years in both taxes and new economic activity.[13]

The Center for American Progress projects that if lawmakers granted legal status, not even full citizenship, to the undocumented, over the next ten years, "the cumulative increase in income of all Americans would be $470 billion," thus benefiting immigrant and native-born workers alike.[14]

Migration: Economic Tool or Human Right?

But the economic arguments constrain the frame of the debate on both the right and left: pushing liberals to tout how immigration fulfills the promises of neoliberal prosperity, rather than the value of having a more just and humane immigration policy.

The neoliberal approach to immigration reform comes at the expense of the issues most crucial to immigrant families and communities. The Senate plan would cut back the family reunification visa program at the same time it expands employment-based visas, with major potential demographic as well as social consequences. Reunification visas are a principal way for women to enter the United States. Although many immigrant women work, they are more likely to be employed in informal sectors, such as domestic work. Reflecting general discrimination in the workforce, women immigrants also earn less in many cases, which would likely make it more difficult to qualify for provisional status on the basis of earnings or employment status—even if they are the main providers for their families, just "off the books."

By privileging formal wage work, the Senate bill prioritizes male workers over their female colleagues along with their partners and relatives. While there may be an economic rationale to this gender gap, it is blind to the social complexities of migrant communities. For immigrant workers who see labor as a means to support their families, cutting families out of the reform equation undoubtedly misses the point.

The reform plan has alienated more radical strands of the labor and pro-migrant movements, because it fails to address the global inequalities at the root of migration. Some on the labor left challenge the entire concept of national borders as economic gateways. The structural inequality built into the borders of the capitalist nation-state is most explicitly codified in "free trade" deals like the North American Free Trade Agreement, which have invited the free flow of companies and capital across borders, but clamped down on human movement of those who seek to follow the prosperity accumulating on the other side of the border.

Some binational activists advocate a radical transborder policy that accepts freedom of movement—twinned with the free migration of labor—as a human right. Gaspar Rivera-Salgado, a professor at the University of California, Los Angeles and former coordinator of the Binational Front of Indigenous Organizations, told *The Progressive*, "We want rights for migrants in the U.S. and at the same time development that makes migration a choice rather than a necessity—the right to not migrate. Both are part of the solution."[15]

The immigration reform debate reflects a constant tension between migration as a right and migration as an economic policy. The idea of freedom of movement as a human right is essentially at odds with the idea of conditional citizenship; subjecting migration rights to the regulation of the state and corporations produces a system that systematically exploits and devalues their labor and strips them of basic human dignities.

Washington seeks to invite migrants as probationary workers, not fellow humans. Advocates for labor and human rights must ask themselves whether this is the kind of "path to citizenship" that the country wants to enshrine in law.

Notes

1. See, for example, Liz Halloran, "Gang of 8 Champion Plan, Declare 'Year of Immigration Reform,'" *NPR.org* , April 18, 2013, available at <www.npr.org/blogs/itsallpolitics/2013/04/18/177780665/bipartisan-senate-gang-prepares-to-sell-immigration-plan>

2. Michelle Chen, "Carwash Workers and Capitol Hill: Immigration in Limbo," *In These Times*, September 11, 2013, available at <http://inthesetimes.com/working/entry/15563/carwashes_and_capitol_hill_immigration_in_limbo>

3. Jennifer Gordon, "Subcontractor Servitude," *New York Times*, September 1, 2013, available at <www.nytimes.com/2013/09/02/opinion/subcontractor-servitude.html>; National Guestworker Alliance, "Guestworkers to U.S. Reps in FL: Pass Immigration Reform to End the Abuse We Faced," August 19, 2013, available at www.guestworkeralliance.org/2013/08/guestworkers-to-u-s-reps-in-fl-pass-cir-to-end-the-abuse-we-faced-8-19-13

4. Jessica Yellin, "Sides Reach Broad Agreement on Immigrant Guest Workers," *CNN.com*, April 1, 2013, available at <www.cnn.com/2013/03/30/politics/immigration-guest-workers>; Immigration Policy Center, "A Guide to S.744: Understanding the 2013 Senate Immigration Bill," Immigration Policy Center, July 10, 2013, available at <www.immigrationpolicy.org/special-reports/guide-s744-understanding-2013-senate-immigration-bill>

5. "Defining 'Desirable' Immigrants: What Lies Beneath the Proposed Merit-Based Point System?" Immigration Policy Center, May 20, 2013, available at <www.immigrationpolicy.org/just-facts/defining-desirable-immigrants-what-lies-beneath-proposed-merit-based-point-system>

6. Robert Lynch and Patrick Oakford, "The 6 Key Takeaways from the CBO Cost Estimate of S.744," Center for American Progress, June 21, 2013, available at <www.americanprogress.org/issues/immigration/news/2013/06/21/67514/the-6-key-takeaways-from-the-cbo-cost-estimate-of-s-7446>

7. "The Fallacy of 'Enforcement First': Immigration Enforcement without Immigration Reform Has Been Failing for Decades," Immigration Policy Center, May 9, 2013, available at <http://immigrationpolicy.org/sites/default/files/docs/borderenforcement.pdf>; Michelle Chen, "'Bargain' on Immigration Would Feed Prison Profits," *In These Times*, July 26, 2013, available at <http://inthesetimes.com/article/15359/bargain_on_immigration_would_feed_prison_profits>

8. Greg Sargent, "In Blow to Immigration Reform, House 'Gang of Seven' Bill Looks Dead," *Washington Post*, September 20, 2013, available at <www.washingtonpost. com/blogs/plum-line/wp/2013/09/20/in-blow-to-immigration-reform-house-gang-of-seven-bill-looks-dead>; Chris Frates, "Inside Boehner's Strategy to Slow Walk Immigration to the Finish Line," *National Journal*, July 30, 2013, available at <www. nationaljournal.com/congress/inside-boehner-s-strategy-to-slow-walk-immigration-to-the-finish-line-20130730>

9. Philip E. Wolgin and Abhay Aneja, "The Top 5 Reasons Why Immigration Reform in 2013 Is Different Than in 1986," Center for American Congress, June 12, 2013, available at <www.americanprogress.org/issues/immigration/news/2013/06/12/ 66208/the-top-5-reasons-why-immigration-reform-in-2013-is-different-than-in-1986>

10. Peter Schey, *Analysis of Senate Bill 744's Pathway to Legalization and Citizenship*, Center for Human Rights and Constitutional Law, 2013, available at <www. centerforhumanrights.org/6-18-13%20CHRCL-Peter%20Schey%20Analysis%20 Senate%20Bill%20Legalization%20Program.pdf>

11. "More than 30 Latino Organizations Call on Democrats and Republicans to Reject S.744 Immigration Reform Bill," Presente.org, July 26, 2013, available at <http://presente.org/press/releases/2013/7/26/more-30-latino-organizations-call-to-reject-S744>

12. Fawn Johnson, "How Immigration Reform Could Create a New Underclass," *National Journal*, August 1, 2013, available at <www.nationaljournal.com/ magazine/how-immigration-reform-could-create-a-new-underclass-20130801>

13. "The Power of Reform: CBO Report Quantifies the Economic Benefits of the Senate Immigration Bill," Immigration Policy Center, June 20, 2013, available at <www.immigrationpolicy.org/just-facts/power-reform-cbo-report-quantifies-economic-benefits-senate-immigration-bill>

14. Robert Lynch and Patrick Oakford, "The Economic Effects of Granting Legal Status and Citizenship to Undocumented Immigrants," Center for American Progress, March 20, 2013, available at <www.americanprogress.org/wp-content/ uploads/2013/03/EconomicEffectsCitizenship-1.pdf>

15. David Bacon, "What Real Immigration Reform Would Look Like," *The Progressive*, July 27, 2013, available at <www.progressive.org/real-immigration-reform>

Hey! Who Left the Border Open?

By Emily Cadei
Newsweek Global, September 25, 2015

On the 2016 campaign trail, immigration has been a flash point unlike any other. But as Donald Trump pushes his scheme to build a wall across America's southern border and Hillary Clinton promises to go further than President Barack Obama in protecting migrants without documentation, a major immigration reform from a half-century ago is a reminder that policy changes often don't go as planned. For today's politicians, perhaps the biggest takeaway of the Immigration and Nationality Act is to expect unintended consequences.

It was back in 1965, during the depths of the Cold War and the peak of the civil rights movement, that the United States overhauled its immigration laws. Working with liberal Democrats and liberal Republicans (who existed back then), President Lyndon Johnson pushed a bill that did away with the "national origins quota" system. The old quota system, in place since the 1920s, determined who could immigrate to the U.S. based on ethnicity, with a heavy tilt toward Western Europeans—especially the English, Irish and Germans. Only small allotments were granted to Eastern Europeans, Asians and Africans.

That became an issue for the United States in the '60s, when new countries were emerging from colonialism, pitting the U.S. and the Soviet Union in a contest for their allegiances. Republican Senator Jacob Javits, a liberal from New York, noted in September 1965 that the immigration system, with its bias toward Western Europeans, "remains today a target for Communist propaganda...making our effort to win over the uncommitted nations more difficult."

The racial discrimination inherent in the quota system clashed with the idealism of the Civil Rights and Voting Rights acts. And most of all, the ethnic limits ran contrary to many Americans' image of their country. "As President Kennedy so aptly stated, we are a 'nation of immigrants,'" Massachusetts Republican Senator Leverett Saltonstall told his colleagues during the debate on the bill. "There is scarcely an area of our national life that has not been favorably affected by the work of people from other lands."

By '65, however, some conservatives in the U.S. House publicly "worried about the size and scale of future Latin American immigration," says Dan Tichenor, a professor of political science at the University of Oregon, "and were trying to put barriers in its way." Liberal lawmakers didn't like that idea, but they doubted that the new restrictions would have much impact. The limits were high enough, Javits conceded, that immigration from the Western Hemisphere under the new law "would be approximately the same as the level reached last year"—a modest 140,000 or thereabouts. Yet the total number of persons of Mexican origin in the U.S. went from 5 million in 1970, the first census after the act, to almost 34 million today.

The Western Hemisphere cap was one key concession that opponents of Johnson's immigration reform were able to extract. The other significant change was that visas be prioritized for migrants with family ties in the United States. Johnson and the bill's supporters backed a system that would have put a priority on skill, which ended up being secondary in the new law.

When Johnson signed the Immigration and Nationality Act at the foot of the Statue of Liberty fifty years ago this October, he declared that the new law undoing the old quota system was "not a revolutionary bill. It does not affect the lives of millions." In fact, it did. The new system, which opened up American immigration to the world, has dramatically shifted the blend of people coming into the country while contributing to the surge in immigrants from Mexico and Latin America entering the U.S. without documentation—neither of which its authors ever intended.

There was "a whole series of consequences unleashed" by this new law, says UCLA law professor Hiroshi Motomura, author of *Americans in Waiting: The Lost Story of Immigration and Citizenship in the United States*. Though the 1965 law eliminated ceilings on visas for specific ethnicities across Asia and Africa, it did keep a cap in place for the Eastern Hemisphere—encompassing migrants from Europe, Africa and Asia. As a compromise, it also set the cap on immigration from the Western Hemisphere for the first time. That's right: The U.S. used to allow unlimited immigration from Mexico. Even as restrictionists had layered on more and more limits on immigrants, starting with the Chinese in the 1880s, the Japanese around the turn of the century, and the rest of Asia, Africa and much of Europe in the 1920s, the U.S. allowed the open flow of immigration from Canada and nations to the south, part of what was considered a "good neighbor" policy.

The conservatives who backed a system that would give a majority of visas to family members of U.S. citizens "thought we would see an expansion in Southern and Eastern European immigration," says Tichenor. "They never really anticipated the dramatic increase in Asian and Latin American immigration" that resulted thanks to family unification rules. Essentially, the new law allowed American citizens to obtain visas for not

> **Urbanization and economic dislocation drove Mexicans and other Central Americans from rural areas north in search of work, while Americans were obtaining higher levels of education and moving away from menial labor.**

only their small children and spouses but also their sisters and brothers and adult children, who then became citizens and began the process over again.

That started a slow but steady progression of Asian and Latino migration, which had only small populations in the United States before '65. In the 1950s, Europeans made up 56 percent of those immigrants obtaining lawful permanent residence in the U.S., while those from Canada and Latin America were 37 percent, and all of Asia accounted for a measly 5 percent, according to Department of Homeland Security statistics. By this past decade, however, Europeans had dropped to just 14 percent of new lawful permanent residents, compared with 35 percent from Asia and 44 percent from the Americas.

One more factor had a major impact: At the same time immigration law was shifting in 1965, a new national workforce policy was kicking in. A year earlier, in 1964, the federal government ended what was known as the Bracero Program, launched during World War II's labor shortages to provide temporary laborers from Mexico to American farms and fields. But the program was rife with worker abuses and ardently opposed by labor unions, which believed the migrants pushed down wages for Americans. That opposition finally succeeded in halting the Bracero Program in '64, to the consternation of the agriculture industry.

Proponents of the move in the Department of Labor and elsewhere believed they could wean farmers off Mexican labor. But "many of the same people who were coming under the Bracero Program or their relatives or the people who were in those networks continued to come," says Boston College professor Peter Skerry, an expert on immigration and ethnic politics. It's just that now they came illegally. Over the ensuing decades, that reality combined with the new caps on migrants from Latin America turned what had been legal migration illegal.

Economic trends in both Latin America and the U.S. also encouraged more migration. As Motomura explains it, 1965 was the "beginning of a mismatch of the legal immigration system and the demands of the economy." Specifically, urbanization and economic dislocation drove Mexicans and other Central Americans from rural areas north in search of work, while Americans were obtaining higher levels of education and moving away from menial labor. "In 1950, more than half of the labor force were high school dropouts. Now it's less than 5 percent," notes Tamar Jacoby, president of the business-backed coalition ImmigrationWorks USA. The law's drafters "didn't foresee that." That's an understatement.

The lesson of unintended consequences is something advocates on both sides of today's immigration debate acknowledge. "The first lesson is: Don't believe everything a politician tells you. As we've seen with all kinds of social innovations from the 1960s and 1970s, the assurances of their promoters turn out to be incomplete or false," says Mark Krikorian, the head of the Center for Immigration Studies, which advocates for tighter controls on immigration. He and Jacoby agree that the family migration provisions have pushed the system out of whack. But they're divided over whether the country still needs robust immigration, and if unmet labor demand is at the root of America's glut of undocumented migrants.

Disagreements on immigration ultimately come down to a debate over what America should be and how its economy should work. Though President Johnson promised the law "will not reshape the structure of our daily lives," the ensuing shifts in population and migration patterns have indeed meant "big changes in American life," says Skerry, for good and for ill. The last time politicians hashed out a new immigration system, they didn't entirely weigh those implications. Today's leaders would be wise to think about the ripple effect before they mess with the borders.

American Limbo

By Jeffrey Toobin
The New Yorker, July 27, 2015

Olga Flores, the seventh of eleven siblings, was born in a small town in the central Mexican state of Hidalgo thirty-nine years ago. "There was no work," she told me recently. "The only thing for a woman to do was to get married, have children, and cook for her whole life." A job in a nearby city would have required a high-school certificate, but her education ended in middle school. So in January of 1998, when she was twenty-one, Flores arranged to come to the United States illegally. She took her first trip on an airplane, to northern Mexico, and made her way to Sonoyta, a town on the Arizona border.

One of her brothers had immigrated to Columbus, Ohio, a few years earlier, and he helped her make arrangements to cross into the U.S. "There were about a dozen of us," she recalled. "It was a small truck, with the seats taken out. They told us to lie down in the back, head to feet, feet to head, so there would be room for everyone." They drove for about three hours, stopped at a mobile home in the desert, then continued on to Phoenix. A friend had set up another ride, which would take them across the country, to Ohio. "It was so cold, and I didn't have a jacket," Flores said. "We slept in the car and ate at McDonald's. It was the first burger I ever had. It was very tasty." When she reached Columbus, she paid her brother a thousand dollars, which he turned over to the guides, or coyotes, who had made the trip possible.

Eventually, Flores got a job as a cashier at a Wendy's. "It was really hard for me, because I couldn't tell what the Americans wanted," she said. "When I learned more English, I started taking orders." She soon met David Flores, who was also in the United States illegally. They got married and had twin boys, David and Luis, in 2000, and a third son, Iker, four years ago. "David has always been a really good person and a really good father," Flores said. "In Mexico, we are used to men not washing dishes and not doing anything around the house, and he is the opposite." Today, David operates a taco truck, which he stations in a parking lot near the small duplex apartment where the family lives, just outside Columbus. David is in the truck from 11 A.M. to 9 P.M. on weekdays, and on Sundays he works at McDonald's. When Olga is not caring for the children, she is in her kitchen, preparing the rice, intestines, and tongue for the truck.

Like many people who have arrived illegally from Mexico, Flores has built a productive life here. She is a longtime resident, has no criminal record, and is the parent of American citizens. Through much of Barack Obama's Presidency, there was a political near-consensus regarding the need to address the status of immigrants like Flores. Under the immigration-reform law passed by the Senate in 2013, she would have had a path to become a citizen; under the executive actions announced by President Obama in 2014, she could have obtained work papers and a driver's license. But the House failed to vote on the Senate's immigration bill, and a federal court in Texas has placed Obama's initiative on hold.

The result is a comprehensive breakdown in public policy. During the Obama Administration, which purports to be dedicated to easing the plight of residents like her, Flores and her peers have faced greater threats of deportation than at any time in decades. Republicans, for their part, have ended their brief experiment, reflected in the Senate bill, in bipartisanship on immigration. The Party is now close to united in opposition to any initiative that might offer Flores and others the chance to become American citizens. Flores, and the roughly eleven million people in similar situations, have no choice but to wait and worry.

Donald Trump, in his speech announcing his candidacy for the Republican Presidential nomination, in June, addressed the issue of illegal immigration from Mexico. "When Mexico sends its people, they're not sending their best," he said. "They're sending people that have lots of problems, and they're bringing those problems with us. They're bringing drugs. They're bringing crime. They're rapists. And some, I assume, are good people." (The crime rate among first-generation immigrants is significantly lower than that of the general population, according to Bianca Bersani, a sociologist at the University of Massachusetts-Boston.) Trump's remarks prompted several of his business partners, including Univision and Macy's, to sever their ties with him, but the comments have led to relatively little examination of the lives of the immigrants themselves.

For many years, Flores's legal status existed for her as a kind of background anxiety, affecting her life in modest ways. Because traffic stops by the police could lead to deportation, she drove the family car as little as possible, and never out of state. "Here, at least, we know the city, we know the streets, we know which are one-way or two-way," she said. "If we go somewhere else, we are scared that we don't know the area." Now her situation has taken on a new urgency. Early this year, her son Iker had a series of infections that proved resistant to treatment. "The first two times that I took him to the doctor, they said it was an ear infection and then a throat infection, and they did not draw blood. On the fourteenth of February, we noticed that he had some red dots on his ears. That's when they drew blood. Four days later, they told me he had cancer of the blood"—acute lymphocytic leukemia. Iker has begun a course of chemotherapy at Nationwide Children's Hospital, in Columbus, which is likely to take three or four years.

"Before I had children, I thought about what if the police would pick me up—I would just leave, go back to Mexico, even though I haven't been there in a long time," Flores told me. "Now that my child is sick, I really do worry. Medicine back home is very different. When you go to the doctor, you have to take money before things happen. He has a higher probability of surviving in the United States. Now we *have* to stay."

When I visited the Floreses' apartment, Olga demonstrated a trick with sour cream that she had learned during a stint working at Chipotle. She emptied a five-pound jar into a metal bowl, then whipped it with a wooden spoon. "If you whip it first, it comes out of the squirt bottles easier," she said. The family's duplex is in a town-house development. There are two refrigerators squeezed into the kitchen, to accommodate the restaurant-size quantities of food that the family must buy and prepare every week for the taco truck. Iker sat on the sofa watching cartoons on a big-screen television. He's an outgoing kid, who moves seamlessly between English and Spanish, but he has been having a tough time with the chemotherapy. He's weak and very thin, and has trouble keeping food down. Lately, he has been struggling to walk up the stairs to his bedroom, so Olga is carrying him around more than she once did. His brothers help out, but at this moment they were at the truck, helping their father.

Shortly after Iker's cancer was diagnosed, Flores went to see Julie Nemecek, an immigration lawyer in Columbus, to ask about her options for establishing a more secure basis for remaining in the United States. Nemecek had handled many similar cases before. "Most of the people I hear from have been in Ohio for a long time, and the vast majority are undocumented, because they snuck across the border," she said. "They have made lives here. They have been in hiding, hoping that when they drive to work or take their kids to school they won't get stopped." Nemecek offers clients like Flores little reassurance.

> **"When immigrants are able to work legally—even for a limited time—their wages increase, they seek work compatible with their skill level, and they enhance their skills to obtain higher wages, all of which benefits State economies by increasing income and growing the tax base."**

"Everything is in limbo, so people are uncertain, and they feel hopeless," she said.

When Barack Obama ran for the Presidency, he pledged to enact comprehensive immigration reform, but he didn't push the issue in his first two years in office, when Democrats had strong majorities in both houses of Congress. Instead, he made what became known as a "down payment" for a bipartisan immigration bill later in his Presidency.

"There was definitely in the Obama Administration an intention to do tough enforcement as a down payment for comprehensive immigration reform later," Marc Rosenblum, of the Migration Policy Institute, a nonpartisan think tank in Washington, said. Rosenblum is the deputy director of the institute's U.S.-immigration-policy program. "The idea was to prove to Republicans that he could be trusted on enforcement, so that he could get a path to citizenship in return."

The first part of the down payment was to toughen enforcement at the Mexican border. Under Obama, a record number of agents are patrolling the border: nearly twenty thousand, roughly five times as many as there were two decades ago. In the light of this change, the Obama Administration has claimed that the number of illegal immigrants crossing the border has reached a forty-year low. (The faltering economy during Obama's first term, which made the United States a less promising destination, was certainly another important factor in the decline.)

The more controversial part of Obama's down payment involved immigrants who had already arrived and settled in the United States. The Administration greatly expanded a program known as Secure Communities, in which information was shared between Immigration and Customs Enforcement and the FBI. Whenever anyone was arrested and booked, his or her fingerprints would be sent to the FBI, as before, but now the information would also go to the immigration authorities. "It was a huge force multiplier," Rosenblum said. "The program was pitched as a tool to find serious criminals, but, at least initially, the vast majority of people were picked up for traffic violations and very minor offenses. A lot of these people ended up being deported." Julie Nemecek recalled, "Around 2010, the number of my Mexican clients increased, with enforcement getting really, really heavy because of Secure Communities. People were getting picked up left and right when their only offense was driving without a license or drunk driving." As a result of tougher enforcement, deportations soared under Obama. Since 2009, removals of illegal immigrants have averaged more than four hundred thousand per year, compared with an average of two hundred and fifty thousand per year under George W. Bush.

Secure Communities had an enormous impact on the day-to-day lives of Latinos in the United States. "There are people who are not a safety threat who are snared into the deportation apparatus," Clarissa Martínez, the deputy vice-president of the National Council of La Raza, a leading Hispanic-rights organization, told me. "Also, when you start deputizing local law enforcement to help apply immigration law, you are going to have abuses, and that's what happened. People feel that regardless of whether you are first-, second-, third-generation American, the folks who are going to be stopped are going to be Latinos." Rosenblum said, "Until the last decade or so, the chances were, if you made it past the border, you were not going to get deported, unless you were committing serious crimes. But, with the crackdown, the broader immigrant community felt under attack. They lived here, and suddenly they were unable to work, unable to drive."

Still, the underlying theory was that Secure Communities would be the stick, and comprehensive immigration reform would be the carrot—and the goal appeared within reach after Obama was reëlected, in 2012. The defeat of Mitt Romney brought Republicans to the realization that they had to broaden their appeal to Hispanics, the fastest-growing group of potential voters in the nation. In March of 2013, Reince Priebus, the chairman of the Republican National Committee, released a report that said the Party "must embrace and champion comprehensive immigration reform." In short order, many Republicans in the Senate, including such prominent figures as John McCain and Marco Rubio, did just that, and a bill that included a path to citizenship for people like Olga Flores passed by a vote of sixty-eight to thirty-two.

The battle over immigration reform presents a clash of fundamentally different visions of the role of the federal government. The President and his allies assert that their position is based on a combination of realism and compassion. They argue that it's impossible to deport all of the country's illegal immigrants. In addition, they say, it's heartless to break up families who are long settled in the United States.

Opponents of reform, who are led by Jeff Sessions, a Republican senator from Alabama, believe that national security, along with the rule of law, compels a different approach. "If everyone who enters the country illegally can stay and become a citizen, that just encourages more people to come illegally," Sessions told me. "If people see that they have nothing to fear after they cross the border and settle here, then that creates an incentive for more people to come, and that's wrong. If they are here illegally, they should be deported." What's more, he argues, a porous border invites criminals, including terrorists, to settle in the promised land of the United States.

Yet John Boehner, the Republican Speaker of the House, and Eric Cantor, the Majority Leader, described themselves as supporters of immigration reform, and it was clear after the 2012 election that the votes were there to pass it. "Boehner promised the President that he was going to bring a bill to the floor," a former White House aide told me. "There's always a significant House-versus-Senate rivalry, so the Senate bill itself was going to be a nonstarter in the House. But some sort of reform bill was sure to pass if it came to a vote." Virtually all of the Democrats in the House, as well as some Republicans, supported comprehensive reform along the lines of the Senate bill, but immigration reform was anathema to the Tea Party. Boehner asked staff from the House leadership to come up with a proposal that modified the Senate bill without gutting it. The result was an outline of recommendations, but conservatives in the House persuaded Boehner to back away from them.

After the passage of the Senate bill, chances for any sort of reform bill in the House began to recede. The government shutdown, for two weeks in October of 2013, poisoned relations between the President and congressional Republicans. Then, on June 10, 2014, Cantor lost a primary to a poorly funded and largely unknown challenger, who focussed his campaign on Cantor's alleged softness on illegal immigration. The victor, David Brat, went on to win the seat. Republican support for reform suddenly vanished. As the former White House aide told me, "There was always this germ of hope, but then Eric Cantor lost his primary. There was probably a five-per-cent chance before that, and it went to zero."

Olga Flores speaks English imperfectly, so some of our conversations were interpreted by Jessica Pantaleon Camacho, who works as an assistant in Julie Nemecek's law office. Pantaleon Camacho was born in Mexico twenty years ago and brought to the U.S. illegally as a three-year-old. "When I started going to high school, I convinced myself that school was the only way I could get my family out of the situation," she told me. "I took all Advanced Placement classes starting in my sophomore

year. I graduated near the top of my class." Her teachers wrote enthusiastic recommendations to colleges, and Pantaleon Camacho was accepted at several schools,
with scholarship offers. "When I was about to graduate, we had to decide what
school," she said. "That's when they told me that I needed a Social Security number.
I wasn't able to provide it."

Pantaleon Camacho is among the "Dreamers," the term that has come to define
the group of people who were brought illegally to the United States when they were
children. The Development, Relief, and Education for Alien Minors Act, known
as the DREAM Act, was presented several years ago as a modest alternative to
the round of comprehensive immigration reform that was stalled in Congress at
the time. The law would provide a path to citizenship for people like Pantaleon
Camacho, who had essentially lived their entire lives as Americans. It failed, and the
President began taking a series of unilateral executive actions designed to ease the
plight of the Dreamers. On June 15, 2012, the Obama Administration announced
the Deferred Action for Childhood Arrivals program, known as DACA. The program
would give as many as 1.7 million people work authorization and a two-year reprieve
from deportation, which was renewable for another two years. In most cases, this
meant that the Dreamers were also eligible for driver's licenses and, in some states,
for in-state tuition at state universities. Almost eight hundred thousand individuals
applied for DACA coverage, and about eighty-four percent of them were approved.

Pantaleon Camacho was one of them. "It has changed my life," she told me. "I
have a Social Security number and a driver's license. I am able to drive without fear
of being pulled over and being sent back to Mexico." Her job in the lawyer's office
is on the books. She was admitted to Bowling Green, a state university in Ohio, but
she is ineligible for any scholarship assistance, so she takes classes at a local community college. "It all comes out of my own pocket," Pantaleon Camacho told me.
Her situation is much improved but still tenuous: her DACA status expires roughly
at the end of the Obama Administration, and no one knows what the next President
will do with the program.

DACA did nothing to help families like the Floreses, in which the parents
came to the U.S. as adults and the children were born here. By 2014, immigration
activists began putting greater pressure on Obama to take executive action to help
more families. "When Boehner pulled out of the process, that's when there was a
total focus on the President, because the legislative door had been shut," Clarissa
Martínez, of La Raza, said. The White House felt the heat. "There was a period in
2014 when the immigration activists gave up on Congress and said it's now on the
President," the former White House aide said. "They started calling him Deporter-
in-Chief. The President brought them all in. He said by criticizing him they were
letting the Republicans off the hook. He said he needed more time. He said, 'I will
do everything I can at the end of the summer.' " But Democratic Senate candidates
in competitive races, like Kay Hagan, in North Carolina, implored the White House
not to take any controversial steps on immigration before the midterm elections.
Obama agreed; activists seethed; virtually all the Democratic candidates, including
Hagan, lost anyway.

Finally, on November 20, 2014, just a few weeks after the elections, Obama launched his long-awaited series of executive actions on immigration. As the President explained in a rare prime-time address from the White House, the centerpiece was an initiative called Deferred Action for Parents of Americans and Lawful Permanent Residents, known as DAPA. This program, which would be run by the Department of Homeland Security, was aimed at the parents of American citizens who were themselves illegally in the country but had been law-abiding residents of the United States since 2010. Following a case-by-case review, they would receive an immigration status known as "deferred action," enabling them to apply for work permits and driver's licenses. DAPA was intended to cover about 3.6 million people, more than thirty per cent of the illegal immigrants in the United States. The D.H.S. made plans to hire as many as three thousand new employees, some of whom would work in Arlington, Virginia, in an eleven-story building that the government leased for $7.8 million a year. (Also on November 20th, Obama expanded eligibility for the DACA program, and replaced Secure Communities with a program that targets serious criminals.) According to Obama's plan, the government would begin accepting applications for deferred action under DAPA in February, 2015.

"DAPA is of tremendous magnitude," Clarissa Martínez said. "It's what Americans want of the undocumented community—that they come forward, go through criminal-background checks, and those who are working do so legally. For the American public, it sounds practical and pragmatic to give people who have deep roots in the community and have good moral character a chance to get right with the law. The announcement of these programs was an incredible step forward and the biggest progress we've seen on the issue in two decades."

The Floreses pride themselves on using fresh, authentic ingredients for their food truck. Olga showed off a large maguey leaf, from a variety of agave, which David was about to cut up, toast, and use as a seasoning for the meat before he grilled it. "The best things," Olga said.

Olga Flores has not closely followed the twists and turns in immigration policy, but, like most immigrants, she was aware of DAPA and planned to take advantage of it. There is a cruel asymmetry to immigration law: the people with the most at stake have the most trouble understanding it. This is because, even for lawyers, immigration law is notoriously complicated. It's related to, but ultimately very different from, other criminal or civil litigation; immigration law has its own traditions and doctrines—and the rules often change. For civilians, the morass is difficult to navigate, and for non-English-speaking immigrants the law can be nearly impenetrable. Still, everyone knew that Obama's November 20th directives were hugely significant. On the night of Obama's speech, many immigration-rights groups around the country held viewing parties to celebrate the news. Flores was hopeful, too. "We were very excited," she told me.

But two weeks after Obama's announcement Texas and sixteen other states sued the federal government to stop the DAPA program. Eight states joined later. The heart of the case against the Administration is the contention that Obama overstepped his authority in establishing the program. "The case isn't about any particular immigration policy; it's about the rule of law," Scott Keller, the Texas solicitor general, told me. "DAPA rewrites the immigration statutes, and the executive does not have unilateral authority to do that. Congress has not granted the executive the power to deem people who are unlawfully in the country to be eligible for work permits, Medicare, unemployment benefits, and access to international travel. Congress has done quite the opposite. The executive can't do it alone."

Obama Administration lawyers fired back from several directions. First, they argued that Texas and the other states lacked standing—that is, that they had no right to file the case in the first place, because DAPA imposed no obligations on the states. "The core of Texas's argument is that they will have to pay for driver's licenses for the beneficiaries of DAPA," an Administration official told me. "But that's not enough to get them standing. It's a very incidental expense, and they could raise their prices to cover it, anyway. States don't get to sue just because they don't like the policies of the federal government, and that's what this case is really about." The plaintiffs have argued that they have standing because DAPA will encourage illegal immigration, which would be an imposition on states. Yet fourteen states and the District of Columbia filed a friend-of-the-court brief in support of DAPA, asserting that the program would actually help, not burden, individual states. "When immigrants are able to work legally—even for a limited time—their wages increase, they seek work compatible with their skill level, and they enhance their skills to obtain higher wages, all of which benefits State economies by increasing income and growing the tax base," the brief explains.

On the merits, too, Administration lawyers argued that the President was within his rights to extend these benefits to undocumented people. "This whole case is a matter of enforcement priorities," the official said. "We can deport four hundred thousand people a year, but we can't deport all eleven million undocumented people here, so the President has a right to establish his priorities for the limited time he is in office. And he's saying that he is not going to deport people with children and ties to the community who are willing to undergo a background check." George H. W. Bush had a similar program for a select group of immigrants, and it proceeded with little fanfare and no legal challenge.

Like the plaintiffs in many civil cases, the Texas solicitor general had wide latitude in choosing the court where he wanted to file the suit. Lawyers often do some judge-shopping if they think it will help them win their cases, and it was quickly evident that the Texas lawyers shopped wisely. Keller's predecessor brought the lawsuit in Brownsville, close to the Mexican border. The local federal judge assigned to the case, Andrew Hanen, had already shown a marked hostility toward President Obama's immigration policies. Hanen had been appointed to the district court in 2002 by George W. Bush, and, in earlier rulings, he had called the President's deportation policy "misguided" and asserted that it "endangers America."

According to the President's plan, the government was going to begin accepting applications for deferred action under DAPA on February 18th. Less than forty-eight hours before the program went into effect, Judge Hanen filed a hundred-and-twenty-three-page opinion issuing a preliminary injunction that put DAPA on hold.

In the case known as *Texas v. United States*, he ruled that Texas and the other states did have standing to challenge the law, and then he ruled against the Administration on an esoteric but important matter. Hanen held that the Administration had failed to follow the correct procedures in putting DAPA into effect; he said that the Department of Homeland Security should have given the public the chance to be heard in what's known as notice-and-comment rule-making before implementing the new policy. The opinion did not directly address the underlying legality of DAPA, but the judge offered clear hints that he was dubious about the program. DAPA "does not represent mere inadequacy; it is complete abdication," Hanen wrote. "The D.H.S. does have discretion in the manner in which it chooses to fulfill the expressed will of Congress. It cannot, however, enact a program whereby it not only ignores the dictates of Congress, but actively acts to thwart them."

In a further rebuff to the Administration, Judge Hanen issued a stay on DAPA covering the entire country, even though his jurisdiction covered only part of Texas. Administration lawyers rushed an appeal of Hanen's stay to the United States Court of Appeals for the Fifth Circuit—one of the most conservative circuits in the country. On May 26th, a panel of the appeals court ruled, two judges to one, that Hanen was correct to enjoin DAPA. Earlier this month, during a hearing before another three-judge panel, the same two judges maintained their skepticism about Obama's immigration initiative. Regardless of what the Fifth Circuit ultimately rules, the losing party will still have the right to appeal to the Supreme Court. As Jeff Sessions, Obama's chief adversary in Congress, put it, "The courts may take longer than the President will be in office." The Department of Homeland Security has put the plan to hire three thousand people to administer DAPA on indefinite hold.

It's always been a key part of the Administration's plan to establish DAPA before the end of Obama's term, making it difficult for any successor to withdraw a benefit that has already been granted. But by delaying his actions until after the 2014 midterms the President may have given his opponents, in Congress and in the courts, the time and the tools to unravel his most important work on immigration.

The oncology and hematology clinic of Nationwide Children's Hospital is a determinedly sunny place. The furniture in the waiting room is colorful, the pictures on the walls cheerful. Entertainment options for the young patients abound. Iker Flores perched himself on an examination table and quickly lost himself in a video game. His prognosis is good; his cancer has a very high survival rate. Iker has become used to the chemo port affixed to his chest. But the treatment sessions, which last as long as twelve hours at a time, are gruelling. This visit was to check his blood to see if he was ready for a chemo session the next day. The doctors decided to put off treatment for a little while to allow Iker to regain some strength.

The strain on the family, financial and otherwise, is considerable. The Flores children have health insurance through a nonprofit company in Ohio called CareSource, and the hospital has not pressed them for additional payments. But Olga had to give up part-time work cleaning houses to take care of Iker. He had been attending a Head Start program when he became sick, but he's had to drop out. "The timing for DAPA was perfect for us," Olga told me. "Even a few days before he was diagnosed, he was going to school nine to two. Now he can't even go to school. I was helping my husband. Now I can't work."

At one point, immigration represented a kind of exception to the polarization that dominates contemporary politics in Washington. Both George W. Bush and Barack Obama pushed Congress to pass comprehensive immigration reform. And the Senate passed its bipartisan immigration bill only two years ago. But, as the Presidential campaign has heated up, the issue has come to split the parties in stark ways. "The experience under Obama and Bush has upped the ante on what we want to hear from candidates that are vying for the Presidency in 2016," Clarissa Martínez said. "Both Obama and Bush said they wanted to get it done, and their hearts may have been in the right place, but they both ran into trouble with Congress. That's why hearing that somebody believes in immigration reform is not good enough. We want to know what they will do on their own as President."

Trump's comments about immigrants from Mexico drew condemnation from many Republicans for his impolitic tone, but, in their substance, his views are widely shared within the Party. At various times, Jeb Bush, the former Florida governor, Marco Rubio, the Florida senator, and Scott Walker, the Wisconsin governor, all supported versions of immigration reform that would allow people like Olga Flores to become citizens. All have tacked right. Bush has talked recently of a path to "legalized status" for undocumented aliens rather than a path to citizenship; he also said recently that he would repeal DACA and DAPA. Rubio has said that he now favors a piecemeal approach to immigration, rather than a comprehensive bill; and Walker recently said, "I don't believe in amnesty" for those who have entered the country illegally. Rubio and Walker have also denounced DACA and DAPA. The other Republican candidates have talked about immigration almost exclusively in terms of border enforcement. Ted Cruz, the Texas senator, recently asked a group of supporters to "imagine a President that finally, finally, finally secures the borders," and he criticized Obama's "lawlessness and the President's unconstitutional executive amnesty."

Hillary Clinton, in contrast, has staked out a position to the left of President Obama. In an appearance in Las Vegas, in May, Clinton said, "We can't wait any longer for a path to full and equal citizenship." She said it was "beyond absurd" to think that all eleven million illegal immigrants in the country could be deported. And she said that she would expand DACA and DAPA. "If Congress continues to refuse to act, as President I would do everything possible under the law to go even further," she said, suggesting, for example, that she would extend protection to the parents of Dreamers.

For now, though, the only certainty for Olga Flores and others in similar situations is more uncertainty. If Clinton wins, and Congress remains in Republican hands, the new President will be reduced to attempting the same kind of piecemeal executive actions as Obama—if the courts even allow those to proceed. If a Republican wins, Flores's chances of deportation will rise. Either way, the issue will remain on the national agenda, even as the opportunity to come to any solution continues to recede.

Miscalculation on Visas Disrupts Lives of Highly Skilled Immigrants

By Julia Preston
The New York Times, October 1, 2015

In early September, the State Department gave exciting news to tens of thousands of highly skilled legal immigrants in the United States who had been stuck for years in visa backlogs, waiting for green cards. On Oct. 1, they would take a big step forward along the path to their documents, a department bulletin said.

Then, just as suddenly and with no explanation, the department reversed course Sept. 25, sending most of the immigrants—including many people from India and China with advanced degrees and professional careers in the United States—back to where they had been in slow-moving visa lines, dashing their hopes and disrupting their lives.

The problem was that immigration officials realized belatedly that they did not have enough green card visas, which are limited by yearly quotas, for all the immigrants they had allowed to apply for them, Obama administration officials said.

"It was a devastating blow for the workers and their families with skills we are trying to retain in the United States," said Lynden Melmed, a lawyer at Berry, Appleman & Leiden in Washington, who was formerly general counsel of the Department of Homeland Security agency that administers immigration with the State Department. Immigrants who were affected filed a federal lawsuit in Seattle, accusing the administration of "arbitrary and capricious action" that cost them millions of dollars.

The bait-and-switch was also a new setback for President Obama's efforts to make fixes to immigration through executive actions he announced last November. His actions to protect immigrants in the country illegally have been held up by federal courts. New guidelines to speed up green card applications for highly skilled workers were another part of his programs.

The turnabout resulted, officials said, from communication failures between the State Department and Homeland Security. After the State Department published its monthly visa bulletin on Sept. 9 under the new guidelines allowing many thousands of immigrants to apply early for green cards, officials did further hurried calculations and saw that under annual limits, not enough visas were immediately available.

"This revision seriously undermines the stability and predictability of our immigration system," Representatives Zoe Lofgren and Michael Honda, both California Democrats, said in a statement.

Officials at the Homeland Security and State Departments and the White House said they could not comment on the matter because it was under litigation.

Many immigrants caught in the boomerang are on temporary H-1B visas. That program has been under fire from Americans who say foreign workers with the visas displaced them from jobs. But immigrants seeking green cards have been working for some time in specialized fields like science, medicine and technology. They have passed a hurdle requiring their employers to show the Labor Department that no Americans were available for their jobs.

"We have been here years, we have kids here, we bought houses," said Vikram Desai, 33, an electrical engineer from India who has worked on temporary visas for 13 years.

"We consider ourselves future Americans, not temporary workers," said Mr. Desai, a leader of Immigration Voice, a legal immigrants' organization.

But they have been mired in green card backlogs. With a cap of 140,000 employment-based green cards each year, the number of applicants has long exceeded the limit. No country can have more than 7 percent of the visas, so immigrants from India and China must wait for a decade or more.

On Sept. 9, the State Department notified them they would be able to advance early to the next step: filing a formal application. They scrambled to have medical tests and hired lawyers and document translators, paying thousands of dollars in fees. Many postponed travel; some changed plans to marry or move.

> **"We consider ourselves future Americans, not temporary workers," said Mr. Desai, a leader of Immigration Voice, a legal immigrants' organization.**

"People made life-altering decisions," said Aman Kapoor, the founder of Immigration Voice, a national nonprofit group. Only a fraction of at least 50,000 immigrants who expected to move forward will now be able to do so.

They are keenly disappointed because they will not receive new benefits that would have come after their applications were filed, while they waited for their green cards. In that period, immigrants can obtain work permits that allow them to change jobs and employers, freeing them from H-1B constraints tying them to the same employer. In some states, their children can attend college at discounted resident rates. They can travel out of the United States more easily.

Sadhak Sengupta, a medical research scientist from India, said that when he heard the first State Department announcement, "my heart was overjoyed." Now Dr. Sengupta may have to close down his research at the Roger Williams Medical Center in Providence, R.I., where he is part of a team developing a treatment for brain cancer using immunology.

Dr. Sengupta, also a professor at Boston University School of Medicine, came to the United States in 2002. Working on H-1B visas, he began the green card process in 2010. His team's research advances have attracted patients from around the world to the medical center, Dr. Sengupta said. He had plans to start his own biomedical company.

But this year, the federal government unexpectedly failed to renew his H-1B visa. With no green card application, he is scrambling to avoid leaving the United States in December.

"I am so disappointed, I don't have words to describe," Dr. Sengupta said. "Instead of hiring workers here, shall I bundle up my research for a cure for brain tumors and take it back to India? Is that what America wants?"

Lawyers said the episode had shaken immigrants' confidence in the system. "It's no wonder people have so little faith in the government," said Gregory Chen, director of advocacy for the American Immigration Lawyers Association, "when they can't even count their visas."

Immigrants sent thousands of bouquets to Homeland Security headquarters in Washington on Thursday as a mild-mannered protest of their treatment.

The Front Line Against Birthright Citizenship

By Jonathan Blitzer
The New Yorker, September 18, 2015

Last month, Maria Isabel Perales Serna, an undocumented Mexican immigrant who's lived in Texas for the past fourteen years, risked deportation to give a signed and sworn statement as part of a lawsuit against the state. Perales's daughter was born last year in McAllen, Texas, but when Perales went to the Department of State Health Services to obtain a birth certificate she was turned away. (In Texas, hospitals issue a provisional document, and Health Services provides the birth certificate.) No one disputed her daughter's legal status. The problem was that Perales herself did not have proof of identity the state would accept. Now her child is an American citizen without the papers to prove it. Hundreds, possibly thousands, of other parents across Texas are in the same bind. "I worry that, one of these days, they might think my daughter isn't mine, and that they could separate me from my baby," Perales said. "If someone kidnaps my daughter, what am I going to do without papers to prove that I am her mother?"

The denial of a birth certificate can have serious consequences. One mother involved in the lawsuit testified that, without her child's birth certificate, her family no longer qualified for public housing. "The rent is now almost triple what it was before," she said. The same was true for Medicaid. "How will I take care of the baby then, if he gets sick?" she asked. Another mother had to fight to get her son enrolled in the public school system. "They said that if we did not present his birth certificate within thirty days they would expel him," she reported. One American child is stuck in Reynosa, a violent Mexican border town. Without a birth certificate (and, in turn, a passport), he is unable to return.

Birthright citizenship has come under fire this year from Republican Presidential candidates, egged on by Donald Trump. Texas hasn't denied the citizenship of these children, but it has effectively stripped away the rights that would go along with it. "Because of Trump, this is turning into a birthright-citizenship case, but that's not what it is or ever was; not even the state can question whether or not these children are American citizens," Efrén Olivares, a lawyer representing the mothers, told me. Joaquín Castro, a Democrat who represents San Antonio in congress, and who spent a decade in the Texas Legislature, said that the denial of birth certificates reminded him of the voter-ID laws that have passed in Texas and other states in recent years. "It's mostly about putting up obstacles and creating impediments," he told me. According to the lawsuit, which was filed by Texas Rio Grande Legal Aid and the South Texas Civil Rights Project, the state has "acted with the intent to discriminate against the Texas-born children on the basis of their parent's immigration status, depriving the children of the rights, benefits, and privileges granted to all other citizen children."

The problem turns on the *matrícula consular*, an identity card issued by the Mexican Consulate which is overwhelmingly used by undocumented immigrants. In Texas, the parents of an American-born child have to produce identification in order to secure a birth certificate. The list of acceptable documents includes a foreign or American driver's license, an electoral card, and a national identity card. For undocumented parents, who may have lost everything en route to the U.S., most of these papers have either been stolen, lost, or expired, or else are impossible to get, making the *matrícula* their only option. (They could, in theory, have a foreign passport, but it would need an up-to-date American visa to be valid.)

For years, local registrars accepted the *matrícula* without incident, according to country clerks and lawyers across the state. In 2008, Texas officials wrote a letter to the Mexican Consulate in Austin, saying that the *matrícula* would no longer be accepted as proof of identity. (The official reason was concern that the *matrícula* could be used in identity theft. The Mexican government has since taken measures to improve the document's security, but they have not influenced state policy.) Even so, local offices continued to exercise their own discretion, accepting *matrículas* and dispensing birth certificates.

Then, in 2013, immigration lawyers in South Texas started hearing from undocumented immigrants that their *matrículas* were being rejected. "These parents were one-hundred-per-cent shut out," Jennifer Harbury, a lawyer with Texas Rio Grande Legal Aid, said. Health Services had begun to enforce a wider crackdown on *matrículas*. A Health Services official later told lawyers that the policy "was changed to keep undocumented persons from gaining legal status in this country." The reports of rejected *matrículas* had started in the Rio Grande Valley, in South Texas, but soon they were coming from as far west as El Paso.

The timing was suggestive. Tens of thousands of unaccompanied children were streaming across the U.S. border from Central America in what President Obama called a "humanitarian crisis." By the end of last summer, the number of children crossing the border alone had surpassed fifty thousand. The resulting strain on the immigra-

> **Joaquín Castro said he believes the state's response to the lawsuit coincides with a broader effort to create a federal court case around birthright citizenship.**

tion system led to an infusion of federal money to help shelter and process the children. It also gave rise to nativist conspiracy theories. Rick Perry, the Governor of Texas at the time, suggested that Democrats had somehow helped the children over the border. "How do you move that many people from Central America across

Mexico and into the United States without there being a fairly coördinated effort?" he told a news program in June, 2014.

This spring, Texas Rio Grande Legal Aid and the South Texas Civil Rights Project filed their lawsuit against the state, representing four families: six children and four parents. "We thought, O.K., they're going to give us the birth certificates for these kids, then quietly dismiss the case," Efrén Olivares said. Instead, Texas fought back. The Attorney General's office, which is representing the Department of State Health Services, requested that the suit be dismissed, invoking the sovereign-immunity provision of the Eleventh Amendment. Over the summer, twenty-one more families joined the lawsuit, and last month the Mexican government filed an amicus brief in support of the plaintiffs, who are requesting an emergency injunction to force the state to allow two forms of identity documents to be used in place of the *matrículas*. "Our argument isn't: yes *matrícula*, no *matrícula*," Harbury told the Texas *Tribune*. "The argument is: What will you take that people can actually get? They have to take something. [The children] were born here. They are American citizens." A hearing before a federal judge is scheduled for October 2nd.[1]

The state's decision to opt for a protracted legal battle over the use of the *matrícula* has raised questions about its intentions in the case. "It's been brought to the attention of everyone who could possibly resolve the situation—even if it was flying under the radar before—and yet it doesn't get resolved," Denise Gilman, a law professor at the University of Texas, said. "This should be a no-brainer of a case that's resolved quickly. That it hasn't says something about reactions at high levels." (The state has maintained that some of these birth certificates exist on file but cannot be given out without the proper documentation from parents.)

Earlier this week, I spoke to Theresa Daniel, the Dallas County Commissioner, who wrote a letter last month to the federal judge hearing the case. "I am concerned about the legal and constitutional issues being raised due to our stance on the refusal to issue birth certificates to persons born in the United States and residing in Dallas County," she wrote. "I am aware of the concerns about the reliability of the consular identification document. However, I am hard pressed to imagine how its use in this context poses any threat of identity theft, fraud, or other abuse." Daniel's office was audited by the Department of Health in June, and she and her colleagues have since had to follow the new protocol.

When we spoke by phone, Daniel was reluctant to cast blame. "I can only guess," she said, when I asked her who might be behind the effort to fight back against the lawsuit. "It's obviously coming from high up," Jim Harrington, the director of the Texas Civil Rights Project, said, about where the order to fight the lawsuit might have originated. "The general counsel for the Health Department has been pushing this. But it's hard to imagine that it's just coming from the Health Department." So far, the Attorney General's office has declined to comment, citing the ongoing nature of the case.

Joaquín Castro said he believes the state's response to the lawsuit coincides with a broader effort to create a federal court case around birthright citizenship. "Texas is a laboratory of conservative rebellion," he told me. (A spokesman for the

Department of State Health Services foreswore any hidden agenda, and simply said that "State and local registrars have a duty to protect [vital records] by insuring they only release records to people who are qualified to obtain them.")

Late last year, Texas led twenty-five other states in a lawsuit against the federal government to halt and dismantle President Obama's executive order on immigration. One part of the order is a program called Deferred Action for Parents of Americans (DAPA), which would protect law-abiding immigrant parents of American children from prosecution. For a parent to become eligible for relief under DAPA, she must be able to prove that her child is a citizen, and for that she needs a birth certificate. Even if DAPA is implemented, Texas may be able to prevent the program from having its full effect. Two weeks after the President released his executive order, the Solicitor General of Texas denounced DAPA and justified his state's opposition. His posture was "not about a particular immigration policy," he maintained. "It's about the rule of law."

Note

1. On October 16, U.S. District Judge Robert L. Pitman denied the request for a temporary emergency injunction requested by the plaintiffs, and instead order a full evidentiary hearing for the case.

2
Immigration Labor, Activism, and Human Rights

A rally organized by the Georgia Latino Alliance for Human Rights and the Georgia-based #Not1More Coalition was held to denounce raids conducted by Immigration and Custom Enforcement (ICE) on January 2, 2016 that targeted immigrant families. Azadeh Shahshahani, legal and advocacy director for Project South, says that the January 2 raids further traumatized families already fleeing violence.

Laboring for Human Rights

Worldwide, more than 232 million people live outside their countries of origin. Migrants travel for jobs, to escape oppression and violence, and for a variety of other reasons, and the choice to migrate has enormous consequences for the cultures and economies of both host and native nations. There are some who believe the right to migrate for work or to escape dangerous political/social upheaval should be a basic human right, while others believe that national security depends on managing, restricting, and monitoring immigration. Immigrant workers play an important role in workers' rights movements in many nations and the treatment of immigrant laborers has become a key human rights issue in the United States, particularly for unauthorized migrants, who lack adequate political and social protections and are therefore especially vulnerable to exploitation and abuse.

Motivations of Unauthorized Immigration

In 2014, there were an estimated 11.3 million unauthorized immigrants living in the United States, constituting an estimated 3.5 percent of the population. Rates of illegal immigration peaked in 2007 and dropped during the financial crisis of 2008–2009. Nearly half of all unauthorized immigrants are from Mexico, though the number of Mexican migrants has been declining in the 2010s as a result of increased border security and a reduction in employment opportunities. A rising number of immigrants have come from the Middle East, Africa, and Central America in the 2010s, partially resulting from political and social upheaval in those regions.[1]

Some sociologists have noted that the cultural patterns supporting border crossing (legal and illegal) have existed since before the first Anglo settlers arrived in North America. Until 1964, initiatives like the Bracero Program welcomed migrants from Mexico and Central America, providing millions of temporary visas that supported a culture of seasonal migration for work. Though the 1965 changes in immigration law were meant to protect this migratory population from exploitation, ultimately immigration reform drastically reduced temporary visa availability and led to a massive increase in unauthorized migration. Finally, trade agreements decimated Mexican and Central American agricultural industries, while bolstering those in the United States, and led to a far stronger economic motivation for northern migration.[2]

Immigrant Rights and Abuse

The motivations for unauthorized migration are so strong that migrants will risk imprisonment, detainment, deportation, and dangerous border-crossing conditions that claim hundreds of lives each year. Along the borders of the United States and

Mexico, immigrants will pay as much as $3000 to members of organized crime groups, called "coyotajes" to smuggle them across borders. As border enforcement increases, the coyotaje gangs have been the primary beneficiaries, earning an estimated $6 billion per year through human trafficking. The rise of the coyotaje gangs has also deepened the immigration rights crisis. Coyotaje sometimes kidnap migrants, holding them for ransom until they receive payment from their families. Women have reported being sexually assaulted, and some migrants have been found murdered in the deserts and remote passages used by the criminal gangs.[3]

In 2014, Human Rights Watch reported that the housing of immigrant detainees awaiting trial has become a serious human rights concern. Current laws place no restrictions on the length of time an immigrant may be held in detention without legal support, and human rights workers have argued that many detention facilities fail to meet minimum standards. Detainees considered potentially dangerous or disruptive can be held in solitary confinement for periods of up to two months, despite United Nations conventions holding that solitary confinement for more than two weeks is a form of torture. Federal investigations further suggest that many detainees suffer from malnutrition and potential mental health issues.[4] In 2011, the American Civil Liberties Union (ACLU) reported 200 allegations of sexual abuse from undocumented migrants held in detention facilities across the nation, though the ACLU estimates that the actual number of instances may far exceed those reported. In some cases, detainees claimed that they had been sexually assaulted by other detainees, while others said they had been assaulted by detention center employees or guards.[5]

In the 2014 book *The Ethics of Immigration*, political scientist Joseph Carens argues that, over time, unauthorized migrants become defacto citizens and he questions the morality of deporting individuals who have been working and living in the nation for extended periods, many having children who have grown up living as Americans. While Carens agrees that the nation has the political right to defend its borders, he also questions the morality of continuing to do so as America, the world's most economically dominant nation, shares a border with a developing nation in which more than half of the population lives in poverty.[6] Supporters of this position argue further that current immigration policies have led to a situation where the United States continues to benefit from immigrant labor but in refusing to give them legal status leaves these populations vulnerable to exploitation and abuse.

Immigrants and Labor

The U.S. labor movement, for most of its existence, sided with anti-immigration advocates on the basis that immigrants depressed wages and took jobs that might otherwise be available to native-born workers. In 2000, the AFL-CIO (American Federation of Labor Organizations) voted to reverse their position on immigration for the first time in the organization's history. In press releases, the AFL-CIO held that immigrants had become an important part of the nation's labor force and that there should be a clear path to citizenship for immigrants currently in the United

States and an increase in temporary labor permits for Latin American workers. Further, AFL-CIO spokespeople argued that the current system allows companies and employers to exploit the illegal status of workers, paying them low wages and offering them little in the form of benefits or worker's compensation.[7]

Economic analyses going back to before the First World War have demonstrated that immigrants make tremendous contributions to the American labor force. In 2010, the Brookings Institution estimated that foreign-born individuals constituted 16.4 percent of the American labor force. In Texas, which has a population of 4.2 million immigrants (both authorized and unauthorized), immigrant owned businesses contributed $4.4 billion to the state's economy in 2011 (one fifth of the total) and contributed $65 billion to the state in wages, salary, and business earnings. Unauthorized immigrants alone contributed more than $1.6 billion in state taxes in 2010. While other states do not enjoy the same degree of immigrant contributions as Texas, New Jersey, and New York—states that attract a disproportionate number of immigrants—both legal immigrants and unauthorized migrants contribute significantly to America's productivity, labor market, and GDP growth.[8] One phenomenon driving the conflation of immigrant and labor interests has been the growing influence of immigrant activism, pushing for workers' rights protections, educational benefits, and immigration reform.

Immigrant Activism

In addition to supporting the broader labor movement, immigrant activism has evolved into a powerful force in American politics. The Florida Immigrant Coalition, for instance, has been instrumental in educational reforms enacted in Florida, such as a 2014 law that gave in-state college tuition rates to Florida's undocumented high school graduates. Across the nation, politicians hoping to reach out to the large and growing Latino/Hispanic voting population have embraced reforms to state immigration policies that reduce penalties and restrictions for young immigrants and the children of immigrants, allowing these populations more freedom to attend schools, pursue higher education, and have access to public services. The 2001 Development, Relief, and Education for Alien Minors (DREAM) Act, has created a new generation of activists, popular across partisan lines because, as young people whose parents made the decision to migrate illegally, the "DREAMers" are typically seen as comparatively innocent. Most notably, some proposals to help this population of undocumented Americans have come from Republican politicians who have otherwise taken a hard stance on the issue.[9]

Immigration activism can take a variety of forms. Immigrant activists in the DREAMer generation have helped to bring the immigration issue onto the web, using videos, Twitter, and social media to publicize their efforts and draw public support. The success of immigrant activism can be seen in the growing number of local immigrant rights organizations in smaller cities around the country, providing outreach, legal aid, and helping to organize political rallies and meetings to lobby state and federal legislators for reform.

Though primarily Latino, the youth activist system embraces the issues faced by immigrants from all nations. Razeen Zaman, whose parents attempted to legally migrate from Bangladesh but later lost their legal status due to dealings with an unethical immigration attorney, is one example of a non-Latino immigrant activist who has been campaigning to change current deportation laws. Zaman argues that even immigrants who are trying to maintain their legal status can find their efforts stymied by unethical lawyers, corruption, or unclear legal procedures. Most of the nation's undocumented population are not those who illegally crossed the nation's borders, but are individuals who, for a variety of reasons, lost their permission to stay. Many, while legal residents, formed families and found jobs and, when their status is revoked, they make the difficult decision to stay in their homes, jobs, and with their loved ones, even though doing so puts them at risk.[10]

Micah L. Issitt

Notes

1. Krogstad and Passel, "5 Facts About Illegal Immigration in the U.S."
2. Planas, "These Are the Real Reasons Behind Illegal Immigration."
3. Eichenwald, "Illegal Immigration: Myths, Half-Truths, and a Hole in Trump's Wall."
4. Urbina and Rentz, "Immigrants Held in Solitary Cells, Often for Weeks."
5. "Sexual Abuse in Immigrant Detention Facilities," ACLU.
6. Gutting and Carens, "When Immigrants Lose Their Human Rights."
7. Gonyea, "How the Labor Movement Did a 180 on Immigration."
8. Beeson, Helmcamp, and Cerna. "Immigrants Drive the Texas Economy."
9. Johnson, "How a New Class of Activists Is Changing Immigration Politics."
10. Diaz, "How 5 DREAMers Are Rethinking Their Role in the Immigrant Rights Movement."

Illegal Immigrant Detention Centers Rife with Abuses, U.S. Civil Rights Commission Report Finds

By Stephen Dinan
The Washington Times, September 17, 2015

The way the government detains illegal immigrants often breaks fundamental constitutional guarantees, and holding whole families in detention is a particularly harsh abuse of human rights, the U.S. Civil Rights Commission said in a controversial new report Thursday, wading deeply into the immigration debate.

Some detention facilities—both government-run and private ones operating on contracts—don't provide good medical care, deny illegal immigrants the chance to try to get lawyers to help them with their cases, look the other way when rape or sexual abuse occurs, don't allow Muslims adequate leeway to celebrate Ramadan, and mistreat transgender detainees, the majority report concluded.

Two of the eight commissioners issued stinging rebuttals, questioning whether the commission even had jurisdiction to look at immigration enforcement, and portraying the report as rehashed innuendo and discredited accusations.

But the majority said the abuses the commission found were so egregious that the administration should immediately release all families being held, and urged Congress to withdraw funding overall, saying the government should find other ways to track illegal immigrants rather than holding them in detention.

"From calling immigrants 'illegal aliens' and 'invading hordes,' to the most recent rantings of presidential candidates spewing anti-immigrant, anti-Latino and anti-Mexican vitriol, we have witnessed the creation of an environment which condones the inhumane treatment of immigrants, especially those coming from Latin America," commission Chairman Martin R. Castro wrote, accusing Homeland Security of subjecting illegal immigrants to "torture-like conditions."

The report was adopted by five of the eight commissioners. One of the eight recused herself, while the two dissenters said the majority got snookered by immigrant-rights advocates.

"It is said that where there is smoke, there is fire. But sometimes where there is smoke, there is only a smoke-making machine, busily stoked by publicists working for activist organizations," said Gail Heriot, one of the dissenting commissioners.

Homeland Security spokeswoman Marsha Catron said they were reviewing the report, but said they take the care of immigrants in their custody seriously. She said they've made steady improvements, including major changes Secretary Jeh Johnson announced in June to speed illegal immigrants through detention as quickly as possible.

"We are transitioning these facilities into short-term processing centers where individuals who claim fear of return to their countries can be interviewed for asylum and other humanitarian protections. Families who establish a credible or reasonable fear of persecution will be released under conditions designed to ensure their compliance with their immigration obligations," Ms. Catron said.

Homeland Security has also agreed not to use detention as a deterrent to other would-be illegal immigrants, and to request lower bonds that illegal immigrants might be able to post.

But Mr. Castro said that is "nothing but lip service," and there has been little change on the ground.

The commission's report comes at a touchy time in the immigration debate.

The findings echo what some Democratic presidential candidates have argued on the campaign trail. But Republican candidates are tilting the other direction, questioning why the Obama administration has been unable to detain and deport more illegal immigrants.

The surge of both unaccompanied illegal immigrant children and mothers traveling with young children, who have jumped the border in record numbers over the last few years, have tested the administration's abilities.

And a federal judge in California has been looking at the family detention facilities, and has issued a preliminary finding that Homeland Security is in violation of a 1997 agreement on how children should be treated when in custody.

Advocacy groups and the Homeland Security Department are still hashing that case out.

U.S. Immigration and Customs Enforcement, the agency that handles detention and deportation, set up thousands of new beds in special facilities designed to hold families, complete with athletic fields, clinics, school rooms and snacks.

Before the additional beds were added, most illegal immigrant families were released into the population, where they were much less likely to show up for their deportation proceedings.

The Civil Rights Commission, though, said the way the government treats families could violate their due process rights, particularly when facilities make it difficult for illegal immigrants to retain or stay in contact with lawyers.

The report had particularly harsh criticism of private facilities contracted to hold illegal immigrants, saying they often appear to run afoul of federal treatment guidelines.

Under congressional mandates, Homeland Security is required to maintain an average of 34,000 detention beds a day—though the administration says it's not actually required to fill them all.

The Obama administration has argued it is often more cost-effective and humane to release illegal immigrants under alternatives to detention, such as ankle-monitoring or having them check in by phone.

Sen. Bernard Sanders, Vermont independent, and three House Democrats introduced a bill

"From calling immigrants 'illegal aliens' and 'invading hordes,' to the most recent rantings of presidential candidates spewing anti-immigrant, anti-Latino and anti-Mexican vitriol, we have witnessed the creation of an environment which condones the inhumane treatment of immigrants, especially those coming from Latin America."

Thursday that would, among other steps, eliminate the 34,000-bed mandate and encourage more use of alternatives.

The Washington Times reported in June that nearly all of those released under electronic monitoring broke the terms of their release, with many of them racking up multiple violations. All told, the 41,000 immigrants put on electronic monitoring notched 300,000 violations in 2014, the *Times* reported.

The commission's report compiles accusations advocacy groups have lodged for years—some of them having already been investigated and dismissed by internal watchdogs such as the Government Accountability Office or the inspector general's office within Homeland Security.

For example, an American Civil Liberties Union complaint listing more than 100 abuses of unaccompanied minors last year was found to be unsubstantiated by the inspector general.

And reports from both the GAO and inspector general found agents going above and beyond their duties to care for some of the children.

Immigrant Labor, Immigrant Rights

By David Bacon
NACLA Report on the Americas, April 10, 2014

In the late 1970s, the U.S. Congress began to debate the bills that eventually resulted in the 1986 Immigration Reform and Control Act (IRCA)—still the touchstone for ongoing battles over immigration policy. The long congressional debate set in place the basic dividing line in the modern immigrant rights movement.

IRCA contained three elements. It reinstituted a guest worker program by setting up the H2-A visa category; it penalized employers who hired undocumented workers and required them to check the immigration status of every worker; and it set up a one-time amnesty process for undocumented workers who were in the country before 1982. Guest workers (i.e. workers whose immigrant status was tied to temporary, specific jobs), employer sanctions, and some form of legalization still occupy the main floor of the debate.

The AFL-CIO supported sanctions, believing they would stop undocumented immigration (and therefore, presumably, job competition with citizen or legal resident workers). Employers wanted guest workers. The Catholic Church and a variety of Washington DC liberals supported amnesty and were willing to agree to guest workers and enforcement as a tradeoff. Organized immigrant communities and leftist immigrant rights advocates opposed the bill, as did local labor leaders and activists, but they were not strong enough to change organized labor's position nationally The Washington-based coalition produced the votes in Congress, and on November 6, 1986, Ronald Reagan signed the bill into law.

Once the bill had passed, many of the local organizations that had opposed it set up community-based coalitions to deal with the bill's impact. In Los Angeles, with the country's largest concentration of undocumented Mexican and Central American workers, pro-immigrant labor activists set up centers to help people apply for amnesty. That effort, together with earlier, mostly left-led campaigns to organize undocumented workers, built the base for the later upsurge of immigrant activism that changed the politics and labor movement of the city. Elsewhere, local immigrant advocates set up coalitions to look for ways to defend undocumented workers against the impact of employer sanctions. Grassroots coalitions then began helping workers set up centers for day laborers, garment workers, domestic workers, and other groups of immigrants generally ignored by established unions.

Over the years since IRCA, a general division has marked the U.S. immigrant rights movement. On one side are well-financed advocacy organizations in Washington DC, with links to the Democratic Party and the business community. They formulate and negotiate immigration reform proposals that combine labor supply programs and increased enforcement against the undocumented. On the other side are organizations based in immigrant communities, and among labor and political activists, who defend undocumented migrants, and who resist proposals for greater enforcement and labor programs with diminished rights.

In the late 1990s, when the Clinton administration acquiesced in efforts to pass repressive immigration legislation (what eventually became the Immigration Reform And Immigrant Responsibility Act), Washington lobbying groups advocated a strategy to allow measures directed at increasing deportations of the undocumented to pass (calling them "unstoppable") while mounting a defense only of legal resident immigrants. Many community-based coalitions withdrew from the Washington lobbying efforts, refusing to cast the undocumented to the wolves.

> **"We have to change the debate from one in which immigration is presented as a problem to a debate over rights. The real problem is exploitation."**

In the labor movement, the growing strength of immigrant workers, combined with a commitment to organize those industries where they were concentrated, created the base for changing labor's position. At the 1999 AFL-CIO convention in Los Angeles, the federation called for the repeal of employer sanctions, for a new amnesty, and for a strong defense of the labor rights of all workers. The federation was already opposed to guest worker programs. The AFL-CIO maintained that position, even after several unions left to form the rival Change to Win federation, until 2009. At that time, a compromise was reached between the two federations, in which they dropped their previous opposition to employer sanctions, so long as they were implemented "fairly."

Over the past decade, a succession of "comprehensive immigration reform" (CIR) bills have been introduced into Congress. At their heart are the guest worker programs proposed by employers. But while the employer lobbies wrote the first bills, they have been supported by a political coalition that includes some unions, beltway immigrant advocacy groups, and some churches. Except for the vacillating and divided position of unions, this is the same political coalition that passed IRCA in 1986. Some local immigrant rights coalitions have also supported the bills, although many others have been unwilling to agree to guest worker programs and more enforcement. Supporters of the comprehensive bills have organized a succession of high-profile lobbying efforts, which received extensive foundation support.

The structure of the bills has been basically the same from the beginning—the same three-part structure of IRCA—guest workers, enforcement, and some degree of legalization. Under the CIR proposals promoted by Washington advocacy groups for several years, people working without papers would continue to be fired and even imprisoned, while raids would increase. Vulnerability makes it harder for people to defend their rights, organize unions, and raise wages. That keeps the price of immigrant labor low.

Enforcement does not stop people from coming to the United States, but it does produce a much larger detention system. Last year over 350,000 people went through privately run prisons for undocumented immigrants, while over 409,000 were deported.

The Washington-based CIR proposals all expand guest worker programs, in which workers have few rights, and no leverage to organize for better conditions. Finally, the CIR legalization measures impose barriers making ineligible many, if not most of the 11 million people who need legal status. They condition legalization on "securing the border," which has become a Washington DC euphemism for a heavy military presence, augmenting 20,000 Border Patrol agents and creating a climate of wholesale denial of civil and human rights in border communities.

A loose network of groups has grown that has generally opposed most CIR bills and their provisions, and that has organized movements on the ground to oppose increased enforcement and repression directed against immigrant communities. Outside the Washington beltway, community coalitions, labor and immigrant rights groups are pushing for alternatives. Some of them are large-scale counters to the entire CIR framework. Others seek to win legal status for a part of the undocumented population, as a step towards larger change. Many support the call for a moratorium on deportations.

One of the alternative proposals is the DREAM (Development, Relief, and Education for Alien Minors) Act. First introduced in 2001, the bill would allow undocumented students graduating from a U.S. high school to apply for permanent residence if they complete two years of college or serve two years in the U.S. military. For seven years thousands of young *"sin papeles,"* or people without papers, marched, sat-in, wrote letters, and mastered every civil rights tactic to get their bill onto the Washington agenda.

Many of them have "come out," declaring openly their lack of legal immigration status in media interviews, defying authorities to detain them. The DREAM Act campaigners did more than get a vote in Washington. They learned to stop deportations in an era in which more people have been deported than ever since the days of the Cold War.

When it was originally written, the bill would have allowed young people to qualify for legalization with 900 hours of community service, as an alternative to attending college, which many can not afford. However, when the bill was introduced, the Pentagon pressured to substitute military for community service, though even with that change, Congress did not pass the bill. In the heat of the 2012 presidential campaign, however, "dreamers" sat in at President Obama's Chicago reelection office and demonstrated nationwide, leading Obama to issue an executive order "deferring" the deportation of DREAM Act-eligible young people. Today, many immigrant rights activists view the DREAM Act as an important step towards a more basic reform of the country's immigration laws, and also see the dreamers' strategy as proof that absent Congressional action the administration has the ability, if not the political will, to end mass deportations.

Supporting the DREAM Act and other partial protections for the undocumented are worker centers around the country. Worker centers have anchored the protests against repression in Arizona, and fought to pass laws in California, New York, and elsewhere, prohibiting police from turning people over to immigration agents. They have developed grassroots models for organizing migrants who get jobs on street corners. These projects have come together in the National Day Labor Organizing Network. The National Domestic Worker Alliance was organized in part using the

---

Alternative Immigrant Demands

The Dignity Campaign, FiOB, and AFSC proposals, are not just alternative programs for changing laws and policies, but implicit strategies of alliances based on mutual interest. They advocate the following:

- Give Permanent Residence visas, or Green Cards, to undocumented people already here, and expand the number of Green Cards available for new migrants.

- Eliminate the years-long backlog in processing family reunification visas, strengthening families and communities.

- End the enforcement that has led to thousands of deportations and firings.

- Repeal employer sanctions, and enforce labor rights and worker protection laws, for all workers.

- End all guest worker programs.

- Dismantle the border wall and demilitarize the border, so fewer people die crossing it, and restore civil and human rights in border communities.

- Respond to recession and foreclosures with jobs programs to guarantee income, and remove the fear of job competition.

- Redirect the money spent on the wars in Iraq and Afghanistan to rebuild communities, refinancing mortgages, and restoring the social services needed by working families.

- Renegotiate existing trade agreements to eliminate causes of displacement and prohibit new trade agreements that displace people or lower living standards.

- Prohibit local law enforcement agencies from enforcing immigration law, end roadblocks, immigration raids and sweeps, and close detention centers.

—DB

---

experience of day labor organizing, to win rights for domestic workers, almost all of whom are women. It won passage of a domestic worker bill of rights in New York and California. Other projects organize groups with a large immigrant contingent, from taxi drivers to garment workers.

Another group advocating an alternative to CIR is the Binational Front of Indigenous Organizations (FIOB). The group has conducted a series of organized discussions among its California chapters to formulate a progressive position on immigration reform, with the unique perspective of an organization of migrants and migrant-sending communities. FIOB campaigns for the rights of migrants in the United States—for immigration amnesty and legalization for undocumented migrants—while also campaigning against proposals for guest worker programs. At the same time, comments Gaspar Rivera Salgado, FIOB's bi-national coordinator, "we need development that makes migration a choice rather than a necessity—the right to stay home. Both rights are part of the same solution. We have to change the debate from one in which immigration is presented as a problem to a debate over rights. The real problem is exploitation."

"The governments of both Mexico and the United States are dependent on the cheap labor of Mexicans. They don't say so openly, but they are," says Rufino Domínguez, former bi-national coordinator of the FIOB and now the director of the Oaxacan Institute for Attention to Migrants. "What would improve our situation is legal status for the people already here, and greater availability of visas based on family reunification. Legalization and more visas would resolve a lot of problems—not all, but it would be a big step," he says. "Walls won't stop migration, but decent wages and investing money in creating jobs in our countries of origin would decrease the pressure forcing us to leave home. Penalizing us by making it illegal for us to work won't stop migration, since it doesn't deal with why people come."

> "Walls won't stop migration, but decent wages and investing money in creating jobs in our countries of origin would decrease the pressure forcing us to leave home. Penalizing us by making it illegal for us to work won't stop migration, since it doesn't deal with why people come."

The FIOB proposal on immigration reform is similar to that advanced by the Dignity Campaign, a loose coalition of organizations around the country that has proposed an alternative to the comprehensive labor-supply-plus-enforcement bills. The Dignity Campaign brings together immigrant rights and fair trade organizations to encourage each to see the global connections between trade policy, displacement, and migration. The group also brings together unions and immigrant rights organizations to spur the growth of resistance to immigration enforcement against workers, highlighting the need to oppose the criminalization of work.

The Dignity Campaign proposal draws on previous proposals, particularly one put forward by the American Friends Service Committee called "A New Path"—a set of moral principles for changing U.S. immigration policy. Several other efforts were also made earlier by the National Network for Immigrant and Refugee Rights to define an alternative program and bring together groups around the country to support it.

The critique shared by all these organizations is that the CIR framework ignores trade agreements like NAFTA and CAFTA, which have undercut workers' bargaining power and employment opportunities in Mexico and Central America. Without changing U.S. trade policy and ending structural adjustment programs and neoliberal economic reforms, millions of displaced people will continue to migrate, no matter how many walls are built on the border.

Changing corporate trade policy and stopping neoliberal reforms is as central to immigration reform as gaining legal status for undocumented immigrants. There is a fundamental contradiction in the bipartisan policies in Congress that promotes more free trade agreements, and then criminalizes the migration of the people they displace. Instead, Congress could end the use of the free trade system as a mechanism for producing displaced workers. That would mean delinking immigration status and employment. If employers are allowed to recruit contract labor abroad, and those workers can only stay if they are continuously employed (the two essential characteristics of guest worker programs), then they will never have enforceable rights.

The root problem with migration in the global economy is that it is forced migration. A coalition for reform should fight for the right of people to choose when and how to migrate. Freedom of movement is a human right. Even in a more just world, migration will continue, because families and communities are now connected over thousands of miles and many borders. Immigration policy should therefore make movement easier.

At the same time, workers need basic rights, regardless of immigration status. Progressive immigrant rights advocates call for devoting more resources to enforcing labor standards for all workers, instead of penalizing undocumented workers for working, and employers for hiring them. "Otherwise," Domínguez says, "wages will be depressed in a race to the bottom, since if one employer has an advantage, others will seek the same thing."

To raise the low price of immigrant labor, immigrant workers have to be able to organize, an activity made easier by permanent legal status. Guest worker programs, employer sanctions, enforcement, and raids make organizing much more difficult. Today, the sector of workers with the fewest benefits and the lowest wages is expanding the fastest. Proposals to deny people rights or benefits because of immigration status make this process move even faster. A popular coalition might push back in the other direction, toward more equal status, helping to unite diverse communities.

Such a political coalition might start by seeking mutual interest among workers in a struggle for jobs and rights for everyone. It is not possible to win major changes in immigration policy without making them part of a struggle for the goals of working class communities. To end job competition, for instance, workers need Congress to adopt a full-employment policy. To gain organizing rights for immigrants, all workers need labor law reform.

Winning those demands will require an alliance among workers—immigrants and native-born. Latinos, African Americans, Asian Americans, and whites. An alliance with employers, on the other hand, giving them new guest worker programs, would only increase job competition, push wages down, and make affirmative action impossible.

The basic elements of this alternative include permanent residence visas for the undocumented and new migrants, protecting family reunification, ending the mass deportations and firings, repealing employer sanctions, ending guest worker programs, demilitarizing the border, and changing trade policies that cause forced migration.

A new era of rights and equality for migrants does not begin in Washington DC, any more than the civil rights movement did. Human rights reform is a product of the social movements of this country, especially of people on the bottom, outside the margins of power. A social movement made possible the advances in 1965 that were called unrealistic and politically impossible a decade earlier. An immigration reform proposal based on human and labor rights may not be a viable one in a congress dominated by Tea Party nativists and corporations seeking guest worker programs. But just as it took a civil rights movement to pass the Voting Rights Act, any basic change to establish the rights of immigrants will also require a social upheaval and a fundamental realignment of power.

Mexican Migration-Corridor Hospitality

By Alejandro Olayo-Méndez, Stephen Nathan Haymes, and Maria Vidal de Haymes

Peace Review: A Journal of Social Justice, April–June 2014

The world total of international migrants has more than doubled in twenty-five years, with roughly 25 million added in just the first five years of the twenty-first century. The number of international migrants is greater today than at any other time in history, with 214 million, or one in every thirty-five persons worldwide living outside their country of birth. Nowhere is the trend of international migration more marked than in North America between Mexico and the United States. With an estimated 4.4 million foreign-born residents, the United States is the country with the largest immigrant population in the world. This figure amounts to 13 percent of the total current U.S. population. In contrast, Mexico leads the world as a source country for international migrants and represents 29.5 percent of the total foreign-born population residing in the United States.

While the United States is primarily a destination country for immigrants, Mexico embodies several other dimensions of the migration phenomenon: emigration primarily to the United States, transit migration mainly by Central Americans in route north, temporary immigration from Central American and other countries, and more recently, growing numbers of repatriated Mexican nationals. The number of Central American immigrants in the United States has nearly tripled since 1990, growing faster than any other Latin American region-of-origin immigrant population in the United States in the last decade and increasing from less than 1 percent in 1960 to almost 8 percent in 2011. Recent increases in deportations from the United States have deepened the migration link between the United States, Mexico, and Central American countries.

Unique risk factors and stressors for immigrants occur before and after migration. These can include pre-migration and migration stressors such as previous traumatic exposure in countries of origin, displacement, human trafficking, organized crime, extreme poverty, and natural disasters, which can be compounded by separation from nuclear family members, disruptions in extended family and social networks, arduous and dangerous transnational journeys, detention, and multiple deportations and clandestine border crossings.

Post-migration stressors can include acculturative stress or stress reactions related to the physical, psychological, spiritual, social, financial, linguistic, and familial adjustment migrants experience as they adapt to unfamiliar and new social norms, customs, language, and way of life encountered in a new context. The process of migration and cultural adaptation can also contribute to significant role disruptions and conflicts in families. Families with children and adolescents are particularly vulnerable. Children are often separated from family for extended periods of time due to migration and may experience psychological distress and difficulties reintegrating into their families. The increasingly hostile context for immigrants in the United States, marked by the passage of anti-immigrant state and municipal policies and aggressive federal immigration enforcement initiatives, such as Secure Communities, have added a tremendous strain on this population.

Immigrants profoundly experience these challenges as they settle into their new host society or adapt to new roles as family members leave for the north. The multiple losses/separation from family, land, language, and home, paired with the difficulty of incorporation into a newly adopted country experienced by migrants and their families pose risks to well being. In particular, social isolation and marginalization, acculturative stress, depression, and migratory grief are all together.

Recent developments have greatly intensified the susceptibility of migrants to violence, economic hardship, and family separation, particularly for irregular or undocumented migrants. These risks are associated with the aforementioned increased rates of detention and deportations in U.S. destination communities, as well as the heightened violence that exists in Mexico and Central America in communities of origin and transit. While irregular migrants have long been prey to crimes such as theft and extortion, particularly in border areas, common crime has now been overtaken by organized crime along the entire migratory route through Central America and Mexico. Abduction, human trafficking, massive homicides, and sexual aggressions now join theft and extortion as violence continues escalating. Furthermore, violence from organized crime not only attacks migratory flows, but also their communities of origin in Mexico and Central America where there are geographical regions completely controlled by organized crime, in which no governmental institutions effectively operate.

Theologians such as Javier Saravia, SJ, Daniel Groody, and [Gioacchino] Campese ground the foundation for the moral principle of welcome, care, and solidarity towards the migrant in the scriptures and Catholic Social Teaching. Saravia calls for solidarity with migrants, that is inclusive and incarnate, in which men and women, in love and commonality engage in works of justice and mercy in the face of the dehumanizing elements of globalization and migration. The final document of the Fifth Conference of the Latin American and Caribbean Episcopate of the Roman Catholic Church held in Aparecida, Brazil in May 2007 makes a similar call. The Conference document states that migration has enriched cultural and religious diversity, but also results from the negative aspects of globalization that privilege market dynamics of absolute efficiency and productivity as central values regulating all human relationships. To address these concerns as they relate to migration, the concluding document of Aparecida proposes several lines of action that reflect the Catholic tradition of hospitality and welcoming of the stranger, including the call to organize pastoral accompaniment of migrants and families; establish appropriate national and diocesan structures that facilitate the migrant's encounter with the Church in the host community; strengthen dialogue and cooperation between Diocese and Episcopal Conferences of origin, transit, and destination to give permanent humanitarian assistance to migrants and their families; and promote the development of lay people to accompany migrants and their families in their communities of origin, transit, and destination.

Various Catholic faith inspired actors have responded to the call for hospitality for migrants, developing initiatives in Mexico and the United States that attend to migrants along the various stages of migration in communities of origin, transit, destination, and return. Not surprisingly, faith and the social and pastoral accompaniment of faith communities are significant protective factors for migrants and their families. These hospitality-based initiatives include support programs for the family members of migrants remaining in communities of origin, shelters that care for migrants in transit, and welcoming centers for recent arrivals, as well as recently deported return migrants.

According to the World Bank, the Mexican migration corridor is one of the top ten migration corridors in the world and constitutes a well-known and much-traveled route for Central American migrants on their way to the United States. Statistics from different organizations estimate that between 150,000 and 400,000 irregular migrants travel along this corridor each year. The shortest route in this specific migration corridor measures approximately 4,300 kilometers, calculated from a starting point at the Southern border of Mexico and a destination point on the border with the United States. The journey itself poses significant challenges and risks. The increase in violence, extortions, kidnappings, mutilations, deaths, and accidents adds to the already physically exhausting experience of traveling on top of freight trains.

This violent and dangerous landscape has elicited a significant humanitarian response from local communities and Mexican nongovernmental organizations (NGOs) that tend to migrants along the journey. In 1987, there was one shelter located at the border, which served mostly Mexican migrants who were trying to cross the border in search of work. By 2006 there were 32 shelters, serving a mix of Mexican migrants trying to cross the border, as well as deported migrants. During these years there was also an increased number of Central Americans reaching for help at the shelters. Currently shelters are also located on the South border of Mexico, as well as in parts of Central Mexico. By 2013, there were 63 faith-based and non-religious Mexican NGOs and six Human Rights centers providing humanitarian relief or advocating for migrants' rights along this corridor. These NGOs joined in a humanitarian aid network to strengthen and facilitate their efforts.

This network of shelters and humanitarian organizations called Dimension Pastoral De La Movilidad Humana (Pastoral Dimension of ´ Human Mobility) has become a prime example of hospitality to migrants in transit, deported migrants, and migrant workers. The aid primarily consists of food, shelter, medical care, and legal assistance, as well as educational instruction on human rights and health (especially

AIDS prevention) and information about the risks and dangers on the route through the corridor. The shelters and humanitarian aid organizations have changed not only in numbers, but also in the types of services they offer. These alterations have emerged in response to the changes in migratory flows and have adapted to the characteristics of the journey and the dynamic political context of the region.

Examples of these adaptations include the addition of special support for the increasing number of highly vulnerable migrant populations, such as women, unaccompanied minors, and injured migrants. Some shelters have increased the length of stay permitted to allow migrants sufficient time to receive financial support from family or to work to earn money as they prepare to complete the journey. Others provide attention to the mounting number of migrants deported to border communities. One such organization is the Jesuit Kino Border Initiative (KBI). Located proximately on both sides of the Mexican-U.S. border in Nogales, Arizona and Nogales, Sonora, KBI provides pastoral accompaniment and direct assistance to men, women, and children that have been deported from the United States to Mexico in the form of two daily warm meals, clothing and personal care items, and referrals and linkage to Mexican government and NGO services.

Transnational family arrangements are becoming more common in North and Central America due to escalating international migration in the region, heightened difficulty in transit due to organized crime, and tightened border security as well as increasingly stringent immigration policies and visa backlogs in the United States. The separation of family members due to these changes in sending, transit, and destination countries have also contributed to longer familial separation. While much of the research on transnational families has focused on the impact of remittances and the economic effects of migration on transnational families, there is growing research on the noneconomic effects of separation due to migration—the socioemotional wellbeing of families. While the economic situation of family members may improve, there are significant health and emotional costs for the wives, children, and elderly parents of migrants that remain in their community of origin.

In response to the needs of such families, some parishes and organizations in migrant source communities have responded with supportive interventions. The Mujer y Familia Migrante program of Jesuit Migrant Services of Mexico, for example, is a comprehensive program attending to the wives, children, and parents of migrants. This program employs a popular education informed approach to develop participant-led mental health support groups, community banks, and small revenue generating projects. The self-help support groups address the emotional loss and stress associated with the separation and changes in family dynamics associated with migration. The community banks, also led by the wives and mothers of migrants, support the efficient investment and use of economic remittances received by the family members as well as support the development of local employment and revenue generating activities that can prevent the need to migrate and possibly contribute to development of local economies.

In communities of destination, NGOs and parishes have provided humanitarian aid, healthcare, social services, and mental health programs to attend to migrants and their families as well as assist in their integration. Furthermore, some sanctuary cities and immigrant-friendly states provide public services to irregular migrants when allowable, offering welcoming centers and basic social service programs. Churches have traditionally practiced hospitality towards immigrants, ranging from sanctuary for irregular migrants to pastoral accompaniment, to the provision of information resources and referrals regarding legal and social services, labor and immigration rights, health fairs, and emergency services.

In recent years, the hospitality offered to immigrant families by parishes and NGOs in destination communities has expanded to address the rising rates of family separation due to detention and deportation. Over 4.4 million Mexican immigrants were repatriated from the United States between 2005 and 2010. In 2013 alone, 368,644 immigrants were deported, with Mexico, Guatemala, Honduras, and El Salvador, the top four countries of citizenship of individuals deported, collectively comprising 94.4 percent of removals. In 2013, U.S. Immigration and Customs Enforcement detained an average of 33,811 immigrants a day. The detentions and deportations often cause extreme financial and emotional hardships and lengthy or permanent separations for families. To address the suffering of families divided by detention and deportation, many churches have developed accompaniment and new sanctuary projects that provide an array of supports that include: attention to basic needs of family members, transportation of family members to detention centers for visits, escorting immigrants in deportation proceedings to court hearings and U.S. Immigration and Customs Enforcement's (ICE) check-ins, prayer vigils at detention centers, and accompaniment of immigrants in detention and their families.

The Mexican migration corridor, its dynamics and complexities, present a unique challenge for any migrant who ventures through this path. The regional migratory policies—especially those related to irregular migration—are divergent, encompassing different priorities and goals. The U.S. policies are focused on sealing its border with Mexico and promoting measures aimed to retain migratory flows south of Mexican territory. The Mexican migration policies, on paper, but not in practice, take a more humanitarian approach to Central American transit migrants. The migration policies of Central American countries concentrate on providing support, especially against human rights violations of their nationals in transit and encourage development of programs to handle deportations from the United States and Mexico.

At the same time, the humanitarian responses in this corridor and in destination communities in the United States present a unique array of expressions of hospitality that address the volume of migration in the region, as well as the needs of migrants and their families at different points in the migratory arc. Private and public forms of hospitality have provided relief to hundreds of migrants in transit, as well as support to those who are at risk of detention, deportation, and family separation. At the level of public awareness, the practice of hospitality has brought to the forefront the plight of irregular migrants and the human consequences of the immigration and economic policies of migrant source, transit, and destination countries. At both the humanitarian and public awareness level, practice of hospitality stresses the dignity of the human person, the rights of the migrant, and the importance of family and a broader solidarity of peoples in a globalizing world.

Recommended Readings

Alba, Francisco. 2013. *Mexico: The New Migration Narrative*. Washington, DC: Migration Policy Institute. Available at <http://www.migrationinformation.org/Profiles/display.cfm?ID=947> , last accessed January 7, 2014.

Alba, Francisco and Miguel Angel Castillo. 2012. *New Approaches to Migration Management in Mexico and Central America*. Washington, DC: Migration Policy Institute. Available at <http://www.migrationpolicy.org/pubs/RMSG-MexCentAm-Migration.pdf>, last accessed January 13, 2014.

Antman, Francisca. 2011. *The Impact of Migration on Family Left Behind*. Institute for the Study of Labor. Bonn, Germany. Available at <http://www.iza.org/MigrationHandbook/16 Antman The%20Impact%20of%20Migration%20on%20Family%20Left%20Behind.pdf>, last accessed December 18, 2013.

Arbona, Consuelo, Norma Olvera, Nestor Rodriguez, Jacqueline Hagan, Adriana Linares, and Margit Wiesner. 2010. "Acculturative Stress among Documented and Undocumented Latino Immigrants in the United States." *Hispanic Journal of Behavioral Sciences* 32(3): 362–384.

Casillas, Rodolfo. 2008. "The Routes of Central Americans through Mexico: Characterization, Principal Agents and Complexities." *Migración y Desarrollo* (First Semester): 141–157.

CIDH (Comisión Interamericana de Derechos Humanos). 2011. "Observaciones Preliminares de La Relatoria sobre Los Derechos de Los Migrantes De La CIDH a México." Mexico City: Comisión Interamericana de Derechos Humanos.

CNDH (Comisión Nacional de Los Derechos Humanos México). 2009. "Informe Especial de la Comisión Nacional de Derechos Humanos sobre Los Casos de Secuestro en contra de Migrantes." Mexico City: Comisión Nacional de Los Derechos Humanos México.

CNDH (Comisión Nacional de Los Derechos Humanos México). 2011. "Informe Especial sobre Secuestro de Migrantes en Mexico." Mexico City: Comisión Nacional de Los Derechos´ Humanos México.

Conferencia General del Episcopado Latinoamericano y Caribeño. 2007. *Aparecida: Documento Conclusivo*. Bogotá, Colombia: Consejo Episcopal Latinoamericano.

Department of Homeland Security. 2013. "FY 2013 ICE Immigration Removals." Available at , last accessed January 13, 2014.

DPMH (Dimensión Pastoral De La Movilidad Humana). 2012. "Informe de Actividades de La Dimensión Pastoral de La Movilidad Humana, en El Periodo 2006-2012." México: Comisión Episcopal para La Pastoral Social: Conferencia del Episcopado Mexicano.

Espin, Oliva M. 1987. "Psychological Impact of Migration on Latinas." *Psychology of Women Quarterly* 11: 489–503.

Groody, Daniel. 2009. "Crossing the Divide: Foundations of a Theology of Migration and Refugees." *Theological Studies*: 638–669.

Groody, Daniel and Gioacchino Campese (eds). 2008. *Promised Land, A Perilous Journey*. Notre Dame, IN: University of Notre Dame Press.

Harker, Kathryn. 2001. "Immigrant Generation, Assimilation, and Adolescent Well-Being." *Social Forces* 79: 969–1004.

Hipsman, Faye and Doris Meissner. 2013. "Immigration in the United States: New Economic, Social, and Political Landscapes with Legislative Reform on the Horizon." *Migration Policy Institute*, Migration Policy Institute: Washington, DC. Available at <http://www.migrationinformation.org/Profiles/display. cfm?ID=946>, last accessed December 18, 2013.

Hovey, Joseph D. and Cheryl A. King. 1996. "Acculturative Stress. Depression, and Suicidal Ideation among Immigrant and Second Generation Latino Adolescents." *Journal of the American Academy of Child and Adolescent Psychiatry* 35(9): 1183–1192.

Ki-Moon, Ban. 2009. Secretary General Remarks to the Third Global Forum on Migration and Development. Vision of Migration as a System of Legal, Dignified, Mobility with Full Respect for Human Rights. United Nations. Available at <http://www.un.org/News/Press/docs/2009/sgsm12587.doc.htm>, last accessed December 4, 2013.

Koser, Khalid. 2009. "Why Migration Matters." *Current History* 108(717): 147–153.

Leon, Ana M. and Sophia F. Dziegielewski. 1999. "The Psychological Impact of Migration: Practice Considerations in Working with Hispanic Women." *Journal of Social Work Practice* 13(1): 69–82.

Marotta, Sylvia A. and Jorge G. Garcia. 2003. "Latinos in the United States in 2000." *Hispanic Journal of Behavioral Science* 25: 13–34.

Marshall, Grant N., Terry L. Schell, Marc N. Elliott, Megan S. Berthold, and Chi-Ah Chun. 2005. "Mental Health of Cambodian Refugees 2 Decades After Resettlement in the United States." *Journal American Medical Association* 294(5): 571–579.

Mazzucato, Valentina and Djamila Schans. 2011. "Transnational Families and the Well-Being of Children: Conceptual and Methodological Challenges." *Journal of Marriage and the Family* 73(4): 704–712.

Meyer, Maureen and Stephanie Brewer. 2010, December. "A Dangerous Journey through Mexico: Human Rights Violations against Migrants in Transit." Washington Office on Latin America (WOLA) and Centro de Derechos Humanos Pro. Available at <http://www.wola.org/publications/a_dangerous_journey_ through_mexico_human_rights_violations_against_migrants_in_transit>, last accessed August 13, 2013.

Passel, Jerry, D'Vera Cohen, and Ana Gonzalez-Barrera. 2012. "Net Migration from Mexico Falls to Zero—and Perhaps Less." *Pew Research Center*. Available at <http://www.pewhispanic.org/2012/04/23/net-migration-from-mexicofalls-to-zero-and-perhaps-less/>, last accessed December 16, 2013.

Pfanner, Toni. 2010, June. "Editorial." *International Review of the Red Cross* 92(878). Available at <http://www.icrc.org/eng/resources/international-review/review-878-urban-violence/review-878-all.pdf>, last accessed December 18, 2013.

Pumariega, Andrés J., Eugenio Rothe, and JoAnne B. Pumariega. 2005. "Mental Health of Immigrants and Refugees." *Community Mental Health Journal* 41(5): 581–597.

Ratha, Dilip, Sanket Mohapatra, and Ani Silwal. 2011. *Migration and Remittances Factbook 2011*. Washington, DC: The World Bank.

Rosales Sandoval, Isabel. 2013. "Public Officials and The Migration Industry in Guatemala: Greasing The Wheels of a Corrupt Machine." In T. Gammeltoft-Hansen and S. N. Nyberg (eds.), *The Migration Industry and the Commercialization of International Migration*. Abingdon: Routledge, 215–237.

Saravia, Javier. 2004. *La Solidaridad Con Los Migrantes: En La Vida y La Biblia*. Collegeville, MN: Liturgical Press.

SCT (Secretaría de Comunicaciones y Transporte). 2011. *Anuario Estadístico Ferroviario*. Mexico City: Secretaría de Comunicaciones y Transporte.

Selway, William and Margaret Newkirk. 2013. "Congress Mandates Jail Beds for 34,000 Immigrants as Private Prisons Profit. Bloomberg Politics." Available at <http://www.bloomberg.com/news/2013-09-24/congress-fuels-private-jails-detaining-34-000-immigrants.html>, last accessed December 2, 2013.

Smart, Julie F. and David W. Smart. 1995. "Acculturative Stress of Hispanics: Loss and Challenge." *Journal of Counseling and Development* 73: 390–396.

Sorensen, Ninna N. 2013. "Migration between Social and Criminal Networks: Jumping the Remains of the Honduran Migration Train." In T. Gammeltoft-Hansen and S. N. Nyberg (eds.), *The Migration Industry and The Commercialization of International Migration*. Abingdon: Routledge. 238–261.

Stoney, Sierra and Jeanne Batalova. 2013. "Central American Immigrants in the United States." *Migration Policy Institute*. Available at <http://www.migrationinformation.org/USfocus/display.cfm?id=938>, last accessed November 15, 2013.

Valdés Montoya, Vladimiro. 2012, May 12. Loyola University Chicago School of Social Work Commencement Address. Personal Communication.

How Immigrant Activists Changed L.A.

By Manuel Pastor
Dissent Magazine, Winter 2015

Once known as the "wicked city" for its vicious anti-labor politics, Los Angeles has, particularly over the last decade, gained a reputation as a bastion of progressivism. In L.A., one of the few places in the United States where private-sector unionization saw steady gains before the 2008 recession, activists have organized across racial lines for community benefits agreements, job training programs, and transit justice. They have also elected progressive mayors like former community organizer Antonio Villaraigosa in 2005—eight years before Bill de Blasio's victory in our (friendly) rival city, New York—and Eric Garcetti, the city's youngest mayor in more than a century, in 2013.

Why the dramatic shift in L.A.'s tone and policy? Any success has many parents (or, at least, people who claim to be its parents), but there seem to be three main causes: the rise of a progressive labor movement with electoral ambitions and skills, the emergence of regional community-based organizing with a sharp analysis of power, and—the concern that lies at the heart of this essay—the creation of an immigrant voice that has gained both the confidence and the capacity to effect change.

While the importance of immigrants in L.A. has not gone unnoticed, they are often depicted largely as a complementary force to labor (see Ruth Milkman's *L.A. Story*) or community-based organizing (see our own *L.A. Rising*). But immigrant rights organizers and advocates—often immigrants, themselves—have not just played supporting roles in the progressive make-over of L.A. Rather, they have had their own organizations, agendas, and political battles to improve the quality of daily life in a region in which nearly one-tenth of residents are undocumented and where one in five children have at least one undocumented parent.

At the same time, immigrant rights organizations and their leaders have been deliberate in joining the progressive pull in California's Southland. So a better understanding of the contribution of these advocates—and how they came to see themselves as tied to a broader progressive project in Los Angeles—can help illustrate how other cities in the United States can promote immigrant integration, stronger movements for social justice, and a better future for all.

The "Los Angeles Riots" of 1992 were a breaking point in L.A.'s political history. While cataclysmic violence cast into stark relief the deeply conflictual relationship between the police and the community (and eventually led to major reforms in the Los Angeles Police Department), the unrest was not only connected to police abuse. The fact that the wave of looting and arson occurred in areas where per capita incomes were half that of the rest of the city highlighted the contradiction between a rapidly deindustrializing economy and the anemic response of a five-term African-American mayor, Tom Bradley, to poverty in the city's black and Latino neighborhoods.

Indeed, the "civil unrest"—as it is referred to by many on the left—bolstered a progressive critique that the Bradley strategy, which had focused on boosting downtown development and generating more government positions for people of color, could not by itself address inequalities in income and opportunity. From this analysis grew one of the country's first battles for a living wage and, to achieve this, the creation of the Los Angeles Alliance for a New Economy (LAANE). Birthed from the County Federation of Labor (known as the "Fed"), LAANE now boasts a staff of about fifty. But its mission remains laser-sharp in its focus on working poverty and it continues to work closely with the Fed.

It was not just a focus on broadening economic opportunity that emerged from the ashes. The 1992 unrest also revealed that the region had rapidly and dramatically "Latinized," and nowhere was this more apparent than in South Central, the historic heart of black Los Angeles. While television commentators and pundits seemed surprised at seeing Latinos in the riot-torn streets—and even more surprised when post-riot analysis revealed that about half of the people arrested during the widespread looting were Latino—it was no big shock to statisticians like myself: while South L.A. was roughly 80 percent African American in 1970, it was 45 percent Latino in 1990 and is about two-thirds Latino today.

One of the main drivers of that change was immigration. In 1980, 22 percent of L.A. County residents were foreign-born, a figure that rose to 33 percent in 1990 and has since leveled off (36 percent in 2000 and 35 percent in 2010). The largest numbers came from Mexico and other Latin-American countries. Often undocumented, the newcomers expanded the ranks of the working poor as good jobs in durable manufacturing slipped during nationwide deindustrialization and lower-paid service sector and non-durable manufacturing jobs filled the void. Spilling out of traditional entry neighborhoods like Pico-Union, Westlake, or East L.A. into other parts of the city like South Central, chain migration soon further swelled their ranks.

The new immigrants expanded the community and labor base for left-leaning politics in Los Angeles, particularly as organizers sought to channel the rage that had burned down part of the city into something more socially productive. Through the 1980s and 1990s, union organizers found that immigrants brought a repertoire of practices that included familiarity with labor organizing—and immigrant janitors, hotel workers, and others proved themselves willing to stage dramatic strikes and public actions (such as marching through major commercial corridors) to secure new contracts. The impacts of these organizing efforts can be seen in the data: from 2000 to the Great Recession of 2008, U.S. private-sector unionization dropped from 9 percent to 7.6 percent, while in the greater Los Angeles metropolitan area (the so-called Combined Statistical Area) those rates went from 8.9 percent to 10.6 percent.

Of course, making change also requires political voice. While Latinos comprised nearly 40 percent of the city's population in 1990, they made up only about 10 percent of L.A.'s registered voters, partly because of immigration status and partly because they were (and are) a younger population. However, immigrants became part of the army of precinct walkers who expanded the number of pro-labor voters even when they themselves could not vote. Such immigrant-involved electoral organizing was facilitated by union contracts that included "lost time payments" for members to do union work, thus giving the central labor council access to the best worker organizers. And while labor took the lead in this type of campaigning, it was partially built on a set of grassroots get-out-the-vote efforts from the mid-eighties— originally put in place by community organizers seeking to shift spending from military to civilian purposes—known as the Jobs with Peace campaign.

Meanwhile, local groups, often starting from a strong base in black neighborhoods, similarly found that immigrants could be loyal members of broad-based coalitions for economic and social justice. These included drives to win less expensive and more accessible mass transit (that is, the Bus Riders Union–led campaign against the L.A. County Metropolitan Transportation Authority that secured a 1996 consent decree to expand bus service and hold the line on fares), better job training (such as the Strategic Concepts in Organizing and Policy Education–led campaign that won a private-sector-funded workforce de-

> **"There was a nuanced process in which immigrants, the labor movement, and progressives wound up pulling traditional politicians, including Latinos, in their direction, instead of just the other way round."**

velopment program from DreamWorks in 1999), and community benefits agreements that held developers accountable to the communities in which they built (like the 2001 campaign at the Staples Center led by Strategic Actions for a Just Economy and LAANE, with a surprising role for immigrant organizers usually assumed to be witnesses and not participants in such key decisions). In short, the L.A. progressive renaissance had much to do with immigrant energy and enthusiasm, and the weaving of new multi-racial coalitions for social change.

So goes the story of how immigrants helped fuel labor and community-organizing in progressive Los Angeles. But there is a broader tale to be told in which immigrant rights work had its own unique and parallel arc toward justice. For while 1992 was a crucible for a rebirth of progressive politics in Los Angeles, 1994 was an equally momentous year for immigrant rights: California voters enacted Proposition 187, a measure designed to bar undocumented immigrants from using nearly every public service, including education for their children. The courts later struck down most of its provisions but it managed to spark an autonomous immigrant-rights movement.

Moreover, the campaigns for and against Prop 187 made two important things clear. First, the Republican decision to embrace the nativist reaction eventually marginalized the party as the state's demographics and political attitudes shifted. The second but less appreciated consequence of the campaign was that it revealed a growing tension between recent immigrants and many traditional Latino political officials (nearly all of whom were then Mexican-Americans).

The initial flash point for the latter came in the fall of 1994 when such officials criticized a march against Prop 187 that included participants boisterously flying Mexican flags. For immigrant organizers, this critique seemed to miss the point of the march—which was not so much to win an election as it was to inspire immigrants to take independent political action. It was a striking idea—immigrants as actors, not subjects—and it triggered a debate about who should be in control of the strategy to defend their rights.

The uneasy and uncertain relationship between immigrants and U.S.-born Latino leaders is actually a key feature of Latino political ascendance in L.A. While the rising share of immigrants (and the wave of naturalizations that came in reaction to Prop 187's victory) propelled Latino politicians, it was not a passive process of accumulating voters and assimilating immigrants into ethnic politics; indeed, several of the rising Latino officials, including Antonio Villaraigosa and Gil Cedillo, found themselves learning Spanish to better communicate with newcomers who had their own hopes and demands.

And this non-traditional approach to ethnic politics was also demonstrated in the ways in which campaigns played out. For example, Marty Martinez, a pro-business Latino Democrat, was thrown out of Congress in 2000 when L.A.'s Central Labor Council complained he was not supportive enough of its concerns. The council mobilized its union and immigrant bases to win the seat for Hilda Solis (who later became President Obama's Secretary of Labor—the first Latino to hold that post—and is now on the Los Angeles County Board of Supervisors).

And being Latino was not enough to guarantee success with immigrant voters and activists. In 2000, Jackie Goldberg, a Jewish, lesbian city council member who led the fight for the living wage, ran for state assembly against a Latino opponent supported by political figures who complained that she was competing in a "Latino" district. The 45th Assembly District was more than 70 percent Latino. But Goldberg won with strong support from labor, progressives, and immigrants, all of whom cared more about her agenda than her ethnic background.

It was a similar coalition—and not simply demographic change—that helped Villaraigosa become the city's first Latino mayor since 1872. After all, while the city went from about 39 percent Latino in 1990 to 47 percent in 2000, the election of Villaraigosa occurred in a decade during which the percentage of Latinos barely budged (it was 48 percent in 2010). Instead, there was a nuanced process in which immigrants, the labor movement, and progressives wound up pulling traditional politicians, including Latinos, in their direction, instead of just the other way round.

Immigrant electoral politics was bevvied by a number of immigrant rights organizations that combined demands for immigrant rights with gains at the workplace—often outside of a traditional union structure. They included the Coalition for Humane Immigrant Rights of Los Angeles (CHIRLA), the Koreatown Immigrant Workers Association (KIWA), the National Day Laborer Organizing Network (NDLON), the South Asian Network (SAN), and the Central American Resource Center (CARECEN). Activist groups like these made sure that immigrants were not simply providing "boots on the ground" for a newly mobilized labor movement and its electoral ambitions. Rather, their members helped shift the stance of organized labor both locally and nationally.

In 1999, breaking from organized labor's historically anti-immigrant stance, the AFL-CIO, with heavy influence from the Los Angeles County Federation of Labor, officially adopted a platform supportive of immigrant rights and comprehensive immigration reform. The following year, a labor-sponsored hearing to demonstrate support for the importance of immigration reform—one of a series of forums across the nation—drew an overflow crowd of about 20,000 at the L.A. Sports Arena. "If someone had told me three or four years ago that we'd be taking this position today," John Wilhelm (then president of HERE) told the *L.A. Weekly* of the AFL-CIO's reversal on immigrant politics, "I'd have thought they were out of their minds."

Meanwhile, the immigrant rights groups themselves jumped into direct electoral work when in 2003, a statewide bill repealed the right of undocumented immigrants to obtain driver's licenses. The next year, a new statewide multiethnic collaborative called Mobilize the Immigrant Vote (MIV) began registering, educating, and mobilizing residents to vote and became part of a larger set of efforts to encourage infrequent voters to cast their ballots. MIV's impact extends beyond Los Angeles County.

Yet the real "coming out" of immigrant organizers occurred on May 1, 2006. Across America, immigrant activists and their allies in labor, the left, and faith communities (most prominently, the Catholic Church) came together to protest the proposal of the Sensenbrenner-King bill in Congress. Among its other draconian provisions, this bill would have criminalized any assistance to undocumented immigrants. While the turnout was dramatic all over the country, the largest crowd gathered in Los Angeles: here, half a million people clogged downtown streets.

And unlike in 1994, this time—and at the insistence of immigrant organizers themselves—many marchers waved American flags and encouraged one another to become citizens and to vote. Indeed, a popular chant in that May Day march was "Hoy Marchamos, Mañana Votamos" ("Today, We March; Tomorrow, We Vote"). A surge of naturalizations did occur, as lawful permanent immigrants realized the best way to defend their relatives was to show up on election day. Soon, Republican office-holders became as scarce in Los Angeles as a rainy day in August.

The multiethnic nature of this organizing showed that this was a movement and not a special interest group. Groups like the Asian Pacific American Legal Center (since renamed Asian Americans Advancing Justice, a telling switch) was critical to showing that this was not a matter of Latino politics. Other organizations like the Pilipino Workers Center helped Asian immigrants engage with the labor movement, particularly since their members were (and are) low-wage, often undocumented workers in homecare and other exploited occupations.

African-American politics in L.A. changed too. While the aforementioned Latinization of South Central fueled certain conflicts and fed into some nationalist impulses, the most successful organizations in the new landscape were committed to—indeed, *had* to be committed to—black-brown coalition building, including around issues of education, neighborhood quality of life, jobs, and immigrant rights. In return, the largely Latino (and often immigrant) SEIU deliberately organized a largely black security guard sector while a similarly Latino-dominated union, the Hotel Employees and Restaurant Employees Union (HERE), secured provisions in new contracts to ensure outreach to and hiring of black workers who were once so prominent in the sector but had since been eclipsed by Latino numbers.

So where will L.A. be in 2015? A strong progressive movement with prominent immigrant voices has given Mayor Garcetti an opportunity both to reboot the Office of Immigrant Affairs—which was established by Mayor James Hahn (2001–2005) but lay dormant under Villaraigosa (2005–2013)—and to advocate what is likely to be the nation's most significant increase in a city's minimum wage. (Seattle's $15 will be higher, but Mayor Garcetti's proposed $13.25 will cover more people given the extent of working poverty in L.A.)[1]

Los Angeles has become a city where a progressive think tank can propose a measure to address inequality and have it swiftly put on the books: LAANE developed a policy package to adopt a competitive franchise system for waste collection that would simultaneously reduce the city's trash, improve the environment, and create green jobs. The city council adopted it relatively quickly, considering the fierce opposition from businesses that led to what the *L.A. Times* deemed "a battle royale" at city hall over the issue. L.A. is also a place where unions can still improve conditions for union and non-union workers alike—as has been the case for workers in big hotels who will, starting in July 2015, be paid a minimum wage of $15.37.

Local politicians have also done the right thing to aid immigrants in legal limbo. In July 2014, the Mayor and the LAPD announced they would no longer honor "detainer" requests from ICE, the federal agency responsible for immigration and customs. Detainers are government attempts to jail an undocumented man or woman arrested for a non-immigration-related offense, such as a minor driving violation, for up to two extra days beyond their release date (either because they posted bail or because the charges were dropped) in order to transfer him or her to the ICE. This has been a huge relief for families whose lives have been disrupted by deportation.

Los Angeles has become a city where immigrants routinely lobby public officials not only to end such detainers or the towing of cars driven by undocumented (and, as a result, unlicensed) drivers but also pressure policymakers for better land-use planning, improved education, and enhanced job training. City officials have also encouraged naturalization, joining New York and Chicago in a Cities for Citizenship campaign that aims to increase the number of immigrants eligible to vote and use public services. Even public libraries have gotten into the act, creating "citizenship corners" that provide information to immigrants where they live.

L.A. is also one of the centers of the DREAMers movement, which seeks to legalize the status of undocumented immigrants who came to the United States as children. One sign of the progressive nature of the movement's local branch is the existence of "Dream Summer"—a title that is a nod to the youth of the civil rights movement. It places these young migrants in organizations that work for LGBT rights, climate justice, and a variety of other issues. Dream Summer nudges participants to view themselves as part of a wider left while simultaneously helping the groups in which they intern better understand immigrant issues. Tellingly, it is run out of the UCLA Labor Center, an organization traditionally focused on developing union leadership.

Of course, one should not make too much of L.A.'s pro-immigrant surge. The city has lagged behind other big cities in enacting policies that would improve the daily lives of immigrants, such as issuing municipal identification cards (New Haven, Connecticut, took that lead). Moreover, L.A. County frequently heads in a direction different than the city; for example, its Board of Supervisors recently reaffirmed a policy to have the County Sheriff hand off immigrant detainees to federal authorities. Still, this is a remarkable change from the past and it holds hopes for an even more welcoming future.

That immigrant politics would tilt in a progressive direction in Los Angeles—or anywhere else—was not a foregone conclusion. Certainly, activists saw their work as advancing a universal ideal of human rights, which is essential to defending those without papers. The prior involvement of some immigrants in labor and leftist movements in their homelands also created a basis for political engagement. However, emphasis on individual initiative, the conservative pull of cultural traditions, and the desire to avoid the overt discrimination faced by African Americans are also factors that can drive immigrants to the right of the political spectrum.

The question of how Latino immigrants identify themselves by their race is one part of this equation. Some commentators predict that most Latinos will eventually identify themselves as "white"—helping America become a "post-racial" society without solving the problem of racial inequality at all. But research on Southern California Latinos actually suggests that the longer Latino immigrants are in the country, the less "white" they feel. Some of that is due to the way in which the contemporary hostility to immigrants creates a sense of being "other." But it is also the case that key campaigns, such as those around transit justice or domestic workers' rights, have created coalitions in which participants are self-identified "people of color."

In any case, progressive identification by immigrants must be nurtured, not assumed. According to Angelica Salas, executive director of one of L.A.'s most well-known immigrant rights groups, the Coalition for Humane Immigrant Rights of Los Angeles (CHIRLA), the choice of a progressive identity for CHIRLA was intentional, not accidental. While the organization cut its teeth protecting day laborers and continues to lobby on issues relating to local, state, and federal policy toward immigrants, it has recognized that what will most improve immigrant lives are policies that should appeal to other Americans, too: a stronger and more inclusive economy, a cleaner and more sustainable environment, and an educational system that leads to economic security, rather than a path to the criminal justice system.

Working in coalition on all these matters helps to build alliances with progressives, and the logic flows in the other direction as well. In Los Angeles—and across the country—progressives have to work hard to secure the loyalties of immigrants by proving their own solidarity with immigrant concerns. It is remarkably easy for the immigrant agenda to slip off the table; witness the president's postponement of executive action on immigration until after the November election and the reluctance of congressional Democrats to force the issue. While the eventual decision to defer deportation for millions of undocumented residents was a welcome victory for immigrant advocates and their allies, it's important to remember what is always at stake in delays and decisions: the future political alignment of both immigrants and their children and the way that that could create a different—and progressive—new American majority

After all, it is not just progressives who are cultivating an immigrant following. In Los Angeles and elsewhere, evangelical Christians are increasingly waking up to their undocumented congregants and have started to back some version of immigration reform. Right-leaning megachurches view this strategy, in part, as a way of increasing their numbers. The Mormon Church has worked to limit the worst nativist impulses and civic leaders in the very red state of Utah have agreed to a "Utah Compact" that would improve the lives of immigrant residents in that state. (Utah also secured driver's licenses for undocumented residents long before progressive California, and also secured in-state tuition for that same group a mere one year after the Golden State.)

So progressives need to take the lead on creating a welcoming atmosphere for immigrants, particularly in metropolitan areas that are politically to the left. We should help protect families from the threat of deportation, encourage naturalization and other forms of civic engagement, promote English classes and job training, and continue to include immigrants in broader movements for economic and environmental justice. The political payoff for the progressive agenda will come in unexpected ways: for example, Latino voters in California are actually more concerned about climate change than white voters (and this sentiment is even stronger on the part of those Latinos who are Spanish-dominant and so, likely to be immigrants), and they are therefore a key component of addressing our climate crisis.

Coalition-building at the local level is especially important as long as immigration reform is stuck in Congress. But it may not be stuck forever. Consider that the next electoral redistricting will occur in 2021, right after a presidential election in which there will be more Latinos, Asians, and black people (in addition to immigrants and their children) in the electorate. The resulting remapping could release us from the current gerrymandered Congress in which Tea Party Republicans hold undue influence and are therefore plugging the dike against a potential tide of change.

Will progressives be ready to seize that moment? It will require many things: a more compelling narrative about the ills of the economy; a willingness to connect issues such as marriage equality, immigration reform, and women's reproductive rights to an economic justice agenda; and a clear-eyed strategy to both win elections and govern effectively. Immigrants and their children are a vital part of the progressive coalition, but the alliance is not predestined. As immigrants see progressive politicians as a wise option and as those political actors work in collaboration with immigrant rights organizers—as they have in contemporary Los Angeles—we will build an America that is more inclusive and more equitable for us all.

Editor's Note

1. On May 19, 2015, the Los Angeles City Council voted fourteen to one in favor of an ordinance to increase the city's minimum wage from $9 per hour to $15 per hour by 2020, gradually phasing in the rate over the next five years.

Deadly Human Trafficking Business on Mexico-US Border

By Axel Storen Weden
Al Jazeera, January 24, 2016

One single road cuts through drowsy Altar, an hour's drive south of the American border at Sasabe, Arizona. At first glance, the town seems a sleepy outpost. But this look is deceiving.

Foot soldiers of the drug cartels, young, tough-looking men on bikes, patrol the blocks. Men in pick-up trucks with fully tinted windows and no licence plates drive up and down the one main road menacingly.

A migrant pulls his jacket over his head and trots into a shop. But his attempt to make himself invisible is of little use. No one gets in—or out—of Altar without the permission of the cartels.

The migrant hub

"You can't trust anyone here," says Juan, a 38-year-old migrant who hopes to find work in the US. He is a widower and father of six children from the southern Mexican state of Chiapas, staying at a church-run shelter for migrants. The shelter offers a safe place to stay and a meal for migrants who've undertaken a difficult and dangerous journey.

After the US tightened border security controls following the September 11, 2001 attacks, Altar was transformed into a hub for migrants seeking to enter the country illegally through remote desert routes.

In this small town the shops, exclusively geared towards migrants, offer everything from "coyotes"—as the human traffickers here are known—to camouflage, sand-coloured clothing and anti-snakebite kits.

But these days, the little town plaza is no longer crowded. Local authorities and shop owners say up to 3,000 people once arrived here every day from all over the world in the hope of reaching their American dream.

Today, however, the flow of people is reduced significantly. Yet everyone here agrees that dangers lurk at every corner for the few migrants who take the risk to travel through this town.

The drug cartels, locally referred to as "la mafia," control an extensive network of human traffickers and informants. They extort for money, kidnap and kill migrants at

"Deadly Human Trafficking Business on Mexico-US Border" by Axel Storen Weden. Originally published by *Al Jazeera*, January 24, 2016.

will. The locals think they have infiltrated the local branches of the police and government structures.

> **Human trafficking accounts for an increasing part of the income for the cartels. It is a safer way of making money.**

The ongoing conflict over trafficking routes between two rival factions of the Sinaloa cartel, "Los Memos" and "Los Salazar," means that there is increased competition over the migrants that do arrive.

Pay or be killed

To cross the Sasabe desert and go on to Arizona, migrants are told they must pay about $4,500 to the coyote, who is appointed by the cartels. They are also forced to pay an additional $700 in a separate "tax" to the criminal groups themselves.

At the church-run shelter, there were rumours that the week before, two Honduran migrants were murdered after they took the fatal decision to embark on the journey north without paying.

Juan, the migrant from the south of Mexico, is left without any money after his long and perilous journey through the country.

Now he has been offered to get over the border "mochilando"—as a drug mule, carrying a backpack filled with at least 30 kg of marijuana.

But Juan is hesitant and well aware of the stories about how migrants are killed once the merchandise is delivered.

"I'm afraid. Every single day I try to come up with something else. But if I don't send any money home soon, my children will die of hunger," he says, his eyes filled with tears.

Decreased crossings

Figures of the number of those apprehended by the US border patrol indicate that fewer and fewer migrants are risking the crossing than in previous years.

According to US Border Control data, from 1983 through 2006, more than one million migrants were detained trying to cross the US-Mexico border. But the number has come down significantly in recent years, with only 337,117 apprehensions in 2015, the lowest since 1971.

Marc Rosenblum, deputy director of the US immigration programme at the Migration Policy Institute, attributed this decrease to the stricter border security policies in the US.

And this decrease is having a significant effect on the small town that depends on the commerce of migrants.

"Pretty much all the stores geared towards the migrants have had to close. The same thing goes for the hotels and flophouses. Almost 60 percent of Altar are without work," says the newly appointed mayor, Everardo Martínez, from Mexico's governing party the Institutional Revolutionary Party.

Martínez rejects the notion that Altar is dangerous and that drug cartels still pose a problem here.

"Extortions, kidnappings and killings of migrants are not an issue anymore. It's something that belongs to the past," he says.

Weddings for security

Prisciliano Peraza, a catholic priest and a well-known activist for migrant rights, laughs at the denial presented by the mayor. "What does he know?" he says. Peraza thinks the mayor is downplaying the influence of the criminal networks because he is involved in them.

"The mayor may have a new job, but he hasn't given up drug and human trafficking," Pereza says.

As a part of his routine, Pereza travels around the villages surrounding Altar to conduct weddings, baptisms and religious services for "la mafia" and their loved ones.

He speeds through the unforgiving desert landscape just a few kilometres from the American border in his Chevy pick-up truck every weekend. "I do this for my own security," says the priest.

"Although they sell drugs and kill people at will, they're still concerned about being in the good graces of God," he says hiding his gaze behind aviator sunglasses and a cowboy hat.

Human trafficking accounts for an increasing part of the income for the cartels. It is a safer way of making money, according to the priest.

"The sentences are shorter, and no matter what, the migrants will always pay," Peraza says.

Not afraid of death

"When you know the kind of life you can have in the US, it's worth risking your life to obtain it," says Dagoberto, a migrant from Honduras, a country plagued with gang violence.

The 53-year old had already lived in the US twice previously. He has two grown children who live in Washington, DC. But, he was deported during his last stay there. This time, he plans to head to Atlanta, Georgia.

He has spent a month and a half traversing Central America and Mexico. He recounts that on his journey, he has been robbed by criminals and has been extorted for money and his clothes by the police.

When the blisters on his feet heal, he will once again try to cross the border. But without money, he may have to take the potentially fatal risk of a backpack stuffed with narcotics on his back.

But he says he does not fear death.

"I've had a long life. If it's my turn to go, the time will be right."

3
Popular Conceptions, Stereotypes, and Biases

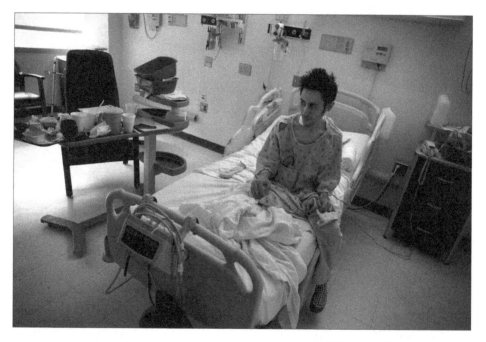

A Syrian refugee, Samir Maani, 32, receives much-needed medical care for a serious heart condition in his hospital room at University of Chicago on November 20, 2015. Maani, whose family is all back in Syria and scattered in Europe, was unable to receive adequate medical attention in war-torn Syria. While many Americans welcome Syrian refugees, others, fearing terror, argue for tightening restrictions.

Immigration Myths and Misconceptions

Prejudices and stereotypes about immigrants have changed little in 200 years, though different groups of immigrants may be targeted in each generation. Politicians and anti-immigration activists have blamed immigrants for rising crime rates and economic turmoil while millions of immigrants have been detained or deported out of fear of foreign influence, terrorism, and/or espionage. Often, anti-immigration movements are motivated by isolationism or racism, as some Americans feel that foreign individuals threaten the values and/or distinctiveness of American culture. In each generation, anti-immigration advocates use xenophobia and fear to rally voters against immigration, and this has created persistent myths and misconceptions about immigrants that are pervasive in American pop culture.

The Immigrant Crime Wave

Controversial presidential candidate Donald Trump ignited controversy in 2015 when he suggested that immigration was correlated with higher crime rates. In a July 5, 2015 segment on Fox News' "Media Buzz" program, Trump stated that "The Mexican government is forcing their most unwanted people into the United States. They are, in many cases, criminals, drug dealers, rapists, etc."[1] Trumps arguments are not a new feature of the debate and have been repeatedly used to justify anti-immigration policies since the 1800s. By definition, unauthorized migrants are criminals, as they violate U.S. law by crossing borders and/or remaining in the country illegally. Border control expenditures cost an estimated $18 billion each year, and hundreds of thousands of unauthorized migrants are arrested each year.

A 2011 study by the Government Accountability Office found that a total of 2.89 million criminal offenses were attributed to undocumented migrants (half of which were for immigration-related offenses) between 2003 and 2009. The report listed 42,000 robberies, 70,000 sex crimes, 81,000 auto thefts, and 213,000 instances of assault. The Department of Homeland Security estimates that 20 percent of the U.S. prison population are foreign born.[2] Pew Research Statistics show that while first generation immigrants commit few crimes in comparison to the native population crimes rates among the children of immigrants increase dramatically.[3]

However, critics argue that, though immigrants commit thousands of crimes each year, immigration contributes little to overall crime rates. The American Immigration Council found that between 1990 and 2013 the foreign-born population increased from 7.9 percent to 13.1 percent (and the unauthorized immigrant population rose from 3.5 million to 11.2 million), while violent crime declined by 48 percent across the country and property crime fell by 41 percent.[4] Police statistics indicate that 90 percent of immigrants arrested by the police are either charged with immigration offenses or drug crimes.[5] Sociologists have also pointed to cities like El Paso, Texas, a border city with a population of more than 600,000 that has one of the highest populations of undocumented immigrants in the nation but statistically has lower crime rates than many other cities of the same size. In 2009, as immigration rates spiked in El Paso and surrounding communities, El Paso was the second-safest city in the United States.[6]

The Foreign Menace

Since 2014, the rise of the Syrian terrorist group ISIS (also known as ISIL and IS) has created a massive refugee crisis in Syria and Iraq. Thousands of Syrians and Iraqis are fleeing their native nation, hoping to escape the violence that has destroyed their cities and communities. In the United States, some anti-immigrant advocates, like Donald Trump, have proposed that the United States should either restrict or completely prohibit immigration and tourism of all Muslims or at least individuals from Syria, Iraq and other nations associated with Islamist radicalism. Opponents, including the Obama Administration, have argued that the United States has a moral obligation to extend aid to all suffering populations, including Syrian and Iraqi refugees.

Anti-Islamic immigration sentiments are similar to those of the 1870s–80s Workingmen's Party of California, which adopted the political motto "The Chinese Must Go!" and was influential in President Arthur's decision to sign the Chinese Exclusion Act of 1882, the first federal law specifically banning the immigration of an ethnic group. The Exclusion Act was later abandoned, and has since been seen as an unfortunate example of political policy being influenced by racial bias.[7] During World War II, similar lobbies opposed proposals to accept millions of Jewish immigrants fleeing the holocaust and called for the detainment and political marginalization of Japanese Americans out of a fear that they might be spies for Axis forces. Today, similar sentiments are resurging due to pervasive and highly generalized fears about Islamic terrorism.

Fears of immigrant-related terrorism are not entirely unfounded. Accepting Syrian refugees could potentially result in the unwitting admittance of extremist individuals and there remains a possibility, though many national security experts consider it unlikely, that terrorists could enter Mexico and illegally cross the U.S.-Mexico border. However, many national security experts argue that border control and immigration restrictions will not significantly hinder terrorism. Supporting this position is the fact that in the 14 years since the 2001 terrorist attacks, there have been 19 terrorist incidents in the United States committed by native-born extremists, including white supremacists and anti-government radicals. Statistics indicate that the threat of domestic terrorism is more than twice as high as the threat of foreign terrorism.[8]

In December 2015 at the National Archives, President Obama gave a statement against the recent wave of anti-immigration sentiment from Republican candidates, saying, "In the Mexican immigrant today, we see the Catholic immigrant of a century ago. In the Syrian seeking refuge today, we should see the Jewish refugee of World War II."[9] In 2015, a number of U.S. governors passed measures to ban

Syrian refugees, fearing that terrorists could be hiding among them. Critics argue that terrorists have many other ways of entering the nation other than hiding among refugees and that the refugee process is so long and bureaucratic that it is unlikely terrorists will seek to enter the nation by hiding among legitimate refugees. Further, while there are a variety of motivations involved in terrorism, experts agree that terrorists tend to be individuals who have felt marginalized, traumatized, and are searching for identity and belonging. Some therefore argue that refusing to aid Syrian refugees might actually exacerbate the problem, further marginalizing an already vulnerable population and leaving many Syrians with few options other than joining extremist organizations.[10] At its core, refugee policy forces Americans to weigh the possible moral value of helping people in need against the perceived national security benefits of isolationism.

Assimilation or Exploitation

During the 2016 Presidential race, several media reports have criticized candidates for their use of the term "anchor baby" to refer to immigrants who have children in the United States as a way to increase the likelihood that they will be allowed to stay in the country or immigrate to the country in the future. Such rhetoric has contributed to a minority lobby seeking to end birthright citizenship, a set of laws that essentially hold that a person born in the United States is eligible for U.S. citizenship. The exploitation of birthright citizenship is a stereotype similar to the "welfare mothers" stereotype concerning mothers who have children to derive additional revenue from the welfare system. While extreme examples of both phenomena exist, neither is common enough to dictate national policy. While some Republican anti-immigration advocates have argued that as many as 400,000 "anchor babies" are born in the United States each year, the CDC and Census Bureau argue that this number is 44 higher than legitimate estimates.[11]

The birthright debate touches on another myth about immigrants; that they take advantage of America's economy and social welfare, while contributing little. To support this view, advocates cite statistics indicating that migrants send billions of dollars to their native nations each year in the form of remittances. Many immigrants come to the U.S. hoping to earn enough to support not only themselves, but their families and friends back home. While some see this as exploitation, others argue that there is humanitarian value to this process, as remittances and migration support developing communities, easing the burdens of poverty and violence for millions around the world.

Whether or not immigrants come to the United States for political or economic reasons, surveys by Pew Research found that 93 percent of immigrants surveyed ultimately wanted to become citizens, though many felt hampered by linguistic difficulties and the cost of naturalization.[12] While it helps immigrants to learn the laws, language, and mores of American culture, the success of this endeavor also depends on the willingness of U.S.-born citizens to assist in this difficult process. The failure of immigrants to assimilate is related to the resistance of local populations to accept them as equal and valued members of society. Ultimately, it is also important to recognize that there is no "general immigrant" personality or persona. Immigrants, like native-born Americans, are a diverse population with an equally diverse set of goals and hopes. Whether immigration is curtailed or expanded in the future, generalization, racism, and stereotypes are inappropriate in the construction of policy. It is increasingly important that Americans learn to abandon stereotypes in favor of more nuanced, informed views of the issue to make the best and most productive decisions for future policy.

Micah L. Issitt

Notes

1. Ye Hee Lee, "Donald Trump's False Comments Connecting Mexican Immigrants and Crime."
2. Frum, "The Problem with Downplaying Immigrant Crime."
3. Morin, "Crime Rises Among Second-Generation Immigrants as they Assimilate."
4. Ewing, Martinez, and Rumbaut, "The Criminalization of Immigration in the United States."
5. Eichenwald, "Illegal Immigration: Myths, Half-Truths and a Hole in Trump's Wall."
6. "El Paso Still Safe Although Next to a War Zone," NBC News.
7. Wang, "Muslims are to Trump as the Chinese were to President Arthur in 1882."
8. Shane, "Homegrown Extremists Tied to Deadlier Toll than Jihadists in U.S. Since 9/11."
9. May, "Obama: Syrians Seeking Refuge Like 'Jewish Refugees of World War II."
10. Stockton, "Turning Away Refugees Won't Fight Terrorism, And Might Make it Worse."
11. Barro, "Just What Do You Mean by 'Anchor Baby'?"
12. Lopez and Gonzalez-Barrera, "If They Could, How Many Unauthorized Immigrants Would Become U.S. Citizens?"

More Than Half the Nation's Governors Say Syrian Refugees Not Welcome

By Ashley Fantz and Ben Brumfield
CNN.com, November 19, 2015

More than half the nation's governors say they oppose letting Syrian refugees into their states, although the final say on this contentious immigration issue will fall to the federal government.

States protesting the admission of refugees range from Alabama and Georgia, to Texas and Arizona, to Michigan and Illinois, to Maine and New Hampshire. Among these thirty-one states, all but one have Republican governors.

The announcements came after authorities revealed that at least one of the suspects believed to be involved in the Paris terrorist attacks entered Europe among the current wave of Syrian refugees. He had falsely identified himself as a Syrian named Ahmad al Muhammad and was allowed to enter Greece in early October.

Some leaders say they either oppose taking in any Syrian refugees being relocated as part of a national program or asked that they be particularly scrutinized as potential security threats.

Only 1,500 Syrian refugees have been accepted into the United States since 2011, but the Obama administration announced in September that 10,000 Syrians will be allowed entry next year.

The Council on American-Islamic Relations said Monday, "Defeating ISIS involves projecting American ideals to the world. Governors who reject those fleeing war and persecution abandon our ideals and instead project our fears to the world."

Authority over admitting refugees to the country, though, rests with the federal government—not with the states—though individual states can make the acceptance process much more difficult, experts said.

American University law professor Stephen I. Vladeck put it this way: "Legally, states have no authority to do anything because the question of who should be allowed in this country is one that the Constitution commits to the federal government." But Vladeck noted that without the state's participation, the federal government would have a much more arduous task.

"So a state can't say it is legally objecting, but it can refuse to cooperate, which makes thing much more difficult."

Kevin Appleby, director of migration policy at the U.S. Conference of Catholic Bishops, said one tactic states could use would be to cut their own funding in areas such as resettling refugees. The conference is the largest refugee resettlement organization in the country.

But "when push comes to shove, the federal government has both the plenary power and the power of the 1980 Refugee Act to place refugees anywhere in the country," Appleby said.

More than 250,000 people have died since the violence broke out in Syria in 2011, and at least 11 million people in the country of 22 million have fled their homes. Syrians are now the world's largest refugee population, according to the United Nations. Most are struggling to find safe haven in Europe.

In announcing that his state would not accept any Syrian refugees, Texas Gov. Greg Abbott tweeted Monday on his personal account, "I demand the U.S. act similarly," he said. "Security comes first."

In a letter to President Barack Obama, Abbott said "American humanitarian compassion could be exploited to expose Americans to similar deadly danger," referring to Friday's deadly attacks in Paris.

> **"So a state can't say it is legally objecting, but it can refuse to cooperate, which makes thing much more difficult."**

In a statement from Georgia's governor, Republican Nathan Deal, he said Georgia will not accept Syrian refugees "until the federal government and Congress conducts a thorough review of current screening procedures and background checks."

Alabama Gov. Robert Bentley also rejected the possibility of allowing Syrian refugees into his state and connected refugees with potential terror threats.

"After full consideration of this weekend's attacks of terror on innocent citizens in Paris, I will oppose any attempt to relocate Syrian refugees to Alabama through the U.S. Refugee Admissions Program," Bentley said Sunday in a statement.

"As your governor, I will not stand complicit to a policy that places the citizens of Alabama in harm's way."

There is currently no credible threat against the state, the governor's office said, and no Syrian refugees have been relocated to Alabama so far.

As the list of states blocking refugees grows, at least one state, Delaware, announced that it plans to accept refugees.

"It is unfortunate that anyone would use the tragic events in Paris to send a message that we do not understand the plight of these refugees, ignoring the fact that the people we are talking about are fleeing the perpetrators of terror," Gov. Jack Markell said in a statement.

WHICH GOVERNORS OPPOSE NEW SYRIAN REFUGEES?

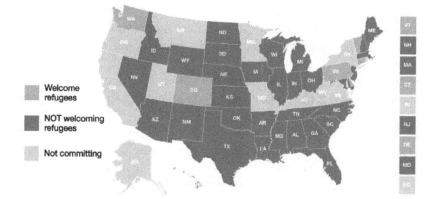

Welcome refugees

NOT welcoming refugees

Not committing

States whose governors oppose Syrian refugees coming in:
—Alabama
—Arizona
—Arkansas
—Florida
—Georgia
—Idaho
—Illinois
—Indiana
—Iowa
—Kansas
—Louisiana
—Maine
—Maryland
—Massachusetts
—Michigan
—Mississippi
—Nebraska
—Nevada
—New Hampshire
—New Jersey
—New Mexico
—North Carolina
—North Dakota
—Ohio
—Oklahoma
—South Carolina
—South Dakota
—Tennessee
—Texas
—Wisconsin
—Wyoming

States whose governors say they will accept refugees:
—Colorado
—Connecticut
—Delaware
—Hawaii
—Pennsylvania
—Vermont
—Washington

***

Michigan Gov. Rick Snyder said the state would "put on hold our efforts to accept new refugees."

"Michigan is a welcoming state and we are proud of our rich history of immigration. But our first priority is protecting the safety of our residents," he said in a statement.

Snyder demanded that the Department of Homeland Security review its security procedures for vetting refugees but avoided blanket suspicion of people from any region.

"It's also important to remember that these attacks are the efforts of extremists and do not reflect the peaceful ways of people of Middle Eastern descent here and around the world," Snyder said.

And Arkansas Gov. Asa Hutchinson posted on his official Twitter account that he would "oppose Syrian refugees being relocated to Arkansas."

Mississippi, Ohio Bristle at Taking Refugees

The governors of Ohio and Mississippi announced their states would not allow Syrian refugees.

Jim Lynch, a spokesman for Ohio Gov. John Kasich, issued this statement:

> "The governor doesn't believe the U.S. should accept additional Syrian refugees because security and safety issues cannot be adequately addressed. The governor is writing to the President to ask him to stop, and to ask him to stop resettling them in Ohio. We are also looking at what additional steps Ohio can take to stop resettlement of these refugees."

Kasich is a Republican presidential candidate.

Mississippi Gov. Phil Bryant wrote on Facebook that he was working with the state's homeland security department to "determine the current status of any Syrian refugees that may be brought to our state in the near future.

"I will do everything humanly possible to stop any plans from the Obama administration to put Syrian refugees in Mississippi. The policy of bringing these individuals into the country is not only misguided, it is extremely dangerous. I'll be notifying President Obama of my decision today to resist this potential action."

Louisiana: 'Kept in the dark'

Louisiana governor and GOP presidential candidate Bobby Jindal complained bitterly in an open letter to Obama that the federal government had not informed his government about refugees being relocated to his state last week.

"It is irresponsible and severely disconcerting to place individuals, who may have ties to ISIS, in a state without the state's knowledge or involvement," Jindal said in his letter Saturday.

He demanded to know more about the people being placed in Louisiana to avoid a repeat of the Paris attacks and wanted to know whether screening would be intensified for refugees holding Syrian passports.

And he suggested Obama hold off on taking in more refugees.

"It would be prudent to pause the process of refugees coming to the United States. Authorities need to investigate what happened in Europe before this problem comes to the United States," Jindal said.

Republican candidate Donald Trump called accepting Syrian refugees "insane."

"We all have heart and we all want people taken care of, but with the problems our country has, to take in 250,000—some of whom are going to have problems, big problems—is just insane. We have to be insane. Terrible," Donald Trump said at a rally in Beaumont, Texas.

It's not clear why Trump used the 250,000 figure.

The Obama administration has previously announced plans to take in 10,000 Syrian refugees next year.

While addressing reporters on Monday, Obama called out Republican candidates who have objected to admitting refugees to the United States.

> "When I hear a political leader suggesting that there should be a religious test for which a person who is fleeing from a war torn country is admitted… when some of those folks themselves come from families who benefited from protection when they were fleeing political persecution, that is shameful," the President said. "We don't have religious tests to our compassion."

New York: 'Virtually no vetting'

A senior White House security official attempted to allay concerns about the vetting of Syrian refugees.

On NBC's "Meet the Press" Sunday, White House Deputy National Security Adviser Ben Rhodes said, "We have very extensive screening procedures for all Syrian refugees who have come to the United States. There is a very careful vetting process that includes our intelligence community, our National Counter Terrorism Center, the Department of Homeland Security, so we can make sure that we are carefully screening anybody that comes to the United States."

New York Rep. Peter King, speaking on Fox News, cast doubt on Rhodes' comments.

> "What he said about the vetting of the refugees is untrue. There is virtually no vetting cause there are no databases in Syria, there are no government records. We don't know who these people are."

On Sunday, investigators said that one of the Paris bombers carried Syrian identification papers—possibly forged—and the fear of Syrian refugees grew worse.

"It's not that we don't want to—it's that we can't," Florida Sen. and Republican presidential hopeful Marco Rubio told ABC's George Stephanopoulos. "Because there's no way to background check someone that's coming from Syria."

Turning Away Refugees Won't Fight Terrorism, and Might Make It Worse

By Nick Stockton
Wired, November 17, 2015

French authorities announced that a passport belonging to a Syrian refugee was next to the remains of one of the suicide bombers who attacked Paris last week. Fingerprints match, but it might be a forgery. Either way, the American response was swift. As I type, 25 US governors have closed their borders to Syrian refugees, even though the US committed to taking in 10,000 people fleeing the civil war in Syria.

That raises an ethical question, of course—do Americans deserve peace of mind more than Syrians refugees deserve safety? The more practical question though, is whether blocking Syrian refugees will stop terrorism.

Defined narrowly, the answer is a qualified yes: A Syrian refugee moratorium would block the narrow subset of terrorists who also happen to be (or are posing as) Syrian refugees.

Broadly, the answer is a far less qualified no. Research at every link of this chain suggests that keeping refugees out probably doesn't stop any terrorists, and letting them in might keep people—or their kids—from taking up arms.

Believe it or not, the main reason is crummy American bureaucracy. Getting into this country is tough. According to the US State Department's website, the average wait time for processing an asylum request is a year to 18 months. For refugees from the Middle East, it takes longer. People from places there, if they're engulfed in conflict, tend to lack adequate documentation. That makes background checks difficult. And when in doubt, the Department of Homeland Security tends to deny the request.

The US refugee process is so long, so thorough, that it is probably the least efficient way for a potential terrorist to enter the US. "Why would an ISIS terrorist sit and wait to be a refugee for three years to get into the US, when they could get a radicalized European citizen and fly here on a visa waiver and then live here under the radar?" says Anne Speckhard, director of International Center for the Study of Violent Extremism. Or maybe the terrorist isn't a European citizen. "They can fly to Mexico and get across the border and it's a much faster way than the refugee route," says Speckhard.

Who needs the grief, in other words. But then again, "You can have a thousand people come in and 999 of them are just poor people fleeing oppression and violence," said presidential candidate and senator Marco Rubio (R-FL) in a November 16 speech. "But one of them is an ISIS fighter—if that's the case, you have a problem."

In a way, he's right. Psychiatrists, psychologists, and conflict experts who study terrorism generally agree that everyone who becomes a terrorist does it for different reasons. "If you're looking at terrorists' motivations, it is always going to be contextual," says Speckhard, who is also the author of *Talking to Terrorists*. (She has interviewed over 400). "If you are Moroccan, it's going to be about living in a society that doesn't really welcome you and gravitating towards something that gives you identity and a feeling of self-worth. If you you're Chechen, your motivations are trauma and revenge."

Forced to generalize, the researchers I spoke with described terrorists as traumatized, marginalized, looking for justice, identity, or meaning. And in that sense, Rubio is wrong. The problem is, those words could apply to most refugees, and most refugees are not terrorists. According to the Bureau of Population, Refugees, and Migration, of the 3 million refugees admitted to the US since 1975 (785,000 since 9/11), roughly a dozen have been arrested or removed due to security concerns. Generalization doesn't work.

Think about mass shootings in the US, says Rochelle Davis, cultural anthropologist at Georgetown who studies Middle Eastern refugees. The perpetrators might share similar profiles, but those similarities are statistically insignificant when compared to all the disaffected, antisocial, mentally troubled, young men who do not pick up a gun, or a bomb, or many guns and bombs. "We may try to explain them, but for the most part each one is an exceptional event," she says.

If you insist on profiling Europe's terrorists, maybe start closer to home. Besides the errant Syrian passport, most of Europe's terrorists are European. Terrorists, or at least the brand of religious zealot attracted to ISIS, Al Shabaab, or Al Qaeda, tend to be from marginalized communities. "If you look at the Charlie Hebdo attacks, those individuals were not immigrants or

> **Research at every link of this chain suggests that keeping refugees out probably doesn't stop any terrorists, and letting them in might keep people—or their kids—from taking up arms.**

refugees," says Simond de Galbert, a visiting fellow at the Center for Strategic and International Studies. "They were French citizens, the sons or grandsons or great-grandsons of immigrants who arrived in France."

Europe's marginalized Muslim communities descended from people invited to the country as laborers (because the continent's birth rate is so low). In the simplest terms, the current troubles with radicalized minorities are bits of baggage left over from both Europeans' and the immigrants' reluctance to assimilate each others' culture.

In that light, the answer is not to leave refugees to fester—marginalized. It doesn't matter if that marginalization occurs in first world countries, or Lebanese (1.2 million Syrians) and Jordanian (700,000 Syrians) camps.

But still: the Syrian passport. Though the document was likely forged, the fingerprints match those of the remains near where it was found. The fact is, if one or more of the Paris attackers was actually also a Syrian refugee, it should have little to no bearing on how the US determines its immigration policy. In fact, doing so would be more in line with what the actual terrorists seem to hope will happen—for the US to close its shutters and let ISIS continue to make life hell for millions in the Middle East.

The roots of terrorism are deep and tangled. The patterns are also familiar, if you look for them. The Syrian story doesn't have to go that way this time—if the policymakers look at the data.

Report Aims to Debunk Anti-Immigration Myths

By Yasmin Anwar
Futurity, September 23, 2015

Immigration is shaping up to be among the top wedge issues in the 2016 presidential race. GOP front-runner Donald Trump is stoking the debate with
threats to build a wall between the United States and Mexico and eliminate
birthright citizenship.

A recent Gallup poll shows that one in five registered voters say they will support
the candidate who shares their views on immigration.

A new report that discusses how well immigrants have adapted to US society
in the last 40 years makes the case for collecting broader and better data on immigrants and their descendants.

"Our goal in writing this report is to provide a state-of-the-art synthesis of the
best social science evidence so that politicians and policymakers can make more informed decisions," says Irene Bloemraad, professor of sociology and Canadian studies at University of California, Berkeley. "Donald Trump should definitely read it."

She discussed the report with university writer Yasmin Anwar.

WHY SHOULD WE CARE ABOUT THE STATE OF IMMIGRATION?

There are more than 41 million immigrants living in the United States and another 37
million Americans have at least one foreign-born parent. That translates into one in
four people in the United States who are first-or second-generation immigrants. The
consequences of integration thus touch everyone, from neighbors and co-workers,
to our school systems, the technology sector, health care institutions, and more.

WHAT WERE SOME OF THE REPORT'S KEY FINDINGS? ANY SURPRISES?

Immigrant integration is happening at the same pace or even faster than prior waves
across a wide range of measures such as education, employment, earnings, poverty,
language, and intermarriage. Immigrants are becoming more and more similar to
other Americans over time and across generations.

A lot of people might be surprised to know that if we look at new immigration
to the United States, people from Asia now surpass Latino immigrants in terms of

numbers. Also, the undocumented population, counting about 11.3 million people, is smaller now than back in 2007, when it was over 12 million.

English is virtually universal among second-generation immigrants today, which wasn't the case a century ago. Improvements in the educational outcomes for children with parents from modest backgrounds are striking. And unlike in the past, a significant proportion of immigrants are highly educated, with more years of education than the average American.

These immigrants move immediately into professional occupations and entrepreneurship. Interestingly, regardless of level of education, immigrant men tend to work at rates higher than the native-born.

HOW ARE UNDOCUMENTED IMMIGRANTS FARING?

They are integrating to the extent that they are working, they are learning English, they are involved in their religious communities, and so forth. However, integration is slowed down by a lack of legal status or a precarious immigration status.

For example, the panel found evidence that a lack of legal status not only affects immigrants, but it slows integration among citizen children. There are negative effects on cognitive development for young children, higher levels of anxiety and depression for adolescents, and lower levels of overall schooling for young adults with undocumented parents compared to children with legally secure parents. Over 5 million children in the United States live with at least one undocumented parent, so this is a significant concern.

Another striking finding was that only about half of all immigrants naturalize, even though most immigrants say they wish to be US citizens. Over 7 percent of the US population are not citizens, so that means they cannot vote or run for office, impeding political integration. The US naturalization level is also much lower than in other high-immigration countries, such as Canada and Australia.

WHAT IS HOLDING THEM BACK?

Since the last report in 1997, there has been a proliferation of many distinct legal statuses that immigrants can hold, from permanent to temporary to precarious status, as well as not having papers, and each carries very different implications for work, post-secondary education, a path to citizenship, and access to public services at the federal, state and local level.

> **"...integration is slowed down by a lack of legal status or a precarious immigration status."**

It is remarkable how incredibly complex the laws have become and the difficulty in changing status. However, resolving the legal complexities and passing new legislation is a political, not a scientific matter. I do hope that the panel's findings will help inform the public debate.

WHAT ARE SOME OF THE MYTHS THAT THIS REPORT DEBUNKS?

That immigrants bring crime. In fact, neighborhoods with higher percentages of immigrants have lower crime rates. But with integration across generations, the descendants of immigrants become more and more like other Americans, and incarceration rates go up.

It's the same story when it comes to health. Immigrants are less likely to die from heart disease and cancer than the native-born, and on average, they have lower rates of depression, alcohol abuse, and smoking, as well as higher life expectancy. But we again see "integration" to American norms with time spent in the country and across generations so these health advantages dissipate.

As for language acquisition, although a majority of immigrants don't speak English at home, two-thirds report they can speak English well or very well, and by the second generation English proficiency is very high. Indeed, linguistic integration happens more quickly now than a century ago. Still, there is a need for high quality English language instruction, among school-aged children and for adults.

Four and a half percent of US households are linguistically isolated, which means no adult in the household speaks English. Funding has not kept pace with rising numbers, however. In fact, federal and state support for adult English-as-second-language classes has declined.

DOES THE REPORT EXAMINE BIRTHRIGHT CITIZENSHIP?

We did look at birthright citizenship in the context of civic and political integration and concluded that it is one of the most powerful mechanisms of formal political and civic inclusion in the United States. Birthright citizenship helps mitigate the inter-generational transfer of integration barriers produced by undocumented and precarious or temporary legal status, though it does not seem to erase them entirely.

BROADLY SPEAKING, HOW IS IMMIGRATION CHANGING AMERICA'S LANDSCAPE?

From our investigation, it is clear that immigration is contributing to demographic renewal, an important process given the retirement of the Baby-Boomer generation. Immigration is also changing social relations, sometimes in the most intimate spheres of life. Immigration to the United States has always been a patchwork quilt of backgrounds, but today that quilt is more intricate than ever.

WHAT CAN PRESIDENTIAL CANDIDATES AND ELECTED OFFICIALS LEARN FROM THIS REPORT?

The country receives an incredible diversity of immigrants from all corners of the world, of many different cultural and religious backgrounds, from those with very modest levels of education to the very highly educated. Overall, with time, and from one generation to the next, we find evidence of significant integration, in education, speaking English, where one lives, and so forth. This could be reassuring for policy-makers.

Yet the complexities of integration due to legal status, the challenges of racial integration, the fact that some integration makes immigrants less well-off, and the relatively low levels of citizenship acquisition are all areas of concern.

The Carnegie Corporation of New York, the Russell Sage Foundation, National Science Foundation, the US Citizenship and Immigration Service, and the President's Committee of the National Academies funded the report.

Immigrants and Crime: Crunching the Numbers

By Catherine E. Shoichet
CNN.com, July 8, 2015

With a presidential election looming, politicians on both sides of the aisle are sparring over immigration in a battle that shows no sign of stopping.

Some are pointing to a recent case—a woman in San Francisco who was killed, allegedly by an undocumented immigrant who'd already been deported five times—as another sign that the U.S. system is in serious need of an overhaul.

But what are the numbers behind the rhetoric?

Here's a look at some of the statistics, where they come from and what people on different sides of the debate say about them.

11.2 million

That's the latest estimate of the number of unauthorized immigrants in the United States, according to the Pew Research Center. And it's less than 4% of the total U.S. population.

The number peaked in 2007, according to Pew, when there were an estimated 12.2 million unauthorized immigrants in the country. But since 2009, it's "remained essentially unchanged," Pew reports, as the numbers of undocumented immigrants entering and leaving the United States "have come into rough balance."

177,960

The number of undocumented immigrants deported last year who were convicted criminals, according to Immigration and Customs Enforcement.

That's 56% of last year's total number of deportations, according to ICE, and it's a group that the agency says it's putting first when it comes to deciding which cases to prioritize.

Ask someone like Republican presidential contender Donald Trump about this number and you'll get an earful about how this statistic and others show rampant crime among undocumented immigrants.

Immigrant advocates say that's far from the truth, adding that it's important to look at how the term ICE uses when it talks about convicted criminals—"criminal alien"—is defined.

"Government statistics on who is being removed from the country can be somewhat deceptive," says Walter Ewing, a senior researcher for the American Immigration Council who helped author a report released this week that argues immigrants are less likely to be criminals than native-born U.S. citizens.

"Immigrants who experience even the slightest brush with the criminal justice system, such as being convicted of a misdemeanor, can find themselves subject to detention for an undetermined period, after which they are expelled from the country and barred from returning," the report says. "In other words, for years the government has been redefining what it means to be a 'criminal alien,' using increasingly stringent definitions and standards of 'criminality' that do not apply to U.S. citizens."

121

The number of people released from immigration custody who were later charged with murder between 2010 and 2014, according to figures from the Department of Homeland Security cited in a recent letter from two U.S. senators. That's about a thousandth of a percent of the total estimated number of unauthorized immigrants in the United States.

Sen. Jeff Sessions and Sen. Chuck Grassley, both Republicans, have been pointing to this number as they push federal authorities for answers, arguing that "countless innocent Americans every year are the victims of crime perpetrated by deportable criminals."

And the recent San Francisco shooting has added fresh fuel to the debate over whether authorities are doing enough to keep harmful offenders off the streets—and kick them out of the United States.

But other officials have stressed that it's important to look at the big picture and not to make knee-jerk decisions based on individual cases.

"On the issue of immigration," California Attorney General Kamala Harris said this week, "our policy should not be informed by our collective outrage about one man's conduct."

73,665

The number of inmates in state and federal prisons who are not U.S. citizens, according to the latest prison population report from the Bureau of Judicial Statistics. That's about 5% of the total prison population.

In his recent push for building a massive wall on the southern U.S. border, Trump has said that there are "hundreds of thousands" of undocumented immigrants in the nation's state and federal prisons. It was a claim that the PolitiFact fact-checking website gave a "mostly false" rating.

"The basic claim is at best unsustainable or more likely pure fiction. A fact created out of thin air," Ramiro Martinez, a criminal justice professor at Northeastern University, told PolitiFact.

The bottom line, PolitiFact says, is that it's unclear just how many undocumented immigrants are currently in prison, because the available statistics don't provide details about inmates' immigration status.

Analysts on both sides of the immigration debate do agree on one thing: There's a lack of good data about this. But as to how likely it is for immigrants to commit crimes, that depends on who you ask.

In a 2009 report arguing that immigrants have "high rates of criminality," the Center for Immigration Studies pointed to statistics that non-U.S. citizens represent a quarter of the U.S. prison population.

This week's report from the American Immigration Council counters that immigrants are less likely to commit crimes and are overrepresented in the federal prison system. Citing the American Community Survey, the report also notes that the percentage of foreign-born men in the United States who are incarcerated (1.6%) is less than the percentage of U.S.-born men who are imprisoned (3.3%). And the reason they're behind bars is often tied to immigration offenses.

> **"Immigrants who experience even the slightest brush with the criminal justice system, such as being convicted of a misdemeanor, can find themselves subject to detention for an undetermined period, after which they are expelled from the country and barred from returning."**

"While some may be there for committing a serious criminal offense, a great many more may be there because of an immigration violation," the report says.

1 million

The number of so-called detainer requests issued by Immigration and Customs and Enforcement and sent to local authorities from 2008 to 2012, according to the Transactional Records Access Clearinghouse at Syracuse University.

More than three-quarters of those were for immigrants who had no criminal convictions on their records. For the ones who'd been convicted, only 8.6% were charged with serious offenses, based on federal standards.

Federal immigration authorities use detainers to ask local agencies to hold unauthorized immigrants and eventually hand them over to the Department of Homeland Security.

It's a controversial approach that's long drawn fire from immigrant rights advocates, who argue that the feds have used the tool inappropriately to detain and deport people who don't deserve it.

As a result, some places—like San Francisco—call themselves sanctuary cities and say they won't honor those requests, demanding that federal authorities go through the courts.

It's a situation that's been in the spotlight with this month's shooting in San Francisco. Critics of the city argue that officials there erred when they didn't let Homeland Security know they were releasing suspect Juan Francisco Lopez-Sanchez.

In an interview with CNN on Tuesday, Democratic presidential hopeful Hillary Clinton said San Francisco should have listened to the Department of Homeland Security and made a mistake when it didn't send Lopez-Sanchez packing.

"I have absolutely no support for a city that ignores the strong evidence that should be acted on. . . . If it were a first-time traffic citation, if it were something minor, a misdemeanor, that's entirely different," she said. "This man had already been deported five times. And he should have been deported at the request of the federal government."

San Francisco Sheriff Ross Mirkarimi said his city has a good reason for their approach.

"Because of what has not been reconciled on the federal level," he says, "local governments and state governments are devising new laws."

10,182

The number of ICE detainers state and local enforcement authorities declined to honor last year.

"This required ICE to expend additional resources attempting to locate, apprehend and remove criminal aliens who were released into the community, rather than transferred directly into custody," ICE said in its report on last year's deportation statistics.

But when it comes to immigration detainers, there's a long history of distrust between local and federal agencies, says Ruben Rumbaut, a professor of sociology at the University of California at Irvine.

"The majority of people that were put in ICE detainers were in the end deported out of the country for reasons that have nothing to do with crime," Rumbaut said. "It's become very controversial."

For Illegal Immigrants with Babies, the Anchor Pulls in Many Directions

By Pamela Constable
The Washington Post, September 20, 2015

The pregnant Latina women who come for checkups and guidance at Mary's Center in Northwest Washington say that they understand that their babies will become anchors in their lives—but not the kind of anchors that Republican presidential candidate Donald Trump disparages on the campaign trail.

The newborns—who will be U.S. citizens even if their parents are in this country illegally—are a mixed blessing for their mothers: another mouth to feed, another obstacle to finding or keeping a precious low-wage job, another complication in an already complex life that, in many cases, includes providing for older children left behind in Central America.

"I didn't come here to have a baby. I came to have a better future and help my daughter back in my country," said Nellis Najera, 27, a kitchen worker who was attending a breast-feeding class. "Babies come because it is part of life. But it makes your life harder, because you have to choose between the baby and work."

The number of children born to immigrants who are in this country illegally has declined steadily in recent years, according to data from the Pew Research Center, as the undocumented population here has leveled off. After peaking at 360,000 in 2007, such births fell to 295,000 in 2013, the center said.

At the same time, an Obama administration proposal to allow the parents of U.S.-born children to avoid deportation has provided new ammunition for critics like Trump, who say babies born to people here illegally should be denied citizenship and, along with their parents, forced to leave this country.

The issue has inflamed the 2016 presidential primary contest, with Trump's provocative rhetoric pushing him to the top of GOP polls even as his rivals try to sidestep the topic for fear of alienating Hispanic voters.

"A woman gets pregnant. She's nine months, she walks across the border, she has the baby in the United States, and we take care of the baby for 85 years," Trump said at the GOP candidates' debate Wednesday, shaking his head in apparent disgust. "I don't think so."

Last week, he told a cheering Dallas crowd that the United States has become a "dumping ground" for violent gang members and "anchor babies."

Although U.S. hospitals near the Mexican border have reported that they regularly deliver babies whose mothers live in Mexico, experts at several research organizations in the district said that the vast majority of undocumented immigrants who have babies here have lived in the United States for at least several years. They also said most of the women came here to work and escape lives of poverty and violence, not to raise a family.

The true "anchor baby" problem, these experts said, is not that undocumented immigrants are giving birth in the United States in order to increase their chances of staying and accessing social programs. It is that starting a family here inevitably changes the parents' long-term goals.

Over time, the arrival of children weakens family ties to the homeland and cements the parents' bonds with the United States. And once their children have learned English and become used to life here, many immigrant parents said that they could not imagine bringing them back to the dirt-poor, gang-plagued countries that the parents fled.

"This is not birth tourism," said Mark Krikorian, executive director of the Center for Immigration Studies in the District. "It's not so much about inducement or enticement, but about people coming here to work, meeting someone, then the birds and the bees happen, and they have kids."

"And once you have kids," he said, "it becomes less likely that you will leave on your own or get deported."

'Nobody gives me anything'

In the Mary Center's waiting room one day last week, Maria Canas, 35, struggled to quiet her shrieking 2-year-old son and corral her feisty 5-year-old daughter.

Canas came to the United States from El Salvador in her 20s, illegal and illiterate, leaving behind a young daughter. She cleaned hotel rooms and offices, cooked burgers and fries, and sent as much money home as she could.

Meanwhile, she met and married a Salvadoran construction worker. They had two children, who, as U.S. citizens, qualified for an array of public benefits and services. But juggling work shifts and child care has sapped Canas's strength and strained the family's budget.

> **Experts at several research organizations in the district said that the vast majority of undocumented immigrants who have babies here have lived in the United States for at least several years. . . .[and] came here to work and escape lives of poverty and violence, not to raise a family.**

"If they say we come here to have children and take people's jobs, it's not true," said Canas, who never attended school. "Nobody gives me anything. I have done any work I could find. I want my children to have what I couldn't. What's wrong with that?"

Trump and other immigration hard-liners argue that children born to undocumented immigrants should not be rewarded with access to public schools and other taxpayer-funded benefits, including Medicaid and social service programs for those whose incomes are low enough to qualify.

"It's like saying a complete stranger walks into your living room, gives birth in your house, then suddenly the child is a member of your family, and you are obligated to provide all sorts of things for that child," said Ira Mehlman, head of the conservative Federation for American Immigration Reform.

Trump has proposed deporting all 11 million people who are in this country illegally—an idea most of his rivals dismiss as impossible and inappropriate. He questions whether the 14th Amendment guarantees U.S. citizenship to the children of undocumented immigrants and says that such "birthright citizenship" should be prohibited by law.

Those who advocate for immigrants and their children counter that the right to citizenship is enshrined in the Constitution and is a core American value. They also argue that illegal immigrants contribute to the U.S. economy and social safety net more than many Americans realize. Undocumented workers sustain numerous industries, such as meatpacking and farming, often doing dirty and dangerous jobs that American-born workers shun, advocates and researchers say. They pay sales taxes, many pay income taxes and a significant number pay into Social Security—even though they, unlike their U.S.-born children, stand little chance of receiving retirement payments.

National surveys of undocumented Hispanic immigrants echo the stories told by the Latina mothers at Mary's Center, almost all of whom are from Central America. Most do not become pregnant until they have been here for several years and have formed new romantic or marital relationships—often without anticipating the burdens that a new child will bring.

A majority of the women interviewed at the center, both legal and undocumented, were receiving services through the federal Special Supplemental Nutrition Program for Women, Infants and Children. Their older children were attending public schools. But the women said that having a U.S.-born child had not entitled them to any individual benefits—and that they had not expected that it would.

"Even if our children are born here, we still have no documents," said Laura Flamenco, a 33-year-old Salvadoran woman who got married after four years in the United States and was about to have her first baby. "I came here to support my parents back home, but I had to stop work because of the baby. Now I have less to send them, even though they still need it," Flamenco said. "The people who judge us have no human feeling. We do all the hard and heavy work. We need them, and they need us."

A fraction of U.S. births

Birth tourism does exist, in small numbers, at both ends of the economic scale, immigration experts say. There is a thriving cottage industry that helps affluent, pregnant foreigners fly to the United States on visitors' visas, stay at hotels until they deliver, and return home with a newborn U.S. citizen. And among the thousands of people who come to the United States on multi-year work or student visas, some become parents during their stays.

In communities north of the Mexican border and cities, such as Los Angeles, with large Latino populations, hospitals often deliver babies for Mexican mothers, although some of those mothers are commuters who work on the American side of the border or have roots in both countries.

But all those births make up a fraction of the babies born to illegal immigrants in the United States each year. And experts say there is little evidence that significant numbers of Latinas are deliberately crossing the border to give birth.

According to Mark Lopez, the director of Hispanic research at Pew, the typical immigrant living illegally in the United States today has lived here for at least 10 years. For those with U.S.-born children, it is at least 15 years. Some U.S. citizens born to undocumented Hispanic mothers since the 1980s are now having children of their own.

One was Jessica Melendez, a DC resident whose parents fled El Salvador years ago. Born in Texas, Melendez met her husband, an undocumented Salvadoran, in 2004; three years later, their daughter Viviana was born. But things went wrong during the delivery. The baby's oxygen supply was cut off, and she suffered severe brain damage and physical disabilities. She has received extraordinary medical care ever since, including a nurse who accompanies her to school, much of it paid through the federal Supplemental Social Security program.

"If she had been born in El Salvador, she would be dead," said Melvin Melendez, 33, who works as a restaurant cook and now has temporary legal amnesty.

Regardless of the family's legal status, Melendez said, the couple has earned the benefits that help keep their daughter alive.

"For nine years, my wife took the bus every morning at 4 to work at McDonald's, and as soon as she came home at night, I went to work. We lived in shifts and never took a vacation," Melendez said. "We didn't plan for this to happen to our daughter. But thank God it happened here."

The Telling Way White Americans React to Pictures of Dark-Skinned Immigrants

By Jeff Guo
The Washington Post, January 12, 2016

It's the lashing-out theory of Trumpmania. President Obama, Sen. Bernie Sanders, and others have speculated that working class whites are signing on to Donald Trump and his inflammatory anti-immigrant rhetoric out of a deepening anxiety over their place in the 21st century American economy.

Some political scientists, however, say antagonism toward immigrants is being driven by a more primal instinct: mistrust of outsiders—or even racial prejudice, either of the conscious or unconscious variety.

A body of academic research has tried to deconstruct why some Americans are skeptical about immigrants. Are they driven by policy concerns, about economics, or security? A general dubiousness about foreigners? Or a deep-seated aversion to people of a different skin tone?

A study forthcoming in the journal *Political Psychology* sheds new light on these questions. Political scientist Mara Ostfeld, who will be an assistant professor at the University of Michigan, randomly assigned white, non-Hispanic people to read different fictional stories about an immigrant family.

In one version of the story, the immigrants are sitting at a diner eating buffalo wings and discussing baseball. In another, the immigrants are at an ethnic food market eating spicy goat meat and talking in their native tongue.

After seeing the stories, the people were asked broad questions about immigration policy.

People who read about the American-acting immigrants expressed more positive feelings about immigrants and immigration policy *in general*—they were more likely to believe immigrants are helping America, more likely to support increasing the number of immigrants, and less likely to support building a fence on the Mexican border.

In other words, Ostfeld showed that people's attitudes about immigration can be nudged just by having them read stories about immigrants who behave in traditionally American ways.

These effects were modest, though statistically significant, and not too surprising. So far, these results were in line with past experiments showing that people feel positively toward immigrants who they think have made an effort to fit in.

Hidden fears

Outfeld wanted to go deeper, though.

In previous studies, researchers have found that people's views on immigration policy are affected generally by the ethnicity of the immigrants being discussed, but they did not find an effect based on skin color. In other words, showing people pictures of darker-featured Latinos as opposed to lighter-featured Latinos doesn't change how they feel about immigration policy.

In her experiment, Outfeld took another angle. After showing subjects pictures of either light-skinned or dark-skinned families, she also asked more personal questions. How would they feel having the immigrants from the story move into the neighborhood? Work alongside them? Marry somebody in the family?

On all these measures, respondents shown the darker-skinned immigrants were less likely to be accepting. Asked for their feelings about these scenarios a scale of 1 to 10, people given the darker pictures were about half a point less enthusiastic on average.

It's hard to detect racial prejudice in surveys because people tend to censor themselves when a stranger asks directly. But by comparing subjects who were randomly shown different pictures, Ostfeld got to measure people's knee-jerk biases.

Ostfeld's study shows that context matters to the immigration debate. "It's really important we understand that our perceptions of threat are different, whether we're thinking about immigration in the abstract or in our own communities," she says.

When the discussion is about immigration policy in general, people are mostly concerned with [the] way immigrants act, not the way they look. Will the newcomers fit in? Will they adopt American ways of life, or change what it means to be American? But if you get specific—if you talk about immigrants moving in next door—then people's racial biases also start coming to the fore.

The political implications

This issue has become particularly salient as immigration takes center stage in the GOP presidential primary. Trump has rallied supporters by inflaming their anxieties about immigrants, calling some Mexicans rapists and Syrian refugees terrorists. Trump's platform makes this a local issue, talking about the impact of immigration on "communities, schools and unemployment offices."

Earlier this month, the *New York Times* published data suggesting that the most racist places in America—where people tend to make the most "racially charged" Google

> A massive report from the National Academies of Sciences, Engineering and Medicine has shown that today's immigrants are integrating as swiftly as their predecessors, if not faster. They are more likely to speak English than past immigrants, are more educated, and neighborhoods with lots of immigrants tend to have less crime.

searches—are often the same areas where Trump has the strongest support among conservatives.

Researchers have found that racism tends to predict anti-immigrant views. Public opinion surveys, for example, show that whites who hold negative stereotypes about blacks are also more likely to oppose immigration, and to support making English the official language of the United States. This is a "surprising" result, the authors note, because most immigrants these days are not black, but Latino or Asian.

While many have blamed economic stress for causing Trump voters to direct their anger at immigrants, these and other studies show that views against immigration are often guided by deeper instincts.

"In fact, the evidence suggests there's more to the view that it's all about culture—that people are threatened by different ways of life, different religions, and different languages," says Shanto Iyengar, a political science professor at Stanford. "You have a bunch of other people speaking other languages, with brown skin, going to temples and mosques, and that is what is making people oppose immigration."

Trump, Iyengar says, has been particularly enthusiastic at highlighting this cultural divide. The candidate scored points at a Republican debate in September when he scolded Jeb Bush for speaking Spanish on the campaign trail. "We have to have assimilation to have a country," Trump later told *Politico*.

"[Trump] features all kinds of culturally dissimilar people in his rhetoric. He mentions specific nationalities, goes out of his way to point out this [immigration] is coming from a different country, a different way of life," Iyengar says. "He is absolutely playing to this notion of assimilability."

Many Americans seem to share the view that immigrants are dedicated to maintaining a different culture. A Pew poll in April, for instance, showed that 59 percent of the nation believes immigrants aren't learning English fast enough, while 66 percent say that immigrants these days want to hold onto their customs instead of adopting American ones.

These beliefs aren't accurate. A massive report from the National Academies of Sciences, Engineering and Medicine has shown that today's immigrants are integrating as swiftly as their predecessors, if not faster. They are more likely to speak English than past immigrants, are more educated, and neighborhoods with lots of immigrants tend to have less crime.

So why do so many Americans believe otherwise? Perhaps there is also some underlying bias, like what Ostfeld's research uncovered. Anxiety over immigrants not assimilating might not reflect racism per se, but it is influenced by a similar (and very human) impulse: suspicion of people who look and act differently. And sometimes, perhaps, a complaint about clashing cultures is really a complaint about race in disguise.

These sentiments have deep roots in America's past. In 1751, for instance, Benjamin Franklin griped about German settlers in Pennsylvania and their "swarthy" features, contrasting them to the "white" English. "Why should Pennsylvania, founded by the English, become a Colony of Aliens, who will shortly be so numerous as to Germanize us instead of our Anglifying them, and will never adopt our Language or Customs, any more than they can acquire our Complexion," Franklin wrote.

"But perhaps I am partial to the Complexion of my Country," he added, "for such Kind of Partiality is natural to Mankind."

4

Education, Culture, and Families

© Jose M. Osorio/TNS via ZUMA Wire

Students work on their math in their fourth grade classroom at Carman-Buckner Elementary School on January 22, 2016 in Waukegan, Illinois. Ten years ago, schools with high populations of Hispanic students spent this time of year scrambling to catch up students who had returned from long absences after their families spent Christmas and the following weeks in Mexico. But today, educators say the long trips have significantly diminished due to a number of factors: changes in immigration enforcement, landscaping businesses keeping parents employed through the winter, and a growing understanding by immigrant families of the importance of school attendance.

Immigrant Family Value

One of the most controversial facets of the immigration debate concerns federal and state policy on the treatment of immigrant children, minors, and families. The United States and many other nations have adopted specialized laws and policies to protect the rights of children and parents with dependents.[1] The U.S. Juvenile Justice System, for instance, was established in the late 1800s as legislators and justice department policy makers increasingly recognized that minors, because of their inexperience and other biological/sociological factors, should be treated differently than adult offenders. The U.S. justice system also has special provisions designed to keep families together, and such policies reflect the widespread belief in the central importance of the family in human culture. When it comes to immigration, legislators and judicial representatives disagree about the degree to which unauthorized immigrant minors and families, who are not citizens under U.S. law, should be treated differently than adult immigrants without dependents. As the population of immigrant minors and families with young children increases, the U.S. government is forced to contend with new challenges in attempting to balance legal standards with humanitarian values.

Unaccompanied Minors and Immigrant Families

Between 2011 and 2014, the United States saw a massive increase in the number of unaccompanied immigrant minors arriving from Mexico and Central America. In 2014, for instance, 52,000 unaccompanied children either surrendered to or were apprehended by border patrol officers while attempting to migrate into the United States. The massive influx overwhelmed state and federal agencies, resulting in what some characterized as an urgent humanitarian crisis.[2] While many unaccompanied minors were detained and/or deported, advocacy groups have urged for a more humane solution. As of 2016, the issue remains controversial. The United Nations Commissioner for Refugees conducted a series of interviews with children arriving from Honduras, El Salvador, Guatemala and Mexico and found that, in 58 percent of cases, the primary reason for leaving was gang violence in their home communities.[3]

To border patrol officers, politicians, and justice department officials, the influx of unaccompanied minors forces them to weigh child welfare against their duty to protect national borders. With gang violence increasing in Mexico and Central America, families are increasingly willing to risk migrating illegally despite the danger of detainment or arrest, human trafficking gangs who have been known to kidnap young migrants to extort money from their parents, and a variety of other potentially life threatening hazards. Despite these dangers, conditions in many poor Mexican and Central American communities have deteriorated to the point that parents and children will risk migration, though in many cases it means that the family will need to be separated. As of 2016, politicians and justice department officials are undecided as to whether minors and families fleeing gang violence qualify as refugees under U.S. law, a distinction that is typically used for those fleeing war or military conflict. Some argue that, by helping unauthorized immigrant minors, governments may be unwittingly supporting the human trafficking industry.[4]

Immigration and justice department officials also face a challenge determining how to house/detain immigrant minors and families with young children while they are waiting to plead their case in court. The Obama Administration began constructing a series of new federal facilities to house immigrant minors and families, but federal investigations found that the facilities fail to meet minimum hygiene and safety standards for the long-term detention of children.[5] Immigration service estimates have found that approximately 90 percent of women and children in detention centers may qualify for political asylum, and yet bureaucratic backlog and political opposition to reform continue to complicate the situation. Children and families may wait months or years before appearing in court.[6] For unaccompanied minors granted asylum, providing housing, food, and other necessities remains a problem. Host families and group housing facilities are in short supply, forcing some immigrant minors to wait in detention for extended periods, even after being granted refugee status.

The status of immigrant minors raises deeper questions about the morality of immigration restrictions. When, for instance, is it ethical to deport someone who arrives in a country unlawfully? In cases where refugees are fleeing war torn countries, federal laws support a fast track to political asylum. However, current laws do not extend the same opportunities to the millions of immigrants fleeing poverty or a lack of employment opportunities, despite the fact that these factors can have an equally devastating effect on well being. Such considerations continue to motivate proposals to liberalize immigration law, especially in cases that involve immigrant minors. However, opponents argue that such reforms, however good intentioned, might encourage further unauthorized migration, thus straining an already overburdened system.

Education and Family Support

The growth of the immigrant population since the 1990s placed increasing strain on public schools, and many schools and school districts have responded by creating new ESL, immigrant and family outreach, and other programs designed to encourage assimilation and integration. However, immigrant children often face discrimination exacerbated by common stereotypes depicting immigrants as unwanted or unsavory members of American society. Also damaging is the stereotype that immigrants typically want to maintain native traditions and resist assimilating with American laws and mainstream culture. In sharp contrast, surveys and studies of immigrant families routinely show that the vast majority of immigrants want to assimilate and become or be seen as Americans.[7]

A related problem concerns the thousands of children brought to the United States as undocumented migrants who then grow up attending U.S. schools and finding employment in U.S. businesses. Young adults and children in this category face a significant problem when it comes to their ability to pursue higher education as some states prohibit undocumented students from enrolling in local colleges while others allow undocumented students to enroll but force them to pay far more expensive out-of-state tuition rates. The DREAM Act, proposed in 2001, would have provided educational support, including in-state tuition rates, for undocumented students and also proposed that the federal government would defer deporting the children of undocumented migrants meeting certain criteria. The DREAM Act failed to win approval in Congress, and subsequent efforts to pass similar legislation also failed. Most recently, President Obama announced the Deferred Action for Childhood Arrivals (DACA) Act, which would allow undocumented migrants who arrived before their sixteenth birthday to receive work permits, obtain state IDs and driver's licenses and to be exempted from deportation. While a majority of U.S. states have agreed to comply with DACA, legislators and politicians in a few states, most notably Arizona and Nebraska, have refused to grant driver's licenses to undocumented applicants and have protested other aspects of the federal proposal.[8]

Many legislators who otherwise support strict adherence to immigration law, including numerous conservative Republican politicians, have supported efforts to provide aid and educational support for minors and the children of undocumented immigrants. In some cases, politicians have justified this position by noting that the children of undocumented migrants and underage migrants themselves have reduced culpability in the decision to migrate and should therefore not be punished for the decisions of their parents. In addition, there is a political angle to the issue, especially as many of the young undocumented students have begun to make an impact in immigrant activism and political movements. Struggling to appeal to a demographic that has justifiably seen them as the enemy, the Republican Party has been reaching out to the children of undocumented immigrants demographic in hopes of increasing the party's traction with Latino voters in future elections.

Language and Cultural Diversity

Among those who oppose immigration, there is a small but passionate minority who argue that immigration dilutes or threatens a perceived American culture. Though the concept of American culture is difficult to define, especially given that there are few aspects of American culture that have not been influenced by immigration, several lobbyist groups have attempted to push for legislation that would preserve American culture from foreign dilution or influence. One example is the "English-only" language movement, which seeks to promote a federal amendment, or state/federal laws that establish English as the official language of the United States. Surveys of immigrant culture indicate that most first generation immigrants and the vast majority of second generation immigrants already put significant effort and energy into becoming fluent in English. The American Psychological Association released a report concluding that there was no clear benefit to the English-only movement, and that some of the proposed laws could have negative psychological and educational consequences for the number of immigrant Americans already struggling to become fluent.[9]

Outside of the English-only movement, bilingualism and bilingual education are important issues in the immigrant debate. According to demographic data collected by the Census Bureau, there might be as many as 39 to 43 million Spanish speakers in the United States by 2020,[10] and Spanish (with 37 million speakers) is the most spoken non-English language in the United States. Most Latino Americans feel that maintaining fluency or at least familiarity with Spanish is important to the continuation of their culture, but a majority of Latin American immigrants also use English at home and make efforts to ensure that their children become fluent in English as well.[11] Despite the continued high levels of immigration from Spanish speaking countries, Pew Research studies indicate that fluency in Spanish declines in immigrant households. In third generation immigrant households, for instance, most families speak English, though some of the family is likely to maintain some familiarity with their native language.

Debates over immigration and language raise interesting ideas about cultural diversity versus assimilation. While U.S. residents practice a variety of ethnic cultural traditions, some customs are not tolerated—for instance genital mutilation and childhood marriage—because they infringe on what U.S. law protects as basic human rights. U.S. law does, however, protect the rights of American citizens and legal residents to practice a wide variety of cultural, religious, and ethic traditions that do not violate U.S. law or the rights of others. Whether these traditions are tolerated, respected, and accepted by the American public is a different story, and a nativist, anti-foreign sentiment continues to prevail among certain communities across the country. Ultimately, many argue, the introduction of new cultural traditions by immigrants has a positive, broadening effect on U.S. culture, and cultural, ethnic, and racial diversity have wide-ranging and long-lasting positive effects in educational and professional environments. Indeed many sociologists have posited that the diversity of American society is one of the key reasons that the United States is culturally innovative and has become one of the world's most powerful nations both economically and culturally. From this perspective, immigration and assimilation might be seen as building blocks of a new, more culturally-diverse society, rather than destructive forces threatening existing American culture or traditions.

Micah L. Issitt

Notes

1. Convention on the Rights of the Child, *OHCHR*.
2. "Under-age and On the Move," *Economist.*
3. Nazario, "The Children of the Drug Wars."
4. Abdullah, "Immigrants or Refugees? A Difference With Political Consequences."
5. Carcamo, "Judge Orders Prompt Release of Immigrant Children from Detention."

6. Sakuma, Amanda. "The Failed Experiment of Immigrant Family Detention."

7. Thompson, "Where Education and Assimilation Collide."

8. Luzer, "Dreamers Deferred."

9. Padilla, et al, "The English-Only Movement."

10. Konnikova, "Is Bilingualism Really an Advantage?"

11. Lopez and Gonzalez-Barrera, "What is the Future of Spanish in the United States?"

Schools Brace for Influx of Immigrants

By Lesli A. Maxwell
Education Week, July 9, 2014

As the federal government scrambles to respond to an unprecedented surge of un-accompanied minors streaming across the U.S.-Mexico border, the wave of young immigrants arriving alone from Central America has already begun to surface in communities and public schools far from the Southwest.

In Miami, a nonprofit agency that provides legal services to unaccompanied mi-nors has served 1,600 such children since the beginning of the calendar year, the same number it served in all of 2013. Last month, the Miami-Dade County school board approved Superintendent Alberto Carvalho's request to seek additional feder-al funding to help the district cover the costs of educating what he called "a spike in the number of foreign-born students from Central America, specifically Honduras."

In San Francisco and Oakland, Calif., as well as in suburbs of Washington, edu-cators report that the number of unaccompanied minors has been rising steadily for several months in their high schools.

And in New York City, educators are beginning to coordinate with city agen-cies and nonprofit groups to address the needs of some 3,000 undocumented chil-dren and youths who have arrived there in the past few months.

"There are so many noneducational needs that need tending to for these young people before they can even begin to focus on their education," said Claire Sylvan, the executive director and president of the Internationals Network for Public Schools, a New York City-based group of 17 high schools around the country that serve newly arrived immigrants and English-language learners.

'Humanitarian Crisis'

Since last October, more than 50,000 child migrants—most of them from El Salvador, Guatemala, and Honduras—have been detained by U.S. Border Patrol agents. That's more than twice the number detained in all of 2013. Most of the deten-tions have occurred in the Rio Grande Valley region along the border between Texas and Mexico.

Under federal law, immigration authorities cannot turn away any children arriving from noncontiguous countries.

The ballooning numbers prompted the Obama administration in late May to declare a humanitarian crisis and to open three emergency shelters, in California,

Oklahoma, and Texas, to add to the federal government's stable of 100 permanent shelters that house unaccompanied minors while they wait for immigration hearings and possible reunification with family members already in the United States. The administration has also asked Congress for $2 billion in new money to open more detention facilities and to hire more immigration judges to accelerate processing of a growing backlog of asylum and removal proceedings.

Many of the children and youths say that escalating violence and gang activity in their home countries, as well as the desire to reunite with parents in the United States, are driving them to make the grueling 1,000-mile trek through Mexico to the Texas border, where they are turning themselves over to Border Patrol agents.

Also contributing to the flow is the widespread belief in Central America that a change to U.S. immigration policy in 2012 allows young immigrants who make it to the border to stay. The Obama administration has aggressively countered that notion as Republican lawmakers have charged that the president's Deferred Action for Childhood Arrivals policy, which suspended deportation for many immigrants brought to the United States illegally as children before 2007, as the main driver of the new migration.

In the Shelters

With hundreds of children and youths crossing the border daily, federal officials have struggled to provide shelter, food, and other basic services to them while they are detained. After taking the children and youths into custody, immigration officials have three days to transfer them to the federal Office of Refugee Resettlement, which is responsible for their care in longer-term shelters while attempts are made to place them with relatives or guardians as they await deportation proceedings.

While in the shelters overseen by the Office of Refugee Resettlement, nonprofit organizations provide unaccompanied minors English-as-a-second-language classes, along with arts-and-crafts and recreational activities both inside and outside the shelters, said Kenneth Wolfe, a spokesman for the U.S. Department of Health and Human Services, the agency that houses the refugee office. The average length of stay in the longer-term shelters is 35 days, Mr. Wolfe said.

By the time the young migrants reach U.S. communities like Miami, San Francisco, New York, and Prince George's County, Md., many have already been released from federal custody to stay with a parent or an extended-family member. Some have been released to adult sponsors who are not relatives.

"I've never seen so many of these children coming at once, and I've never seen so many young ones on their own," said Cheryl Little, the executive director of Americans for Immigrant Justice, a legal-services agency in Miami that provides free representation to unaccompanied children and youths.

"By the time we are seeing them, they may have already been in the country for weeks," she said. "Many of them appear to be as young as 9 or 10."

Once children are released to parents or adult sponsors, they are required to enroll in school. And while more polarized debates rage in Washington and around the country about immigration policy and how the Obama administration should handle the surge, district officials say they must be ready to serve the child migrants who arrive at their schools.

Impact in Maryland In Maryland's 125,000-student Prince George's County district—just outside Washington and home to a large Central American immigrant community—educators saw an increase in the numbers of unaccompanied minors in 2012. Before that uptick, the district had around 75 such students, all of them of middle or high school age, said Patricia Chiancone, a counselor in the district's international-programs office.

"We had over 200 unaccompanied minors this past school year," she said. "And we are seeing them at the elementary level, which is new."

The district has teacher professional development on tap this summer to prepare staff members for more of those students, Ms. Chiancone said.

Karen C. Woodson, the director of English-as-a-second-language and bilingual programs for the 151,000-student school system in neighboring Montgomery County, Md., said the trend has been similar there.

"We are finding a much greater need for mental-health support for these students," Ms. Woodson said. "They've endured incredible trauma, and even when they are reunified with a family member, they might be facing a situation where their mom has a new husband and they are living with siblings that they have never met."

Many of the unaccompanied minors—especially those who are of high school age—have had long periods of disruption to their schooling, though some may arrive with records showing they earned a few credits while living in the Office of Refugee Resettlement shelters.

School of Newcomers

At San Francisco International High School—where all 400 students are recently arrived immigrants—the percentage of unaccompanied minors has reached 25 percent of the school's enrollment, up from about 10 percent when it first opened its doors in 2009, said Principal Julie Kessler.

Students' personal circumstances vary, Ms. Kessler said. Some are living with parents and other family members, or in group homes, she said, but many are "navigating all of this on their own."

Her school is set up to connect students to the services they will need, she said, including legal representation, housing referrals, and counseling.

"Our school is really built for these kids," Ms. Kessler said. "They are not marginalized here, and we have the luxury of being able to really focus on what their needs are."

Still, the barriers that unaccompanied minors face both in and out of school are daunting. A majority of them come into U.S. high schools, where graduating within four or even five years, while still needing to learn English and pass state exit exams, seems nearly impossible.

"The pressures are immense on them and on those of us who are working with them," Ms. Kessler said.

At the same time, she said, unaccompanied minors are often the most motivated students in her school.

Case in point: A 22-year-old graduate of San Francisco International recently won a scholarship to a four-year college, even as she was in charge of a household of five younger brothers and sisters.

"It is a superhuman feat," said Ms. Kessler. "These are some of the most resilient and brilliant young people I have ever seen."

In U.S. Schools, Undocumented Youths Strive to Adjust

By Corey Mitchell
Education Week, May 6, 2015

Kevin faced a traumatic journey to the United States in search of a better life.

The 19-year-old undocumented immigrant from El Salvador faced yet another set of challenges when he arrived in the U.S. last year and enrolled in school.

First came the laughs of classmates poking fun at his halting English. Then came the puzzled looks from teachers struggling to understand those same words.

But a new place in the same place has made all the difference for Kevin.

The teenager is one of 200 students enrolled in the first-year International Academy for English-language learners at the District of Columbia's Cardozo Education Campus, a school-within-a-school for students who arrived in the United States within the past 18 months.

The struggles and successes of Cardozo's recently arrived students and English-learners provide a peek into the experiences of the surge of unaccompanied children and youths who streamed across the U.S.-Mexico border and entered American classrooms last fall. The students, many with yearlong gaps in their formal education and suffering from post-traumatic stress disorder, represent a significant new challenge for schools. Many are still in legal limbo as they wait for immigration judges to decide whether they can stay or will be deported. Language barriers can complicate every step of the process.

"When I speak, I am scared," said Ruth, 17, a Salvadoran immigrant who is self-conscious about speaking English aloud.

"That's the problem we all have," added her classmate, 16-year-old Yeykin from Guatemala.

Because of their immigration status, *Education Week* is identifying students only by their first names.

Similar to what's taking place in many other districts, English learners, many of them recent immigrants, are the fastest-growing student population at Cardozo.

The majority of the academy's students at Cardozo fled violence in Central American countries such as Honduras, Guatemala, and El Salvador. Most spoke little English when they arrived, if any at all. In some cases, Spanish is not even students' primary language: The academy also educates students from the Horn of Africa and several nations in Asia. The majority of students in the academy are boys, who made up the overwhelming majority of children who made the treacherous trip to the U.S. border last year.

"Many of them feel like they aren't going to succeed in school, like it's too big of an undertaking," said Margie McHugh, the director of the Migration Policy Institute's National Center on Immigrant Integration Policy.

But the academy has helped ease Kevin's transition to the United States. He's on track to graduate in 2016, his English has improved, and he serves as a translator for classmates who struggle with the language.

"All of us are a part of the community," Kevin said. "We are all equals."

Making a Connection

Cardozo's academy for newcomers is based on a model developed by the Internationals Network of Public Schools, a New York City-based nonprofit that focuses on serving immigrant students. The network has 19 schools in districts from Oakland, CA, to Alexandria, VA.

Close to half the students at Cardozo's academy are 18 or older so they face a tight timeline to learn the language and make up sizable schooling gaps. The students can remain in the public school system until age 21.

Each student belongs to a 25-member cohort that has all the same classes together and the same instructors. The approach allows students and teachers to get to know one another, build trust, and develop deeper relationships, school officials said.

While some English-language programs enforce English-only conversations, the students at the academy are encouraged to use their home language to discuss what they are learning. Those who struggle to speak and write English are paired with peers who have developed a better grasp of the language.

Many of the unaccompanied youths already are saddled with responsibilities and problems—adjusting to life in a new country, holding down jobs to help support themselves, to name a few—outside school that make learning inside school that much more of a challenge.

Most schools are "not equipped and entirely overwhelmed and unable to deal with the social-emotional problems," said Carolyn Sattin-Bajaj, an assistant professor in the department of education leadership, management, and policy at Seton Hall University in South Orange, NJ. "Students need to feel safe and comfortable before learning can take place."

At Cardozo, nearly all the academy's teachers are certified in their content areas, as well as in teaching English as a second language. The academy also has two bilingual counselors.

To connect with students, Associate Principal Megan Sands memorized all their names during the first week of classes last fall. Students with common first names—like José—earn nicknames from Sands and her staff.

The students often return the favor. Many call the academy's dean of students, Antonio Carter, "Grande Chocolate," for "Big Chocolate."

Mr. Carter, who has learned some Spanish, is a constant presence in the hallways, coaxing students to class, defusing flare-ups, and offering counsel. When Ms. Sands is out of the building for a day or two, she said students send her text messages to check on her welfare.

"There's a lot of relationship building before we even get to the academics," said Ms. Sands, a veteran teacher of English-learners. "It's been harder than we anticipated, but the rewards have been great, too."

Student Surge Continues

Last summer's influx of unaccompanied minors isn't a onetime phenomenon.

An estimated 39,000 immigrant children will enter the United States as unaccompanied minors this federal fiscal year, according to a recent analysis from the Migration Policy Institute, a Washington-based research group.

The extrapolation is based on detention figures from U.S. Customs and Border Protection for the first five months of the fiscal year that began Oct. 1. The number would represent a significant decrease from the 68,000 apprehended in fiscal 2014.

The report focuses almost exclusively on migration enforcement and protection policies, but has ramifications for K-12 districts that will likely see the upcoming wave of unaccompanied minors.

Many of the children and youths coming from Central America likely will relocate to districts where established immigrant communities already exist. Federal data show that California, Florida, New York, and Texas have attracted the largest number of unaccompanied minors.

The influx could further tax the resources of school systems welcoming new students who have entered the United States illegally, many of them English-language learners.

At Cardozo, Mary Ball teaches English/language arts to English-learners, with lessons ranging from haiku structure to the works of William Shakespeare.

Ms. Ball's experience at the academy harkens her back to 1987, her first year in the District of Columbia schools, when young refugees fleeing the devastating civil war in El Salvador flooded the city's classrooms.

"When I read their journal entries, I realize this is where they feel safe and comfortable," Ms. Ball said.

While school districts can estimate how many newcomer students they will absorb, many don't know the full scope of the resources they need until the students arrive at their doorsteps. In many districts, students who came to the United States in last summer's surge continued to trickle in, months after the school year began.

> **The students, many with yearlong gaps in their formal education and suffering from post-traumatic stress disorder, represent a significant new challenge for schools.**

Under federal law, all children, regardless of their immigration status, have the right to enroll in public schools. Federal funding dedicates additional money for schools that enroll students who are English-language learners.

Building Bridges

But some districts and schools have struggled to adhere to federal law. After receiving complaints related to enrollment policies across the country, the U.S. Department of Education reiterated last spring that schools cannot turn away students.

The New York State Board of Regents approved an emergency order in December to ensure students are able to enroll in public schools regardless of their immigration status after an investigation last fall found evidence that some districts refused to enroll undocumented youths and unaccompanied minors if they didn't show documents proving guardianship or residency in the state.

New York's new policy prohibits schools from asking about immigration status.

In New York City, schools Chancellor Carmen Fariña issued a memo last fall encouraging principals to connect children in their schools with mental-, medical- and dental-health services either available in schools or nearby school health clinics.

"Some [districts] have taken it in stride, but others had a very difficult time. There's no universal experience here," said Ms. McHugh of the Migration Policy Institute.

Leonol Popol, a bilingual counselor at Cardozo's academy, can relate to his students better than most. A native of Guatemala, he came to the United States at age 25, spending seven years as an undocumented immigrant.

"I am this bridge from where they're coming from and who they could become," Mr. Popol said. "Sometimes, it's about selling hope."

Mr. Popol started building relationships with students last season when he coached the varsity boys soccer team. His counseling office is rarely empty.

"It goes way beyond having someone who speaks the language," said Ms. Sattin-Bajaj of Seton Hall University. "Schools that succeed with these students focus on the basic rights that all kids deserve."

Before Cardozo, Ms. Ball taught at the District of Columbia's Woodrow Wilson High School, where the children of diplomats were often sprinkled among the more traditional English-learners, she said.

The environment is different at Cardozo. At the start of the school year, Ms. Ball had students who struggled to spell their own names. Now, as the school year winds down, sticky notes lining the wall inside her classroom share stories of hopes and dreams, spelled out in English that has steadily progressed.

"I wish to have my family together."

"I wish to finish my studies."

"I wish I finish high school."

Supreme Court Guards Education for Undocumented Immigrants

By Julie Underwood

Phi Delta Kappan, December 2015/January 2016

The right to a public education for those who are not U.S. citizens, legal residents, or living with their parents is not a clear and stable issue. Children who enter the U.S. illegally with or without their parents are at the heart of this question.

Let's begin with the 1954 U.S. Supreme Court decision in *Brown v. Board of Education*, where the court declared state laws denying access to public schools based on race to be unconstitutional under the Equal Protection clause:

Today education is perhaps the most important function of state and local governments. Compulsory school attendance laws and the great expenditures for education both demonstrate our recognition of the importance of education to our democratic society. It is required in the performance of our most basic public responsibilities, even service in the armed forces. It is the very foundation of good citizenship. Today it is a principal instrument in awakening the child to cultural values, in preparing him for later professional training, and in helping him to adjust normally to his environment. In these days, it is doubtful that any child may reasonably be expected to succeed in life if he is denied the opportunity of an education.

But in 1973, in *San Antonio Independent School District v. Rodriguez*, the Supreme Court held that access to public education was not a constitutional right under the U.S. Constitution.

In another case, Chinese-American students with limited English language proficiency claimed the San Francisco school district's failure to provide language accommodation and support for them violated the U.S. Constitution and Title VI of the Civil Rights Act. Finding in favor of the students, in *Lau v. Nichols* (1974), the Supreme Court focused not on the constitutional question but on the Civil Rights Act. Congress codified much of the decision shortly thereafter by passing the Equal Education Opportunities Act.

Plyler Case

In 1982, in *Plyler v. Doe*, the Supreme Court held (5–4) that school districts could not deny access to a public education to resident children whose parents had entered the U.S. illegally. The case arose as a challenge to a 1975 Texas statute that withheld state funds from public school districts for expenses related to educating children who had not been legally admitted into the U.S. The statute also authorized public school districts to deny enrollment to such children (Tex. Educ. Code Ann. 21.031). The Court held that access to education, while not specifically a federal constitutional right, was a significant state benefit. The Court said education "has a fundamental role in maintaining the fabric of our society" by preparing citizens to participate in a democracy. "[T]he public schools [are] a most vital civic institution for the preservation of a democratic system of government and . . . the primary vehicle for transmitting the values on which our society rests. . . . In sum, education has a fundamental role in maintaining the fabric of our society."

> Preserving education rights in the current political environment has been challenging, particularly for undocumented students. There are a number of anti-immigration lobbies and associations.

The Court noted that, if the state intends to deny such a benefit, it should have a sufficiently valid reason. The Court found that denying children an education, not due to their own actions, but the actions of their parents, was not sufficiently compelling to deny children this important public benefit.

In *Martinez v. Bynum*, 461 U.S. 321 (1983), the U.S. Supreme Court ruled (8–1) on another Texas statute intended to close the schoolhouse doors to nonresident children. The student was a U.S. citizen by birth. But, when he was a young child, he and his parents moved Mexico, where is parents were citizens. When he was eight years old, he returned to Texas to live with his sister and attend public school. He was denied tuition-free admission because of a state statute (Tex. Educ. Code 21.031) that denied tuition-free access to students who were not living with their guardians or parents for the primary purpose of accessing an education. Unlike the statute in *Plyler*, this statute did not single out undocumented children but was written to apply to all. The U.S. Supreme Court upheld the statute as a bona fide residency requirement intended to protect the resources of the local school district. The Court stated, "The provision of primary and secondary education, of course, is one of the most important functions of local government. Absent residence requirements, there can be little doubt that the proper planning and operation of the schools would suffer significantly. Thus a district must offer services to all students who reside within its boundaries, unless they are there without the support of their parents or guardians solely for the purpose of receiving an education."

Other Efforts

During the 1990s, the education rights of undocumented PreK-12 students came into question in several state proposals. California and New York considered state provisions that, contrary to the holding in *Plyler*, would have foreclosed access to undocumented students. The California initiative, Exclusion of Illegal Aliens from Public Elementary and Secondary Schools, was part of the Save Our State proposition, passed by California voters in 1994. A federal court issued an injunction against the law in League of United Latin Amer. *Citizens v. Wilson* in 1995. The litigation was abandoned when California elected a new governor, Gray Davis. The U.S. House of Representatives passed a similar provision in 1996 as part of the proposed Illegal Immigration Reform and Immigrant Responsibility Act. However, it was removed from the final legislation.

In 1996, a federal statute, the Personal Responsibility and Work Opportunity Reconciliation Act, passed, precluding undocumented higher education students from applying for federal financial aid and student loans. Further, the Illegal Immigration Reform and Immigrant Responsibility Act prohibited states from offering in-state tuition to undocumented students. In response, starting in 2001, legislation has been introduced that would offer undocumented higher education students conditional residency and access to public higher education on par with other students. The Development, Relief, and Education for Alien Minors (DREAM) Act allows undocumented minors of good moral character who were younger than 16 when they entered the country and who have lived in the U.S. for at least five years to have lawful permanent resident status upon graduation from high school. DREAM students also would qualify for federal financial aid and in-state college tuition. It has been introduced regularly but Congress has not passed it.

Preserving education rights in the current political environment has been challenging, particularly for undocumented students. There are a number of anti-immigration lobbies and associations. The Federation for American Immigration Reform regularly provides its estimates of the costs of educating undocumented children and unaccompanied undocumented children in the public schools. They suggest that these costs are an unreasonable drain on state and local budgets. In this era of declining public education resources, this strategy may appeal to voters, school board members, and administrators. If the current U.S. Supreme Court was called upon to uphold the 5–4 decision in *Plyler*, court watchers are uncertain about the outcome.

Immigration: Assimilation and the Measure of an American

By Stephanie Hanes
Christian Science Monitor, July 7, 2013

If there were such a thing as a classic American immigrant story, it might sound something like the one Arlene tells of her family.

Her immigrant parents each arrived in New York City poor but eager, searching for a better way of life. They found work—and each other—in the garment district; they married, had children, and sent their girls to parochial school where nuns taught proper English.

Arlene's parents told her and her sister that here, in the United States of America, they could do anything. So the girls went to college, became professionals, married, and had children of their own—English-speaking children who would never consider themselves anything but American.

It is a familiar, almost nostalgic, narrative; one that evokes sepia-toned photos of Ellis Island, Little Italy boccie players, German grandmas, or Eastern European deli proprietors.

But there is a twist.

Arlene's last name is Garcia. Her parents came from the Caribbean, not Europe. Today she lives in Lawrence, Mass., a city north of Boston that is more than 73 percent Hispanic. She is fluent in Spanish and English, switching seamlessly one recent morning at work answering the phone at Esperanza Academy, a tuition-free, private school for low-income girls. She is married to a Dominican man (albeit one whose name—Johnny Mackenzie—is far more gringo than hers) and returns regularly to the Dominican Republic (although these days she far prefers the Punta Cana resort area to the villages of her ancestors).

Is she assimilated? She laughs at the question: "Well, it depends on what you mean by 'assimilated.'"

That, it turns out, is a controversial question. And it is one that has moved in recent months to the forefront of public debate, as lawmakers wrestle with immigration reform, and as the Boston Marathon bombings—allegedly perpetrated by two ethnic Chechen immigrants—ushered in a new wave of speculation about newcomers' ability, or desire, to integrate into American culture.

On one side are conservative officials and pundits who worry that a flood of Spanish-speaking immigrants and a reverence for "multiculturalism" have led to a population of immigrants in the US unappreciative of and unconnected to their new country. On the other are a slew of academics, armed with studies from think tanks and longitudinal research projects, who say that assimilation these days is as strong as it has ever been, that immigrants as a group are still more enthusiastic about the country than the native born, that immigrants' children tend to do better than their parents by a host of socioeconomic indicators, and that within three generations an immigrant family fully identifies as American.

This happens across the country, they say, even in regions such as the Southeast that are not traditional immigrant destinations.

Although there has been bipartisan support in Congress's immigration reform efforts for provisions to better integrate new immigrants into US civic and cultural life, as Arlene Garcia and her family show, the notion of assimilation—or "integration," "incorporation," or any word used to describe the process of belonging—is far from straightforward. To evaluate how and whether immigrants—and, arguably more important, their children—are becoming part of this country involves questions of identity, belonging, and the very essence of being American.

Can you measure assimilation?

In 2006, Jacob Vigdor, a professor of public policy at Duke University in Durham, N.C., joined a group of academics in a series of meetings convened by the Manhattan Institute for Policy Research.

The scholars, all with backgrounds in immigration research, were focused on a single question: Is there a way, in the face of an increasingly emotional debate over immigrants in the US, to actually measure assimilation?

This is no simple question. The 2010 US Census found close to 40 million immigrants in the US, making up 13 percent of the population. In 2012, the census determined that 36 million more were "second-generation immigrants," or the American-born children of immigrants. And while much of the public discourse focuses on Latinos—particularly the estimated 11.5 million here illegally—the portrait of America's foreign born is far more diverse.

The country is in the midst of what most scholars refer to as the "modern wave" of immigration, which started when Congress passed the Immigration and Nationality Act of 1965. This law essentially opened the door to Latin Americans, Africans, and Asians who had previously been barred by an immigration quota system that gave preference to northern Europeans. Since then, 40 million immigrants have come to the US, reports the Pew Research Center.

In sheer numbers there are more immigrants today than in prior generations, but as a percentage of the population, first- and second-generation immigrants peaked in the early part of the twentieth century. In 1900, 34.5 percent of the US population was first or second generation; last year it was 24.5 percent.

Today, census data show, 12 million immigrants come from Mexico and 10 million hail from South and East Asia. Almost 4 million come from the Caribbean, while 14.5 million come from Central America, South America, the Middle East, and elsewhere. Within those groups, of course, there are huge differences; that "elsewhere" category, for instance, includes hundreds of thousands from countries ranging from the United Kingdom to Nigeria to Bosnia-Herzegovina.

Categorizing the assimilation of all these different people, Professor Vigdor and the others knew, could prove a daunting task. Even the word itself—"assimilation"—had become contentious; in academia it was associated with nativist pressures on newcomers to assume Anglo sensibilities at the expense of their own culture and history.

But as a social scientist, Vigdor was eager to find evidence in an emotion-laden debate. The key, he says, is in census data.

"When you talk to some people about immigration today, they say, 'Well, my grandmother came here in 1902, and she learned to speak English, and she did all these things, and the immigrants today aren't doing it,'" Vigdor says. "And as it turns out, we were able to get a good sense of whether all the grandmas were really like that."

As early as 1900, the US Census was asking people about where they were born and when they had arrived in the US. Using these markers, as well as other data points such as homeownership, marital status, and citizenship, Vigdor created an index that calculated a statistical difference between immigrants and native-born Americans. Full assimilation, according to Vigdor's work, is when these data points are indistinguishable.

"Assimilation is a process whereby people come to adopt the various manner-isms and behavior of native-born residents of a country . . . ," Vigdor says. "By being able to track immigrants as they spend more time in the US, we can trace out how that process works. And the process actually works in a remarkably similar manner whether you're looking over the past 20 years in the US or looking at immigration from Eastern Europe at the turn of the last century."

In other words, a first-generation immigrant will usually struggle with more cultural differences than his American-born child, who will grapple with more cultural disconnect than his children.

But there are also significant differences between immigrant groups, he points out, more so than between immigrants overall and the native-born population.

In his work, he developed three categories of assimilation—civic, cultural, and economic—and then combined those categories for an overall assimilation score. By his findings, Latino immigrants tend to be least assimilated, particularly on mea-sures of civic and economic assimilation, which include characteristics such as citi-zenship, professional status, and homeownership.

Indians and South Koreans score higher on economic assimilation than on cul-tural assimilation index measures, which include questions about language, marital status, and the number of children in the adult's household.

He has also found that, as a whole, immigrants to the US assimilate far more than those in European countries, but do so less easily than immigrants in Canada.

"It turns out that almost every developed country has worries about immigra-tion," he says. In Europe, immigrants "have a harder time working their way to citi-zenship [and] immigrant unemployment problems are more acute. . . . Even if you look at a basic thing like homeownership—the home-ownership rate for immigrants in most countries is lower than for natives. The disparities in European countries are much more acute than in the US."

In his most recent index, this year, Vigdor found that immigrants to the US today were more assimilated than at any time in the past decade. He attributes this primarily to demographic shifts in post-recession America—new Mexican migrants, who typically score lower on his index, are down in numbers; while Asian migrants, who tend to be from a higher socioeconomic level and score higher on his assimilation index, have increased.

Scholars such as Richard Alba, a sociology professor with the City University of New York who has written extensively on immigration, are more than a little skeptical.

Professor Alba says he is wary of indices of assimilation, which he sees as too simplistic to capture the full complexity and nuance of social integration.

"They might be useful, but they don't exhaust the concept of assimilation," he says. "To take a simple example: We want to know whether people feel like they belong in the United States. How much do they identify with the United States?"

To get at this more im-

> In a survey report released earlier this year on second-generation immigrants, who many scholars say are the true markers of a family's assimilation or lack thereof, Pew found that the children of immigrants are, in general, doing better economically than their parents, are more likely to marry and have friends outside their ethnic groups, and are twice as likely to say they consider themselves to be a "typical American."

portant marker of assimilation, Alba says, you need to find out how immigrants feel. Which is what the Pew Research Center has tried to do in a number of recent studies.

Questioning a 'patriotism gap'

In a survey report released earlier this year on second-generation immigrants, who many scholars say are the true markers of a family's assimilation or lack thereof, Pew found that the children of immigrants are, in general, doing better economically than their parents, are more likely to marry and have friends outside their ethnic groups, and are twice as likely to say they consider themselves to be a "typical American." (Six in 10 Hispanic and Asian-American second-generation immigrants respond this way.)

Meanwhile, second-generation Hispanics and Asian-Americans "place more importance than does the general public on hard work and career success," the Pew research found; they and their parents are more likely than the native-born population—and even more likely than the older adult children of European immigrants from the turn of the last century—to feel optimistic about the direction of the country. More than 80 percent of second-generation Hispanics and Asian-Americans say they can speak English "very well"; 10 percent say they can speak it "well."

"There is a lot of that very positive data in that second generation report," says Paul Taylor, executive vice president of the Pew Research Center. "When you look at values, sense of belonging, things are unfolding the way that a society that opens its arms to immigrants would want it to unfold. Is everything perfect? Of course not. But there is a lot of positive news in that data."

There are other reports about immigrants' feelings, however, that come to a different conclusion. A week before the Boston Marathon bombings, the Hudson Institute, which generally researches conservative issues, released a report claiming a "patriotism gap" between the foreign- and native-born.

Citing a new quantitative analysis of Harris Interactive survey data, the Hudson Institute's researchers determined that native-born citizens are, by 21 percentage points (65 percent to 44 percent), more likely than naturalized immigrants to view America as "better" than other countries rather than "no better, no worse." When given a choice, the native born are more likely to describe themselves as "American" rather than "citizen of the world"; 67 percent of the native born believe the US Constitution is a higher legal authority for Americans than international law, as compared with 37 percent of naturalized immigrants.

These statistics led the researchers to conclude that "America's patriotic assimilation system is broken."

A number of conservative columnists jumped on this finding, seeing proof in news reports that at least one of the Tsarnaev brothers, accused of the Marathon bombings, had felt alienated in and angry at the US.

All of which gets at a bigger issue when it comes to analyzing cultural integration: Who gets to describe the values of a "typical American?"

As Alba points out, a "typical American" changes region to region, family to family. The meaning also changes based on socioeconomic surroundings.

In the 1990s, Princeton University's Alejandro Portes, considered one of the leading thinkers on immigrant integration, helped develop a theory of "segmented assimilation," which at a basic level says that because American society is so unequal, there are a number of social places where an immigrant can fit—including the social underclass.

Often referred to as "downward assimilation," this is when people join gangs and adopt a street culture that is quite American, but not the sort of American that the Hudson Institute had in mind.

Indeed, the pressure for the sort of assimilation described by the Hudson Institute can often backfire, Professor Portes says. (He also takes issue with the word "assimilation," preferring "integration" or "incorporation.")

"Nativists take the position that they don't want any immigrants at all—they want to build fences," Portes says. "The other position is to turn [immigrants] into Americans as quickly as possible—this is forced assimilation . . . . The problem is that the first generation cannot be turned into Americans instantly. And the attempt to do so is often counterproductive. It creates fear and alienation, it denigrates the culture and language of immigrants themselves, and it denigrates it to their kids."

Not only does this put the country as a whole at a disadvantage—after all, Portes says, with the global economy, citizens should understand multiple languages and cultures—it also puts children at the risk of downward assimilation because it hurts their relationship with their parents.

"The idea that the habits and foodways and the religious patterns of immigrants are not worth it and should be eliminated—that is counterproductive," he says. "In the history of this country, groups like Italians and Germans and Poles gradually developed a phased integration into American society. And today, elements of immigrant culture—the Irish, the Italian—are celebrated as positive parts of American culture."

'It's the texture'

In Ms. Garcia's household, there is a regular debate over sleepovers. Her Dominican-born husband cannot, for the life of him, understand why their 14-year-old daughter would want to stay at someone else's house for the night. This is not atypical, she said. Dominicans, and many other Latinos, just don't do sleepovers.

"He'll say, 'You have a perfectly good bed here!'" Garcia says, laughing. "I'll say, 'Johnny, just let her be.' And then he'll say, 'You know, if there's a fire, you know they're not going to be worried about Marleyna. Oh no. They're going to get their own child first.' I'm like, 'Oh my goodness, can you be any more dramatic?' But then I'm awake all night thinking about fires."

She laughs again. It's a far cry from the assimilation debates in her childhood, when the nuns insisted to her father that they speak English at home.

"He said, with that accent of his, 'Seester, out of the home, you da boss,'" Garcia recalls. "'Inside of the home, I dee boss. But I promise you, she will learn to speak good English. But she will also learn to speak our language.'"

Now she worries that her own daughter doesn't know enough Spanish to talk with her cousins.

"But this is what's so wonderful about this country," she says with a smile. "It's the texture. The stories."

Requirements Keep Young Immigrants Out of Long Island Classrooms

By Benjamin Mueller
The New York Times, October 21, 2014

Before dawn breaks and the morning light spills onto his bedroom floor, Carlos Garcia Lobo bounces out of bed, his eyes alight with anticipation, and asks his mother if he can go to school.

Each time, she replies to her 8-year-old son: Not yet.

Four months after fleeing Honduras with a 15-year-old cousin, Carlos has reached what his family said seemed like an impassable frontier. Like dozens of the roughly 2,500 unaccompanied immigrant children who have been released to relatives or other sponsors on Long Island so far this year, Carlos has been unable to register for school.

The impasse has baffled parents, who say their scant resources have proved no match for school district bureaucracies. Required by law to attend school, children are nevertheless stuck at home, despite unrelenting efforts by their parents and others to prove that they are eligible. Suffolk and Nassau Counties, on Long Island, rank third and fifth, respectively, in the United States, after counties centered on Houston and Los Angeles, in the number of unaccompanied minors they have absorbed so far this year; Miami-Dade County is fourth.

Many of the children are barred because their families cannot gather the documents that schools require to prove they are residents of the district or have guardianship—obstacles that contravene legal guidance on enrollment procedures the State Education Department issued in September. Concern over similar deterrents across the country led Attorney General Eric H. Holder Jr. in May to chide districts for "raising barriers for undocumented children," in that way violating a 1982 Supreme Court decision that guarantees their right to an education.

Driven from Honduras by gangs that brandished machetes and robbed his grandmother's home, Carlos trekked to the border in June with his cousin and a guide, bumping along on buses "all day and night," he recalled.

On July 10, Carlos joined his mother, Yeinni Lobo, who came to the United States when he was 11 months old. Since he arrived, Ms. Lobo says she has visited the local school office at least 10 times, toting immunization records. She said she provided her address, and the name of the fellow tenant who collects her rent, to show that she lived in the district. But the school demanded a statement from the home's absentee owner.

So as Carlos tries to decode the schoolwork his older cousins bring home, Ms. Lobo gets an education in red tape. She found her homeowner's Bronx address on property records at a courthouse. A letter she sent pleading for help dropped back through her mail slot, marked "Return to Sender." Carlos's official manila file folder is affixed with a Post-it reading, "Waiting for owner's affidavit." Once, a school secretary suggested that Ms. Lobo fix the problem by moving to a different home. In the school parking lot, she says, she and other mothers cry over the lost weeks.

"They are not giving us a solution," Ms. Lobo said. "I'm worried because he's getting behind."

New York City has recently built programs to guide undocumented children through school and health forms and even finance legal representation. But on Long Island, a small number of low-cost lawyers say they are overwhelmed with hundreds of new cases.

Even children who enrolled in school say they have subsequently been stymied. According to a school document obtained by the advocacy group New York Communities for Change, 33 Hispanic students in Hempstead, many of them recent immigrants, have been signing in for attendance a few times each week, only to be told by administrators they should return home because there are not enough classrooms to accommodate them. The delay prompted the State Education Department last week to order an investigation into the district's procedures and affirm its September legal guidance. School officials said the students would be allowed to start classes at an alternate location this week.

On the margins of Long Island's well-to-do suburbs, where Central American families have long settled, churches have become sanctuaries for the newly arrived.

Carmen Bustillo, who said she left Honduras with her children after a gang repeatedly threatened to kidnap them, seeks advice at St. Brigid's Church in Westbury. Alongside her 12-year-old son, Gendries, and 11-year-old daughter, Linda, Ms. Bustillo waded across the Rio Grande in June, carrying her 3-year-old son over her head. The water lapped at Linda's chin.

Like many immigrants on Long Island, where affordable housing is scarce, Ms. Bustillo rents rooms in a home that illegally lodges several families. To protect himself from scrutiny, the landlord declined to notarize district residency papers. Gendries and Linda were kept out of Westbury schools for about three weeks before they were allowed to enroll.

"I don't know who to trust," Ms. Bustillo said.

Lease agreements or copies of bills are common prerequisites for school enrollment, a practice that is allowed under legal guidance the federal Education and Justice Departments issued in May. Activists say such requirements, when applied to newly arrived children, can impede their access to school and undermine federal law. New York State has asked schools to consider classifying children in shared or temporary housing as homeless, which under federal law allows them to attend school without formal proof of residency.

The updated federal guidance, Mr. Holder said in May, "emphasizes the need for flexibility in accepting documents from parents to prove a child's age and to show that a child resides within a school's attendance areas."

The superintendent of the Westbury schools, Mary A. Lagnado, said the district accommodated new arrivals by making paperwork available in Spanish and looking for "whatever alternative we can" when certain information is unobtainable. As a testament to their success, Dr. Lagnado said, the district has already enrolled 121 more students this year than last.

But especially in a town sensitive to its tax burden, she said, certain residency requirements are rigid. Families like Ms. Lobo's who are subleasing rooms in a home must provide a notarized lease or owner's affidavit, the homeowner's residential deed or mortgage statement, and two home bills.

"We try to make sure that they are a bona fide resident of the school district," she said. "Taxes are very high on Long Island. We have a responsibility to our community and homeowners."

The strain on already-packed classrooms builds because many immigrant children do not speak English and have scant experience in school, Dr. Lagnado said. Integrating them without extra funding makes the perpetual academic competition with nearby districts even harder, she said.

"It's a challenge when you're surrounded by such wealthy districts," Dr. Lagnado said.

Public officials are working to replenish schools' reserves. Representatives Steve Israel, a Democrat, and Peter T. King, a Republican, both from Long Island, recently introduced legislation that would give districts emergency financing for new enrollees, an effort that Mr. Israel said was intended to relieve towns of the burden "to raise taxes or cut other services because the federal government is pursuing humanitarian impulses."

New York City has recently built programs to guide undocumented children through school and health forms and even finance legal representation. But on Long Island, a small number of low-cost lawyers say they are overwhelmed with hundreds of new cases.

Other Long Island districts have deployed extra resources to smooth the transition for new arrivals. Citing schools' obligation not to "make any judgment about the living situation you have," the superintendent of Hampton Bays Public Schools, Lars Clemensen, said staff members knocked on children's doors to certify their residency when more traditional documentation proved elusive.

Still, activists say the obstacles to enrollment on Long Island reflect a wariness toward new arrivals that prevails in schools across the country. The federal Education Department has received at least 17 complaints nationwide since 2011 that led to legal action in school districts, while the Justice Department has evaluated enrollment procedures for 200 districts in Georgia alone. The Southern Poverty

Law Center and a New Orleans advocacy group last week sent letters to 55 schools there that they say were discouraging immigrant children by seeking Social Security numbers or a parent's state identification, documents that illegal immigrants generally would not have.

On Long Island, where some districts in the mid-1990s tried to expel undocumented students or required permanent resident visas to enroll, the re-emergence of "barriers to kids enrolling" has rocked children's unsettled lives, said Patrick Young, legal director for the Central American Refugee Center, based in Brentwood and Hempstead.

"That will be traumatic because then children will enter midsemester," Mr. Young said of immigrants who are turned away. "It kind of stigmatizes them. They don't socialize the same way."

Such restrictions have deepened a cultural cleft in the region between Hispanic and longtime white residents, immigrants say, putting the promise of acceptance and economic opportunity farther out of reach.

Jorge, 16, who fled from El Salvador to Uniondale in 2012 and asked that his surname not be used because of a continuing immigration case, simmers at the memory of a gym teacher's commanding two Hispanic students who had arrived late to class to, as he recalled, "go outside to do 50 push-ups and come back when they were residents."

"I felt stepped on," Jorge continued.

Those feelings resurfaced this month as he and his mother tried to enroll his brother Jonathan, 17, at Uniondale High School. Jonathan traveled from El Salvador by himself in June after a gang attacked him with a tire iron, dislodging his front teeth and leaving scars on his scalp and right shoulder. Despite frequent inquiries at the enrollment office, his mother, Vilma, said the school did not allow him to begin classes until mid-October. She said the school blamed immigration documents with an incorrect rendering of his last name.

"They don't want to see us," Vilma, who works at a fast-food restaurant, said of her neighbors.

On a recent afternoon at St. Brigid's Church, Carlos squirmed on a bench next to Yanira Chacon, the church's outreach worker. He smiled and spoke about going to school to make friends and learn to play the guitar.

Hoping to help him prepare, Ms. Chacon gave Carlos a purple backpack adorned with peace signs that was stuffed with rulers, notebooks and pens.

It lies unused on his bedroom floor.

Bilingualism: When Education and Assimilation Clash

By Melinda D. Anderson
The Atlantic, October 27, 2015

With more than 20 languages spoken in one eighth-grade classroom, Harlem Village Academy West in New York City rivals the vibrant cultural and ethnic mix of the United Nations headquarters, a short trip down the FDR Drive. Spanish, Mandingo, Fulani, French, Arabic, and other languages come together to form a tapestry of nationalities. Yet unlike the U.N., the premier institution representing the peoples of the world, public schools have not always encouraged children to embrace their heritages. Indeed, as non-native English speakers, some of the Harlem Village's middle-schoolers relate feelings of isolation as younger children solely based on their attainment of the English language.

Chelsea, a 13-year-old Spanish-speaker who learned English in the third grade, recalls her earliest years in school as especially difficult amid her struggles to communicate with peers. "I used to get mad and aggravated because I couldn't speak English," she says. "People were looking at me as if I were another type of human being." Her classmates share similar frustrations. "I felt dumb and left out when we did advanced math because my teacher wouldn't let me do it even though I knew I could," says Yaye, a bright 14-year-old who speaks Wolof, the most widely spoken language in Senegal, at home. Yaye says he languished in his K-2 English-as-a-second-language classes, "not progressing or learning." Melyanet, also 14, remembers feeling alienated and lonely when she was in prekindergarten—an age when children often sharpen their social skills through play. "I would try my best to learn English but it was hard," the teen recalls. "No one spoke [Spanish] so I wouldn't make friends. I would sit in the back."

The adolescents at Harlem Village are part of a rapidly growing population of students in America's public schools with diverse linguistic backgrounds. Of the 50 million students currently enrolled in public K-12 schools, almost one in four (12 million) schoolchildren ages 5 to 17 speak a language other than English at home, according to an analysis of census figures. Their numbers have inched up over the last decade, along with the percentage of students participating in English-language-learners programs. Department of Education data shows this segment of the public-school population is steadily climbing. Some 4.4 million students—ranging from those who don't speak English to those transitioning into full proficiency—were classified as English language learners in the 2012–13 school year, an increase of more than 250,000 students over the previous decade.

Even as states struggle to reach a common definition of what it means to be an English language learner, the proportion of these students continues to rise—and with it, the temperature of debate surrounding the purpose and goals of bilingual education. It remains an unsettled issue that continues to challenge America's self-image as welcoming and inclusive: The value of linguistic assimilation is pitted against the values of a culturally diverse na-

A growing contingent of educators are promoting the cultivation of bilingualism.

tion of immigrants, leaving education systems and its students caught in political crosshairs. The divide is exacerbated by financially strapped schools with skyrocketing numbers of English learners—meeting all of the mandates for their education can be expensive—and the national discourse on immigration, which saw the 2016 presidential contender Donald Trump advise his competitor Jeb Bush to "really set the example by speaking English while in the United States."

Many trace today's fraught bilingual-education politics back to the Bilingual Education Act, which was adopted in 1968 to aid local school districts in educating children with limited English. At the bill signing, President Lyndon B. Johnson voiced his enthusiasm for a law that would bring an unprecedented federal role and funds to the education of children whose first language wasn't English:

Thousands of children of Latin descent, young [Native Americans], and others will get a better start—a better chance—in school. . . . What this law means is that we are now giving every child in America a better chance to touch his outermost limits—to reach the farthest edge of his talents and his dreams. We have begun a campaign to unlock the full potential of every boy and girl—regardless of his race or his region or his father's income.

Yet bilingual education's cultural, social, and historical dimensions date back well over a century before Johnson signed his landmark education law. In recounting the history of bilingual education, *Rethinking Schools* chronicles the earliest efforts to teach immigrant students. The first bilingual-education law, enacted in Ohio in 1839, created a German-English language program and was followed by similar laws in Louisiana and the New Mexico area geared around French-English and Spanish-English instruction, respectively. As the trend accelerated, more states and localities began dual instruction in an array of languages, including Polish, Italian, Norwegian, and Cherokee. The onset of World War I—and its accompanying era of xenophobia, discrimination against language minorities, and English-only laws—quickly brought this trajectory to an end. This pattern continued through the 1920s as the tension between forced assimilation and educationally sound practices continued—and as the academic performance of students with limited English skills began to suffer. The passage of the Bilingual Education Act, part of a wave of civil-rights legislation pushed through Congress by the Johnson administration, ushered in a major shift once again and a return to bilingual instruction in many of the nation's schools. But as the Act was reauthorized in the 1980s and '90s and then subsumed under No Child Left Behind in 2002, national policy seesawed between prioritizing multilingual skills and an English-only focus.

Today, schools are still twisting in the wind of politics, with 31 states passing laws naming English the official language over the last two centuries and voters in California, Arizona, and Massachusetts approving ballot measures in recent decades that replace bilingual education with English-only policies. Meanwhile, a growing contingent of educators are promoting the cultivation of bilingualism to support the social and emotional needs of English language learners.

Olga Kagan, a languages and cultures professor at UCLA and director of the university's National Heritage Language Resource Center, has studied the implications of denying students the ability to communicate in their parents' native language. "Many of these students have no literacy in the language they speak," she wrote in a December 2014 *Los Angeles Times* op-ed. "And that is a problem."

Rather than ignoring English in the classroom, Kagan calls for capitalizing on the language skills students already have and taking their background knowledge into account. "I think the main roadblock is societal attitude to bilingualism. . . . We lose much of the nation's capacity in languages by letting go of this resource," she told me recently. And the various benefits for students are evident. Kagan's survey of California college students found many "heritage speakers" wished to study their home language at school to connect with their culture, build their literacy, and strengthen their bonds with relatives.

Driving much of the decision-making in English-language instruction are myths that need debunking, says Rusul Alrubail, an education consultant whose work focuses on English-language learners and pedagogical practices in the classroom. "Banning [a child's] first language often creates a negative impact . . . a sense of divide for students between their first language, often used at home, and English. We see students who refuse to be associated with their first language, or refuse to speak it or acknowledge that they know it, due to them feeling ashamed. . . . This impacts their cultural identity."

Among the consequences, says Alrubail, are when students internalize the notion that their first language is inferior—with English becoming the language of assimilation—and when some immigrant families specifically ask their kids not to speak in their first language at home in an effort to ensure their children conform to Western culture. Interestingly, research finds mixing languages has no impact on children's vocabulary development. But the pressure from teachers and schools, enshrined in policy and practices, can be immense.

"Many teachers believe that in order to learn English one must assimilate to American culture and abandon one's own cultural practices," Alrubail said. "This is always a result of fear and anxiety; when students do not meet their expectation of what it means to be 'American,' it becomes imperative to speak English."

The upshot of this mindset is seen in Amadou, a 13-year-old at Harlem Village who speaks Fulani, a Niger-Congo language spoken by 13 million people in many parts of in West, Central, and North Africa. "Nobody spoke my language except in my home [so] I would only try to speak English so they wouldn't look at me differently. I wanted to fit in with everyone else and be the same," he says. Will his native language, rich in tradition and heritage, soon slip away as the middle-schooler slowly simmers in America's melting pot?

Children of Immigration

By Marcelo M. Suárez-Orozco & Carola Suárez-Orozco
Phi Delta Kappan, December 2015/January 2016

The world is on the move, and today the lives of over a billion people are shaped by the experience of migration. All continents are involved as areas of immigration, emigration, or transit—and often as all three at once. In the 21st century, immigration is the human face of globalization—the sounds, colors, and aromas of a miniaturized, interconnected, and fragile world. During the second decade of the 21st century, over 230 million people are international migrants, about 740 million are internal migrants, and millions more are immediate relatives left behind (U.N. Department of Economic and Social Affairs, 2013). Only China (1.36 billion) and India (1.26 billion) have larger populations than this "immigration nation." The United States has the largest number of immigrants in the world. Currently, 45.0 million (or about 14%) of all U.S. residents are foreign born (Pew Research Center, 2015).

The children of immigrants are the fruit borne of immigration. Today, 25% of children under the age of 18—a total of 18.7 million children—have an immigrant parent. Their growth has been rapid: In 1970, the population of immigrant origin children stood at 6% of the total population of children. It reached 20% by 2000 and is projected to be 33% by 2050 (Suárez-Orozco, Abo-Zena, & Marks, 2015). The children of immigrants are an integral part of the national tapestry. The education and well-being of these youth touches a large swath of our child population. Their story is deeply intertwined with the future of our nation.

Most children of immigrants are born in the U.S. of foreign-born parents. They are U.S. citizens yet many nevertheless are growing up in the shadows of the law (Suárez-Orozco et al., 2011). The most recent estimates suggest that 4.5 million U.S.-born children younger than age 18 are living in the U.S. with at least one parent who is an unauthorized migrant. The number of children who are themselves unauthorized has declined from a peak of 1.6 million in 2005 to about 775,000 in 2012. Altogether, about 7% of all school-aged children in the U.S. have at least one parent who is in the U.S. without authorization.

The current wave of immigration has ushered in an era of hyper diversity. Immigrants are an extraordinarily heterogeneous group. Over 80% originate in Latin America, Asia, Africa, Oceania, or the Caribbean—the rest originate in Europe or

North America. This migratory flow is a significant factor in the U.S., becoming the first high-income country in the world with a majority-minority child population.

Immigrants today are more diverse than ever. They arrive in our country from every continent on earth. The latest data tell a fascinating and dynamic story: Asians now surpass Latinos among those who have been in the U.S. for five years or less. After peaking in the early 2000s, Latino immigration is now at its lowest level in 50 years. New immigration from the Caribbean now exceeds all new immigration from Europe. The number of new immigrants from Africa grew 41% from 2000 to 2013, a significant growth when compared to other new arrivals (Pew Research Center, 2015).

Immigrants vary significantly in levels of education and skill. Some immigrant parents are among the most educated people in our nation, comprising 47% of scientists with doctorates, a quarter of all physicians, and 24% of engineers. In 2013, 41% of newly arrived immigrants had at least a bachelor's degree. Others have low levels of education and gravitate to sectors of the U.S. labor market relying on low-skilled workers, such as agriculture, service industries, and construction. In 2013, 28% of recent arrivals lived in poverty, up from 18% in 1970. According to the U.S. Census in 2014, the official U.S. poverty rate was 14.8% of the population (Pew Research Center, 2015; U.S. Census Bureau, 2015).

With some 460 languages spoken across the land, the U.S. has a deep reservoir of linguistic diversity (Kindler, 2002). New immigrants have certainly added to our linguistic riches. The percentage of children who speak a second language at home has increased from 9% in 1979 to 21% in 2008 (NCES, 2010). Of those speaking a language other than English at home, 62% speak Spanish, 19% speak another Indo-European language, 15% speak an Asian or Pacific Island language, and the remaining 4% speak a different language (Bayley & Regan, 2004; Shin & Kominsky, 2010). Of all immigrant-origin children under age 18, 81% have parents who speak English and another language at home, and 5% live in a home where no parent or caregiver speaks English (Hernandez, 2014).

English language instruction

An important challenge for immigrant-origin children is mastering content while concurrently attaining academic language proficiency in English. Although immigrant-origin children master conversational language relatively quickly, academic language—the ability to detect nuances in multiple-choice tests or argue persuasively in an essay or in a debate—is attained on average after five to seven years of highquality language instruction (Cummins, 2000; Hakuta, Butler, & Witt, 2000). Language mastery is further complicated when immigrant-origin children enter school having had only interrupted or limited schooling. These children also may have weak literacy foundations in the first language, or speak more than one language (Olsen, 1995).

Our nation's inconsistent language-learning policies and practices present a variety of obstacles for learning English (García, 2014; Gándara & Contrera, 2008; Olsen, 2010; Thomas & Collier, 2002). Research on the efficacy of second-language instruction and bilingual programs reveals contradictory results. This should not be surprising given that there are nearly as many models of bilingual and second language programs as there are school districts (Thomas & Collier 2002).

As they enter school, English language learners (ELLs) are often placed in some kind of second-language instructional setting—e.g., pull-out programs, sheltered instruction, English as a second language (ESL), and dual-language instruction. But, in many districts, students are transitioned out of these settings with little rhyme or reason (Olsen, 2010; Suárez-Orozco, Suárez-Orozco & Todorova, 2008; Thomas & Collier, 2002). ESL programs often consist of limited pull-out instruction and academic support as well as immersion in regular classes. Many ESL classrooms have learners from many different countries speaking many different languages. Transitional bilingual programs focus on providing academic support to newcomers as they transition out of their language of origin into English. Dual-language immersion classes involve students' learning half of the time in English and half in a target language (e.g. Spanish, Mandarin, etc.), with half of the class being native speakers of English and the other half native speakers of the target language. Given the predominance of Spanish-speaking ELLs, most program implementation and research in the U.S. has been done on programs targeting this specific language group (Kohler & Lazrín, 2007).

Well-designed and carefully implemented programs ease transitions, provide academic scaffolding, and nurture a sense of community. There is, however, a significant disparity in quality of instruction between settings. Many bilingual programs face implementation challenges characterized by inadequate resources, uncertified personnel, and poor administrative support (U.S. Department of Education, 2002). Because many bilingual programs lack robust support nationwide, they often do not offer the breadth and depth of courses that immigrant origin students need to get into a meaningful college track. There is an ever-present danger that once a student enters the "ESL," "bilingual" track, or English-language acquisition track, he or she will have difficulty switching to the "college-bound track." Schools are seldom focused on meeting the needs of dual-language students—at best, they tend to be ignored, and, at worst, they are viewed as contributing to low performance on state mandated, high-stakes tests (Menken, 2008; Suárez-Orozco et al., 2008).

Assessment

There is considerable debate on the role of educational assessments in general and high-stakes assessments in particular in contributing to unequal outcomes for English language learners (APA, 2012; Solórzano, 2008; Valenzuela, 2005). Standardized tests used to screen for learning differences as well as for high-stakes decisions were largely designed and normed with middle-class populations (Agbenyega & Jiggetts, 1999), or they were adapted from work with those populations. Such tests assume exposure to mainstream cultural knowledge and fail to recognize culture of origin content knowledge. This can lead to underestimates of student abilities and competencies. Timed tests penalize second-language learners who process two languages before they settle on an answer (Solano-Flores, 2008). When culturally or linguistically sensitive approaches aren't used, individual needs often go unrecognized or, conversely, they can be overpathologized (APA, 2012).

Relatedly, we should systematically recognize the sources of bias in assessment, particularly with second-language learners. When students do poorly on tests, it cannot simply be assumed that they lack the skills. Sometimes, students have not been exposed to culturally relevant materials or don't have the vocabulary in English. At other times, retrieval time is an issue; second-language learners may simply need more time to process two languages. Double negatives are an issue for second-language learners. Unfamiliar test formats especially place newcomer immigrants at a disadvantage. Issues of cultural and linguistic fairness in assessment are a critical area of research importance (Solano-Flores & Trumbull, 2003; Solano-Flores, 2008) that must constantly and systematically be addressed when working with this population (APA, 2012).

In the current high-stakes assessment climate, school districts are sometimes pressured to prematurely reclassify students from English language learners to Fluent English Proficient (Escamilla et al., 2003). In other cases, immigrant students languish as "long-term ELLs" (Olsen, 2010). With poorly implemented school assessments and a miscellany of language learning policies, there is wide variability between districts and states in this classification—seldom is reclassification tied to the empirical evidence on what it takes to attain the level of academic language proficiency required to be competitive on standardized assessments (Kieffer et al., 2009). As higher stakes have become attached to standardized tests, this issue has heightened consequences for English language learners and schools that serve them.

Social-emotional supports in schools

As they enter new schools, immigrant-origin children and adolescents, especially newcomers, may face an array of social-emotional challenges, including acculturative stress and rebuilding family relationships following long separations (Suárez-Orozco et al., 2008) and unauthorized status. Some of the challenge of adjustment is related to language acquisition (Olsen, 2010). Before the child acquires the ability to competently express herself, she often goes through a silent phase where she becomes invisible in the classroom (Merchant, 1999). This is a period of time when students can also become vulnerable to peer bullying (Scherr & Larson, 2010; Suárez-Orozco, Suárez-Orozco, & Todorova, 2008; Qin, Way, & Mukherjee, 2008) as well as low teacher expectancies (Weinstein, 2002).

Understanding and then addressing student needs during the critical transition phase for newcomer students is an important area for intervention. Emerging research shows that schools that are strategic in helping newcomer youth adjust to their new environs may be poised to help them be more successful in their psychosocial adaptation and educational performance (Sadowski, 2013; Suárez-Orozco et al., 2013).

For instance, advisory programs that partner students with one another and with older peers can foster communities of learning and emotional support. In these advisory groups, students are encouraged to openly discuss a range of topics, from difficulties with a class to missing families and friends back home to interpersonal issues. As part of classroom instruction, writing prompts also may encourage students to share their personal migration experiences and engage them in class discussions. Activities like these help students recognize that they are not alone in facing the difficulties of transition and also help teachers get to know students (Suárez-Orozco et al., 2013).

State and federal education policies

Immigrant-origin youth are over-represented in highly segregated and impoverished urban settings (Orfield, 2014). These children have little contact with middle-class Americans and are effectively isolated by ethnicity, poverty, and language (Duncan & Murnane, 2013; Orfield & Lee, 2006; Schwartz & Stiefel, 2011). This "triple segregation" is associated with a variety of negative educational experiences and outcomes, including overcrowding, low expectations, low academic standards, low achievement, school violence, and high dropout rates (Gándara & Contreras, 2008; Tseng & Lesaux, 2009). Many immigrant youth are served by Title I schools, which are profoundly influenced by requirements of federal and state policies. It is critical that teachers become aware of the implications of these policies for students.

No Child Left Behind (NCLB) had specific components focused on ELLs. The law required annual English language proficiency exams for ELL students. All students were tested in math and science beginning in their first year of enrollment, though accommodations were made to test ELL students in their mother tongue. More contentious were new federal regulations regarding English language arts (ELA) and reading assessments. In particular, ELLs were not supposed to be tested using the same exam as native speakers, but regulations did not dictate to states the contents of the ELA exam. Though research has consistently shown that, no matter the age, developing academic English language takes time (Cummins, 2000), many states used standard ELA exams after one year of enrollment to assess Adequate Yearly Progress. Thus an impossible benchmark was set that would penalize schools with high numbers of ELLs, placing them at risk of losing standing and funding under NCLB (Escamilla et al., 2003).

> Many bilingual programs face implementation challenges characterized by inadequate resources, uncertified personnel, and poor administrative support. Because many bilingual programs lack robust support nationwide, they often do not offer the breadth and depth of courses that immigrant origin students need to get into a meaningful college track.

Like NCLB, the Common Core State Standards place considerable emphasis on standardized assessments and are highly English-language dependent. Math assessments, for example, require not only solving computation problems but responding to word problems—tasks that require English language skills. This has implications for ELLs, and efforts have begun to adopt interventions to support the Common Core for ELL students (International Reading Association, 2012).

By documenting which groups and sites are doing well in comparison to others and by providing insights into the processes that account for differences, as well as alternative strategies for assessment, teachers and researchers can begin to shed light on practices, programs, and policies that can make a difference for new Americans.

Immigrant-origin youth are the fastest-growing student population in our country. They often arrive sharing an optimism and hope in the future that must be cultivated and treasured; almost universally, they recognize that schooling is the key to a better tomorrow. Over time, however, many immigrant youth, especially those enrolling in impoverished, segregated, and mediocre schools, face negative odds and uncertain prospects. Too many leave schools without developing and mastering the higher-order skills, communication, and cultural sensibilities needed in today's global economy and society.

The shared fortunes of immigrant and native citizens alike will be tied to successfully linking our youngest new Americans to the educational and economic opportunity structure, to civic belonging, and full democratic participation. Embracing immigrant children and cultivating their full potential is the education challenge of our generation. The stakes are high: Their future is our future.

References

Agbenyega, S. & Jiggetts, J. (1999). *Minority children and their over-representation in special education.* EducationIndianapolis, 119, 619–632.

American Psychological Association (APA). (2012). *Crossroads: The psychology of immigration in the new century.* APA presidential task force on immigration. Washington, DC: Author. www.apa.org/topics/immigration/report.aspx.

Bayley, R. & Regan, V. (2004). Introduction: The acquisition of sociolinguistic competence. *Journal of Sociolinguistics*, 8, 323–338.

Cummins, J. (2000). *Language, power, & pedagogy.* Bristol, UK: Multilingual Matters.

Duncan, G.J. & Murname, R.J. (2013). *Restoring opportunity: The crisis of inequality and the challenge of American Education.* Cambridge, MA & New York, NY: Harvard Education Press & Sage Foundation.

Escamilla, K., Mahon, E., Riley-Bernal, H., & Rutledge, D. (2003). High-stakes testing, Latinos, and English language learners: Lessons from Colorado. *Bilingual Research Journal*, 27 (1), 25-49.

Gándara, P. & Contreras, F. (2008). *Understanding the Latino education gap—Why Latinos don't go to college.* Cambridge, MA: Harvard University Press.

García. O. (2014). U.S. Spanish & education: Global and local intersection. *Review of Research in Education* 38, 58–80.

Hakuta, K., Butler, Y.K. & Witt, D. (2000). *How long does it take English learners to attain proficiency?* Berkeley, CA: University of California Linguistic Minority Research Institute.

Hernández, D. (2014, February, 28). Lecture. UCLA Program on International Migration. Los Angeles, CA. UCLA.

International Reading Association. (2012). *Literacy implementation guidance for the ELA Common Core standards.* Newark, DE: Author.

Kieffer, M.J., Lesaux, N.K., Rivera, M., & Francis, D.J. (2009). Accommodations for English language learners taking largescale assessments: A meta-analysis on effectiveness and validity. *Review of Educational Research, 79* (3), 1168–1201.

Kindler, A.L. (2002). *Survey of the states' limited English proficient students and available educational programs and services, 2000-01 summary report.* Washington, DC: National Clearinghouse for English Language Acquisition and Language Instruction Educational Programs.

Kohler, A.D. & Lazarín, M. (2007). *Hispanic education in the United States: Statistical brief,* No. 8. Washington, DC: National Council of La Raza. http://bit.ly/1GBtgWr

Menken, K. (2008). *English language learners left behind: Standardized testing as language policy.* Bristol, UK: Multilingual Matters.

Merchant, B. (1999). Ghosts in the classroom: Unavoidable casualties of a principal's commitment to the status quo. *Journal of Education for Students Placed at Risk, 4* (2), 153–171.

National Center for Education Statistics (NCES). (2010). *The condition of education 2010.* Washington, DC: U.S. Department of Education.

Olsen, L. (1995). School restructuring and the needs of immigrant students. In R.G. Rumbaut & W.A. Cornelius (Eds.), *California's immigrant children: Theory, research, and implications for educational policy* (pp. 209–231). Boulder, CO: Lynne Rienner Publishers.

Olsen, L. (2010). *Reparable harm fulfilling the unkept promise of educational opportunity for California's long-term English learners.* Emeryville, CA: California Tomorrow. http://bit. ly/1MZGHMG

Orfield, G. & Lee, C. (2006). *Racial transformation and the changing nature of segregation.* Cambridge, MA: The Civil Rights Project at Harvard University.

Orfield, G. (2014). *Brown at 60: Great progress, a long retreat, and an uncertain future.* Los Angeles, CA: The Civil Rights Project at UCLA.

Pew Research Center. (2015, September). *Modern immigration wave brings 59 million to U.S., driving population growth and change through 2065: Views of immigration's impact on U.S. society mixed.* Washington, DC: Author.

Qin, D.B., Way, N., & Mukherjee, P. (2008). The other side of the model minority story: The familial and peer challenges faced by Chinese-American adolescents. *Youth & Society, 39* (4), 480–506.

Sadowski, M. (2013). *Portraits of promise: Voices of successful immigrant students.* Cambridge, MA: Harvard Education Press.

Scherr, T.G. & Larson, J. (2010). Bullying dynamics associated with race, ethnicity, and immigration status. In S.R. Jimerson, S.M. Swearer, & D.L. Espelage (Eds.), *Handbook of bullying in schools: An international perspective* (pp. 223–234). New York, NY: Routledge.

Schwartz, A.E. & Steifel, L. (2011). Immigrants and inequality in public schools. In G.J. Duncan & R.J. Murnane (Eds.), *Whither opportunity: Rising inequality, schools, and children's life chances* (pp. 3–23). New York, NY & Chicago, IL: Sage Foundation & Spencer Foundation.

Shin, H.B. & Kominsky, R.A. (2010). *Language use in the United States: 2007.* Washington, DC: U.S. Census Bureau. http://1.usa.gov/1RisGNG

Solano-Flores, G. (2008). Who is given tests in what language by whom, when, and where? The need for probabilistic views of language in the testing of English language learners. *Educational Researcher*, 37 (4), 189–99.

Solano-Flores, G. & Trumbull, E. (2003). Examining language in context: The need for new research and practice paradigms in the testing of English-language learners. *Educational Researcher*, 32 (2), 3–13.

Solórzano, R.W. (2008). High-stakes testing: Issues, implications, and remedies for English language learners. *Review of Educational Research*, 78 (2), 260–329.

Suárez-Orozco, M. & Suárez-Orozco, C. (2013, Fall). Taking perspective: Context, culture, and history. In M.G. Hernández, J. Nguyen, C.L. Saetermoe, & C. Suárez-Orozco (Eds.), *Frameworks and ethics for research with immigrants: New directions for child and adolescent development*, 141, 9–23. San Francisco, CA: Jossey-Bass.

Suárez-Orozco, C., Abo-Zena, M. & Marks, A. (Eds.). (2015). *Transitions: The development of children of immigrants.* New York, NY: New York University Press.

Suárez-Orozco, C., Martin, M., Alexandersson, M., Dance, L.J., & Lunneblad, J. (2013). Promising practices: Preparing children of immigrants in New York and Sweden. In R. Alba & J. Holdaway (Eds.), *The children of immigrant in school: A comparative look at integration in the United States and Western Europe* (pp. 204–251). New York, NY: New York University Press.

Suárez-Orozco, C., Suárez-Orozco, M., & Todorova, I. (2008). *Learning in a new land: Immigrant adolescents in America.* Cambridge, MA: Harvard University Press.

Suárez-Orozco, C., Yoshikawa, H., Teranishi, T., & SuárezOrozco. M. (2011). Living in the shadows: The developmental implications of undocumented status [Special issue]. *Harvard Education Review*, 81, 438–472.

Thomas, W.P. & Collier, V.P. (2002). *A national study of school effectiveness for language minority students' longterm academic achievement.* Washington, DC: U.S. Dept. of Education, Center for Research on Education, Diversity & Excellence.

Tseng, V. & Lesaux, N. (2009). *Immigrant students. 21st century education: A reference handbook.* Thousand Oaks, CA: Sage.

U.N. Department of Economic and Social Affairs. (2013). *Population Division.* New York, NY: Author. http://bit. ly/1VUkc5U

U.S. Census Bureau. (2015). *Poverty.* Washington, DC: Author. http://1.usa.gov/1NeSPfb

U.S. Department of Education. (2002). *1999-2000 schools and staffing survey: Overview of the data for public, private, public charter, and Bureau of Indian Affairs elementary and secondary schools.* Washington, DC: Office of Educational Research and Improvement, National Center for Education Statistics.

Valenzuela, A. (Ed.). (2005). *Leaving children behind: How "Texas-style" accountability fails Latino youth.* Albany, NY: SUNY Press.

Weinstein, R.S. (2002). *Reaching higher.* Cambridge, MA: Harvard University Press.

5
Global and Domestic Economics

© Andrew Lichtenstein/Corbis

Migrant farm workers harvest sweet potatoes on September 20, 2014. The agricultural fields of rural eastern North Carolina produce bountiful crops for America's food markets. These crops are harvested by migrant, predominantly Mexican farm workers, some of whom have seasonal work visas and some of whom are undocumented. Some farm workers settle in the area, while others migrate to Florida for the winter harvest or return to Mexico.

The Economic Impact of Immigration

Each year, millions of immigrants migrate in search of work, often traveling from developing nations to economically-stable societies. Prejudice against immigrants is also often motivated by economic concerns, including the fear that immigrants usurp national resources and jobs that would otherwise go to native-born workers. The administrative costs of the immigration process and the cost of providing health care, social services, and education to immigrants does represent a significant drain on a nation's resources. Immigrants also provide marked economic benefits, including providing a source of affordable labor and massive annual contributions to the growth of host economies. Immigration is also a human rights issue, and those who choose to migrate are often attempting to escape economic hardship in their host nations. Crafting immigration policy, and constructing national attitudes about the value of immigrants, is therefore an issue steeped in economics but also indivisible from the underlying human rights issues that motivate global migration.

The Contribution of Immigrants

Immigrants bring important skills and experience to the U.S. workforce. The percentage of immigrants with PhDs, for instance, exceeds the number of U.S.-born citizens with the same degree by almost double. Immigrants are also far more likely than native-born citizens to become entrepreneurs. Census Bureau data indicates that 26 percent of start-up businesses are immigrant owned, and these provide an important source of employment for both immigrant and native-born workers. At the other end of the spectrum, more than 30 percent of immigrants have less than a high-school education and typically arrive in the United States seeking jobs in farming, labor, or manufacturing.[1]

A 2009 study investigating various immigration reform proposals found that deporting all immigrants would result in a 0.61 reduction in the U.S. GDP, while legalizing all unauthorized immigrants and stopping spending on border control would increase the nation's GDP by 0.53 percent.[2] Unauthorized immigrants currently contribute around $36 billion to the U.S. GDP by increasing the American labor force. By some estimates, if all unauthorized immigrants were given temporary work permits, the GDP could grow by as much as $1 trillion within the first decade.[3]

A 2010 report from the Institute on Taxation and Economic Policy indicated that 50–75 percent of undocumented migrants pay taxes, contributing $10.6 billion each year. If the population of undocumented migrants were to be issued temporary legal work permits, tax revenues might increase by 25 to 50 percent. Unauthorized migrants also contribute $15 billion a year to the Social Security System, despite being unable to access these benefits.[4] The myth that immigrants come to the United

States hoping to take advantage of the nation's welfare system has been repeatedly refuted by economic studies.[5]

Higher rates of immigration, both legal and illegal, have been correlated with lower rates of unemployment. Immigrant entrepreneurs create jobs directly, and foreign-born professionals, technical workers, and students are essential to the continued growth of America's technical and research sectors. For instance, a study of job growth in Silicon Valley in 2000 indicated that immigrants from China and India alone had generated 73,000 jobs and more than $19 billion in revenue.[6] Studies have also found that cities and communities that embrace immigrant laborers, rather than treating them as outsiders, experience higher levels of economic improvement.[7]

The Cost-Benefit Analysis of Immigrants in the Work Force

In some limited cases, immigrant labor reduces income and job availability for certain sectors of the native-born population. A Harvard University economic analysis between 1980 and 2000 suggested that immigrant labor can have a transient effect of reducing wages for U.S.-born workers at the lowest end of the economic spectrum by as much as 4 percent. However, the study also found that, over the longer term, the economy adjusts, negating the detrimental effects of immigration on the labor market.

This potential negative effect on low-wage workers is the primary argument against immigration, but not all economists agree that immigrant labor leads to a measurable reduction in wages. A 2010 study from the National Bureau of Economic Research (NBER) disputed the Harvard Study's findings, suggesting that many immigrants are not directly competing with U.S.-born workers for the same jobs and argued that, if the wages needed to fund a certain job were higher—because native workers command higher pay—than the job might cease to exist.[8] The NBER study suggested that some farmers, if unable to hire immigrant laborers, might consider automating harvesting and other processes, thus removing jobs from the market rather than switching from immigrants to higher-cost native workers.

Both the Harvard study and the NBER study arrived at similar results in the long term, indicating that immigration increases wages for all workers by as much as 2.86 percent by helping businesses to grow and by increasing the size of the population and thus the demand for services, food, and other goods.[9] As a whole, immigrants also lower the cost of many basic services like gardening, cleaning, and child care, benefitting many middle-class families. Studies indicate that even large increases in immigrant populations, called supply shocks in economic jargon, have negligible effects on native employment or wages. The Mariel boatlift, which brought 100,000 Cuban immigrants to Miami in 1980, increased the city's population by 7 percent overnight, but had no significant impact on employment in the city.[10]

The recent development of Arizona's economy demonstrates some of the central issues of the economic immigration debate. Between 2007 and 2012, border control regulations reduced Arizona's population of undocumented workers by 40 percent. The conservative Federation for American Immigration Reform estimated that the undocumented population cost the state $1 billion each year in education, medical costs, and incarceration. However, University of Arizona researcher Judith Gans found that immigrants produced $1 billion more in tax revenues than the population cost the state. In the wake of Arizona's extreme reduction in undocumented labor, some studies found that wages for low-skilled workers increased. However, economic analyses also indicate that the state's GDP has fallen by 2 percent each year. In all, a University of California study found that employment of low-skilled workers decreased during the same period, even while some low-skilled workers saw increases in wages. The Arizona case has been used as a political example by both pro-immigration and anti-immigration groups, but overall supports the general consensus that reduced immigration provides isolated short term benefits but results in slower growth, fewer available jobs, and reduced GDP.[11]

The immigration debate is not clearly divided along partisan lines. While some conservatives favor strict immigration laws, border protection, and more aggressive deportation policies, other conservative groups argue for a more lenient approach based on economic considerations. The American Action Forum, a conservative think tank, produced an analysis indicating that the cost of enforcing current laws—deporting all undocumented immigrants and preventing more from entering—could be $400 to $600 billion, with a resultant $1.6 trillion reduction in the national GDP. Economists, across partisan lines, generally disapprove of the most extreme immigration control measures proposed by conservative anti-immigration groups. The construction of border walls and fences, for instance, represents a massive investment in infrastructure that reduces the likelihood of immigration through some channels, but has little impact when compared to the cost.[12]

The Impact of Remittances

In many cases, immigrants send part of their earnings (remittances) to friends and family in their native nations. According to the World Bank, migrant remittances accounted for more than $550 billion in 2013 and more than $414 billion of this was sent to developing nations, marking the second largest source of income in some developing nations outside of foreign investment. In some of the poorest neighborhoods of Mexico, for instance, remittances can constitute nearly 20 percent of local income. In addition to sending money, migrants send clothing, food, and a variety of electronic devices to their home nations, and the impact of these material remittances may double the overall economic impact of cash remittances for developing communities. Economic analyses further indicate that remittances help to reduce poverty levels by as much as 3.5 percent for each 10 percent increase.[13] A 2014 study from the Inter-American Development Bank indicated that remittances are reducing crime in Mexico, with each 1 percent increase resulting in a 0.05 percent reduction in homicide and a 0.19 percent reduction in street robbery and theft. In time, such changes could lead to a reduction in the need for migration, as illegal industries shrink, allowing legitimate local economic enterprises to grow.[14]

Some have suggested that restricting remittances might limit unauthorized migration, essentially removing one of the chief benefits of migrating for work. Among suggestions in this vein are proposals for increasing taxes on remittance payments or limiting remittances to countries with large levels of unauthorized migration, like Mexico and Central America. The United States currently has low remittance fees, but still charges an average of 5–6 percent on remittance payments sent to Mexico and Central America. However, as remittances help to reduce violence, poverty, malnutrition, and have a stabilizing effect on local economies, critics argue that the remittance issue is an important human rights concern with implications far beyond the goal of deincentivising unauthorized migration. Those most affected by remittance restrictions or increased taxes, whatever the goal of such initiatives, will be poor families living in struggling communities.

Micah L. Issitt

Notes

1. Greenstone and Looney, "Ten Economic Facts About Immigration."
2. Aguiar and Walmsley, "Economic Analysis of U.S. Immigration Reforms."
3. Llosa, "7 Major Immigration Myths Debunked."
4. Santana, "5 Immigration Myths Debunked."
5. Anchondo, "Top 10 Myths About Immigration."
6. Legrain, *Immigrants: Your Country Needs Them.*
7. Jaffe, "More Immigration Means Higher Wages for All Workers."
8. Matthews, "Five Things Economists Know About Immigration."
9. Ottaviano, Peri, and Wright, "Immigration, Offshoring and American Jobs."
10. Matthews, "Five Things Economists Know About Immigration."
11. Davis, "The Thorny Economics of Illegal Immigration."
12. Berman, "The Conservative Case Against Enforcing Immigration Law."
13. Swanson, "Remittances: An Economist's Remedy for Organized Crime in Mexico."
14. Brito, Corbacho, and Osorio, "Remittances and the Impact on Crime in Mexico."

Globalization and NAFTA Caused Migration from Mexico

By David Bacon
The Public Eye, October 11, 2014

Rufino Domínguez, the former coordinator of the Binational Front of Indigenous Organizations, who now heads the Oaxacan Institute for Attention to Migrants, estimates that there are about 500,000 indigenous people from Oaxaca living in the U.S., 300,000 in California alone.[1]

In Oaxaca, some towns have become depopulated, or are now made up of only communities of the very old and very young, where most working-age people have left to work in the north. Economic crises provoked by the North American Free Trade Agreement (NAFTA) and other economic reforms are now uprooting and displacing these Mexicans in the country's most remote areas, where people still speak languages (such as Mixteco, Zapoteco and Triqui) that were old when Columbus arrived from Spain.[2] "There are no jobs, and NAFTA forced the price of corn so low that it's not economically possible to plant a crop anymore," Dominguez says. "We come to the U.S. to work because we can't get a price for our product at home. There's no alternative."

According to Rick Mines, author of the 2010 Indigenous Farm Worker Study, "the total population of California's indigenous Mexican farm workers is about 120,000 . . . a total of 165,000 indigenous farm workers and family members in California."[3] Counting the many indigenous people living and working in urban areas, the total is considerably higher. Indigenous people made up 7% of Mexican migrants in 1991–3, the years just before the passage of the North American Free Trade Agreement. In 2006–8, they made up 29%—four times more.[4]

California has a farm labor force of about 700,000 workers, so the day is not far off when indigenous Oaxacan migrants may make up a majority. They are the workforce that has been produced by NAFTA and the changes in the global economy driven by free-market policies. Further, "the U.S. food system has long been dependent on the influx of an ever-changing, newly-arrived group of workers that sets the wages and working conditions at the entry level in the farm labor market," Mines says. The rock-bottom wages paid to this most recent wave of migrants—Oaxaca's indigenous people—set the wage floor for all the other workers in California farm labor, keeping the labor cost of California growers low, and their profits high.

Linking Trade and Immigration

U.S. trade and immigration policy are linked. They are part of a single system, not separate and independent policies. Since NAFTA's passage in 1993, the U.S. Congress has debated and passed several new trade agreements—with Peru, Jordan, Chile, and the Central American Free Trade Agreement. At the same time, Congress has debated immigration policy as though those trade agreements bore no relationship to the waves of displaced people migrating to the U.S., looking for work. Meanwhile, heightened anti-immigrant hysteria has increasingly demonized those migrants, leading to measures to deny them jobs, rights, or any equality with people living in the communities around them.

To resolve any of these dilemmas, from adopting rational and humane immigration policies to reducing the fear and hostility towards migrants, the starting point must be an examination of the way U.S. policies have produced migration—and criminalized migrants.

Trade negotiations and immigration policy were formally joined together by the Immigration Reform and Control Act (IRCA) of 1986. Immigrants' rights activists campaigned against the law because it contained employer sanctions, prohibiting employers for the first time on a federal level from hiring undocumented workers and effectively criminalizing work for the undocumented. IRCA's liberal defenders argued its amnesty provision justified sanctions and militarizing the border,[5] as well as new guest worker programs. The bill eventually did enable more than 4 million people living in the U.S. without immigration documents to gain permanent residence. Underscoring the broad bipartisan consensus supporting it, the bill was signed into law by Ronald Reagan.

> We come to the U.S. to work because we can't get a price for our product at home. There's no alternative.—Rufino Dominguez, Director of the Oaxacan Institute for Attention to Migrants

Few noted one other provision of the law. IRCA set up a Commission for the Study of International Migration and Cooperative Economic Development to study the causes of immigration to the United States. The commission held hearings after the U.S. and Canada signed a bilateral free trade agreement, and made a report to President George H.W. Bush and Congress in 1990. It found that the main motivation for coming to the U.S. was poverty. To slow or halt the flow of migrants, it recommended that "U.S. economic policy should promote a system of open trade . . . the development of a U.S.-Mexico free trade area and its incorporation with Canada." But, it warned, "It takes many years—even generations—for sustained growth to achieve the desired effect."

The negotiations that led to NAFTA started within months. As Congress debated the treaty, then-Mexican President Carlos Salinas de Gortari toured the United States, telling audiences unhappy at high levels of immigration that passing NAFTA would reduce it by providing employment for Mexicans in Mexico. Back home, he made the same argument. NAFTA, he claimed, would set Mexico on a course to become a first-world nation.[6] "We did become part of the first world," says Juan Manuel Sandoval of Mexico's National Institute of Anthropology and History. "The back yard."[7]

Increasing Pressure

NAFTA, however, did not lead to rising incomes and employment in Mexico, and did not decrease the flow of migrants. Instead, it became a source of pressure on Mexicans to migrate. The treaty forced corn grown by Mexican farmers without subsidies to compete in Mexico's own market with corn from huge U.S. producers, who had been subsidized by the U.S. Agricultural exports to Mexico more than doubled during the NAFTA years, from $4.6 to $9.8 billion annually. Corn imports rose from 2,014,000 to 10,330,000 tons from 1992 to 2008. Mexico imported 30,000 tons of pork in 1995, the year NAFTA took effect. By 2010, pork imports, almost all from the U.S., had grown over 25 times, to 811,000 tons. As a result, pork prices received by Mexican producers dropped 56%.[8]

According to Alejandro Ramírez, general director of the Confederation of Mexican Pork Producers, "We lost 4,000 pig farms. Each 100 animals produce 5 jobs, so we lost 20,000 farm jobs directly from imports. Counting the 5 indirect jobs dependent on each direct job, we lost over 120,000 jobs in total. This produces migration to the U.S. or to Mexican cities—a big problem for our country."[9] Once Mexican meat and corn producers were driven from the market by imports, the Mexican economy was left vulnerable to price changes dictated by U.S. agribusiness or U.S. policy. "When the U.S. modified its corn policy to encourage ethanol production," he charges, "corn prices jumped 100% in one year."[10]

NAFTA then prohibited price supports, without which hundreds of thousands of small farmers found it impossible to sell corn or other farm products for what it cost to produce them. Mexico couldn't protect its own agriculture from the fluctuations of the world market. A global coffee glut in the 1990s plunged prices below the cost of production. A less entrapped government might have bought the crops of Veracruz farmers to keep them afloat, or provided subsidies for other crops.

But once free-market structures were in place prohibiting government intervention to help them, those farmers paid the price. Campesinos from Veracruz, as well as Oaxaca and other major corn-producing states, joined the stream of workers headed north.[11] There, they became an important part of the workforce in U.S. slaughterhouses and other industries.

U.S. companies were allowed to own land and factories, eventually anywhere in Mexico. U.S.-based Union Pacific, in partnership with the Larrea family, one of Mexico's wealthiest, became the owner of the country's main north-south rail line and immediately discontinued virtually all passenger service.[12] Mexican rail employment dropped from more than 90,000 to 36,000. Railroad workers mounted a wildcat strike to try to save their jobs, but they lost and their union became a shadow of its former self.

According to Garrett Brown, head of the Maquiladora Health and Safety Network, the average Mexican wage was 23% of the U.S. manufacturing wage in 1975.

By 2002, it was less than an eighth. Brown says that after NAFTA, real Mexican wages dropped by 22%, while worker productivity increased 45%.[13]

Attracting Investors, Repelling Workers

Low wages are the magnet used to attract U.S. and other foreign investors. In mid-June, 2006, Ford Corporation, already one of Mexico's largest employers, announced it would invest $9 billion more in building new factories.[14] Meanwhile, Ford closed 14 U.S. plants, eliminating the jobs of tens of thousands of U.S. workers. Both moves were part of the company's strategic plan to cut labor costs and move production. When General Motors was bailed out by the U.S. government in 2008, it closed a dozen U.S. plants, while its plans for building new plants in Mexico went forward without hindrance.[15] These policies displaced people, who could no longer make a living as they'd done before. The rosy predictions of NAFTA's boosters that it would raise income and slow migration proved false. The World Bank, in a 2005 study made for the Mexican government, found that the extreme rural poverty rate of around 37% in 1992–4, prior to NAFTA, jumped to about 52% in 1996–8, after NAFTA took effect. This could be explained, the report said, "mainly by the 1995 economic crisis, the sluggish performance of agriculture, stagnant rural wages, and falling real agricultural prices."[16]

> To resolve any of these dilemmas, from adopting rational and humane immigration policies to reducing the fear and hostility towards migrants, the starting point must be an examination of the way U.S. policies have produced migration—and criminalized migrants.

By 2010, 53 million Mexicans were living in poverty, according to the Monterrey Institute of Technology—half the country's population.[17] The growth of poverty, in turn, fueled migration. In 1990, 4.5 million Mexican-born people lived in the U.S. A decade later, that population more than doubled to 9.75 million, and in 2008 it peaked at 12.67 million. Approximately 9.4% of all Mexicans now live in the U.S., based on numbers from Pew Hispanic. About 5.7 million were able to get some kind of visa; but another 7 million couldn't, and came nevertheless.[18]

From 1982 through the NAFTA era, successive economic reforms produced migrants. The displacement had already grown so large by 1986 that the commission established by IRCA was charged with recommending measures to halt or slow it. Its report urged that "migrant-sending countries should encourage technological modernization by strengthening and assuring intellectual property protection and by removing existing impediments to investment" and recommended that "the United States should condition bilateral aid to sending countries on their taking the necessary steps toward structural adjustment." The IRCA commission report acknowledged the potential for harm, noting (in the mildest, most ineffectual language possible) that "efforts should be made to ease transitional costs in human suffering."[19]

In 1994, however, the year the North American Free Trade Agreement took effect, U.S. speculators began selling off Mexican government bonds. According to Jeff Faux, founding director the Economic Policy Institute, a Washington, DC-based progressive think tank, "NAFTA had created a speculative bubble for Mexican assets that then collapsed when the speculators cashed in."[20] In NAFTA's first year, 1994, one million Mexicans lost their jobs when the peso was devalued. To avert a flood of capital to the north, then-U.S. Treasury Secretary Robert Rubin engineered a $20 billion loan to Mexico, which was paid to bondholders, mostly U.S. banks. In return, U.S. and British banks gained control of the country's financial system. Mexico had to pledge its oil revenue to pay off foreign debt, making the country's primary source of income unavailable for the needs of its people.

As the Mexican economy, especially the border maquiladora industry, became increasingly tied to the U.S. market, tens of thousands of Mexican workers lost jobs when the market shrank during U.S. recessions in 2001 and 2008. "It is the financial crashes and the economic disasters that drive people to work for dollars in the U.S., to replace life savings, or just to earn enough to keep their family at home together," says Harvard historian John Womack.[21]

Immigrants, Migrants, or Displaced People?

In the U.S. political debate, Veracruz' uprooted coffee pickers or unemployed workers from Mexico City are called immigrants, because that debate doesn't recognize their existence before they leave Mexico. It is more accurate to call them migrants, and the process migration, since that takes into account both people's communities of origin and those where they travel to find work.

But displacement is an unmentionable word in the Washington discourse. Not one immigration proposal in Congress in the quarter century since IRCA was passed has tried to come to grips with the policies that uprooted miners, teachers, tree planters, and farmers. In fact, while debating bills to criminalize undocumented migrants and set up huge guest worker programs, four new trade agreements were introduced, each of which has caused more displacement and more migration.

Notes

1. Eric Hershberg and Fred Rosen, "Turning the Tide?" in *Latin America After Neoliberalism: Turning the Tide in the 21st Century*, eds. Eric Hershberg and Fred Rosen (New York: New Press, 2006), 23.

2. John P. Schmal, "Oaxaca: Land of Diversity," *¡LatinoLA!*, Jan. 28, 2007, <http://www.latinola.com/story.php?story=3908>.

3. Richard Mines, Sandra Nichols, and David Runsten, "California's Indigenous Farmworkers: Final Report of the Indigenous Farmworker Study (IFS) To the California Endowment," Jan. 2010, <http://www.indigenousfarmworkers.org/IFS%20Full%20Report%20_Jan2010.pdf>.

4. Mines, Nichols, and Runsten, "California Indigenous Farmworkers Final Report of the Indigenous Farmworker Study (IFS) To the California Endowment."

5. Brad Plummer, "Congress Tried to Fix Immigration Back in 1986. Why Did It Fail?" *Washington Post*, Jan. 30, 2013, <http://www.washingtonpost.com/blogs/wonkblog/wp/2013/01/30/in-1986-congress-tried-to-solve-immigration-why-didnt-it-work>.

6. David Clark Scott, "Salinas Plays It Cool After Big Win on NAFTA," *Christian Science Monitor*, Nov. 19, 1993, <http://www.csmonitor.com/1993/1119/19014.html>.

7. Juan Manuel Sandoval, interview with David Bacon, 2006.

8. David Bacon, *The Right to Stay Home: How US Policy Drives Mexican Migration* (Boston: Beacon Press, 2013).

9. Bacon, *The Right to Stay Home*.

10. Bacon, *The Right to Stay Home*.

11. David Bacon, *Illegal People: How Globalization Creates Migration and Criminalizes Immigrants* (Boston: Beacon Press, 2008), 63.

12. Bacon, *Illegal People*, 58.

13. Bacon, *Illegal People*, 59.

14. Elizabeth Malkin, "Detroit: Far South," *New York Times*, Jul. 21, 2006, <http://www.nytimes.com/2006/07/21/business/worldbusiness/21auto.html?pagewanted=all&_r=0>.

15. Paul Roderick Gregory, "Outsourcer-In-Chief: Obama Of General Motors," Forbes, Aug. 12, 2012, <http://www.forbes.com/sites/paulroderickgregory/2012/08/12/outsourcer-in-chief-obama-of-general-motors>.

16. José María Caballero et al. for the World Bank, *Mexico: Income Generation and Social Protection for the Poor, Volume IV: A Study of Rural Poverty in Mexico*, Aug. 2005, (accessed via <https://openknowledge.worldbank.org/handle/10986/8286>), 9-11.

17. Richard Wells, "3 Ways To Compete Sustainably: Lessons from Mexico," *GreenBiz.com*, Oct. 9, 2013, <http://www.greenbiz.com/blog/2013/10/09/3-ways-compete-sustainably-lessons-mexico>.

18. Bacon, *The Right to Stay Home*.

19. Bacon, *Illegal People*, 60–61.

20. Bacon, *Illegal People*, 61.

21. Bacon, *Illegal People*, 64.

The Fear of 'Not Enough to Go Round'

By Bridget Anderson
New Internationalist, January/February 2016

Police confrontations in Macedonia and Calais, suffocation in lorries, drowning at sea and shootings at borders, are, we are told, manifestations of a global migration problem. The 'problem' is not confined to the Mediterranean and the Balkans: consider the Rohingya abandoned in the Andaman Sea in May last year or the swelling refugee camps of Jordan and Lebanon; the detention centres on the Pacific island of Nauru and Australian 'pushbacks' of refugee boats, or deaths in the Sahara desert.

Migration is a 'crisis.' Across the world, states are building walls and passing ever harsher immigration and asylum laws; violence and deaths at borders are increasing. But this idea that migration is a peculiarly contemporary problem does not chime with global history. Thousands of years of mobility for trade, exploration and colonialism—movement to marry, make war, convert or find resources—have shaped our world. The longstanding concern of rulers to control the mobility of the ruled has also played its part. The first immigration controls appeared towards the end of the 19th century, but their origins lie far earlier. In 1388, a labourer in England who strayed outside their area was required to carry an authorization letter that bore the King's seal. By Tudor times in the 15th century, these 'passports' had developed into complex documents and false papers cost between two and four pennies.

Unstable borders

However, while people have indeed always moved, they have not always 'migrated.' It is the spread of nation-states across the world—and the internationalization of citizenship regimes—that has changed mobility into migration. This expansion dates from just after the Second World War—not even a human lifetime ago. Across the world, migration flows continue to fall and shift. Global capital, finance and new technology are also proving highly resistant to state regulation. Despite this instability, international borders are often imagined as natural and fixed. The promise of strong control over immigration appeals to a desire for a national labour market and economy, a stable cohesive national society and representative democratic politics. The figure of the migrant exemplifies the fluidity of the relations between nation, people, and state. In party politics, the presence of migrants has come to be represented as emblematic of waning state power and, in some cases, of mainstream politicians' disengagement with everyday problems. Transatlantic Trends conducts an annual survey of the European Union (EU), US, Russia and Turkey, and consistently finds a core of hostility to immigration.

But who is the 'migrant' that is the subject of such anxiety? All mobility is by no means equivalent, but is constructed and experienced differently. Some is forced and some prevented, while other journeys are encouraged. Not everyone who moves across an international border is considered a 'migrant': students, backpackers, au pairs and expats, for example. As far as public debate is concerned, the US banker working in Sydney or the British footballer coaching in New York does not count as a migrant—but their foreign domestic worker does. In the final analysis, the 'migrant' is a figure that represents the global poor and the desperate.

A logical response

The fear of the 'migrant' is, in part, the fear that 'there is not enough to go around.' These fears should not be dismissed – they are understandable in an ever more unequal world. We are living at a time of unprecedented inequality when the poorest 50 per cent of the world have 6.6 per cent of total global income. The World Bank estimates that three-quarters of income inequality can be attributed to differences between countries. In this context, when wealth and opportunity are tied to birthplace, migration should not be surprising. It is a response to problems shaped by colonial histories—and post-colonial presents—that have led to civil war, violence, and economic systems that in turn render the lives of many people in the world unsustainable and impoverished.

> In this context, when wealth and opportunity are tied to birthplace, migration should not be surprising. It is a response to problems shaped by colonial histories—and post-colonial presents—that have led to civil war, violence, and economic systems that in turn render the lives of many people in the world unsustainable and impoverished.

While wealthy states see migration as the problem, from the perspective of those who move, migration is the solution. For migrants, the problem is the border. It follows people even when they are inside their new country, blocking access to work, hospitals, lecture halls and housing. People are checked for their legality of residence and to ensure that they have not broken their conditions of entry. The responsibility of policing these borders increasingly falls to citizens—employers, lorry drivers and public servants.

Creating difference

Take, for example, the use of immigration controls to 'protect' labour markets. In early 2004, researchers from Oxford research institute COMPAS and the University of Sussex interviewed the agricultural employers of Polish workers. Before EU enlargement in May of that year, many of these workers were on tied visas, and employers were fulsome in their praise of their work ethic, often contrasting them with British citizens who, they said, were lazy and preferred to live on welfare benefits. One year later, when Poles had the same rights as national workers, those same employers complained that Polish people had lost their culture, and become like the British. The National Farmers' Union told Parliament they needed migrants who were on permits, who could be guaranteed to stay in the fields at harvest time.

Immigration laws are typically imagined as a way to weed out unsuitable applicants, but they can also be a way to create differences in the first place. Thus the law and its practice are not neutral taps that turn labour supply on and off, but mechanisms that actively produce certain types of employment relations. Paradoxically, in this case, tied visas designed to protect British jobs in fact served to make those subject to immigration controls more desirable as employees than national workers.

Citizens fall foul

The consequences of immigration controls and enforcement can weigh heavily on migrants. They affect employment and living conditions and their personal lives, particularly those who are living under threat of deportation. Citizens are not immune to these consequences. US Law Professor Jacqueline Stevens has found that approximately 20,000 US citizens were detained or deported as aliens between 2003 and 2010. She noted that the group of illegally deported US citizens were overwhelmingly Black, with little education, and often with mental-health difficulties.

More routinely, citizens are directly affected by immigration controls when their parents, children, and loved ones are taken from them by immigration powers—such as detention or deportation—or when they are prevented from living with them by immigration requirements. For example, in most EU states it is now necessary to be earning over a set income threshold before a partner can join you.

Anxiety about immigration can give rise to security measures which target not only migrants, but the population more generally. In Hungary it is now possible for state officers to enter any home where it is suspected a 'migrant' might be sheltering, and most states punish citizens who harbour or employ undocumented workers, knowingly or unknowingly.

Yet there are discernible shifts. The contradictions between human rights and deaths at borders and between democracy and mass document checks are becoming more exposed—and untenable. In Melbourne, plans announced in August 2015 by the Australian Border Force to check visas on the streets prompted a public backlash and a large spontaneous demonstration, which resulted in their cancellation. In Europe, the 'Refugees Welcome' mobilizations meant that some states, such as Britain, had to backpedal on their hostility to Syrian refugees. Trade unions worldwide are organizing irrespective of immigration status, and health professionals in Spain are refusing to check their patients' documents. Some social services departments are offering support to all children, not only those whose parents have papers.

All these efforts suggest that a world where justice and equality is not bordered can be carved out, even in the most challenging conditions.

Let the Kids Stay

By Franklin Foer
The New Republic, August 12, 2014

There was a time in the not-so-distant past when a swath of the American right was obsessed with an antique British parliamentarian, William Wilberforce. During the exhausted final moments of the Bush presidency, this nineteenth-century crusader—an evangelical, an advocate for animal rights, and an opium addict—suddenly became the subject of numerous celebratory op-ed columns, biographies, and slogans. To social conservatives in particular, Wilberforce seemed to embody the possibility that a politics drenched in morality might ultimately prevail, despite the many recent setbacks in the culture wars. After all, he had pressed his lonely crusade against the slave trade so persistently that he managed to abolish it from the British Empire in 1807, despite the vociferous opposition of moneyed interests.

Of all the Wilberforce revivalists, the most dogged was Sam Brownback, then a senator from Kansas. At seemingly every turn, he tagged himself a "Wilberforce Republican." When the musty biopic *Amazing Grace* appeared in 2007, Brownback stumped for the film. Later that year, in a tribute to his idol, he introduced the Wilberforce Act, which was intended to curb the modern-day incarnation of slavery: human trafficking.

The primary subjects of Brownback's legislation were women and children forcibly transported across the world into sexual servitude and various other states of coerced labor. Inside the Wilberforce Act, however, was another provision, unheralded at the time, but which now looms quite large. Just as the bill relaxed immigration laws to provide more sympathetic treatment to victims of trafficking, it created a set of similarly generous procedures for kids who illegally arrived at the border without their parents. The implicit moral logic of the Wilberforce Act held that unaccompanied children and sex slaves were the most helpless of new arrivals. It would be intolerably cruel to cast them out without ensuring their safety.

Almost nobody—only two House Republicans at first—opposed the Wilberforce Act. That's because it seemed like a cost-free gesture. It was difficult to imagine that more than a small handful of children would ever set out on such dangerous journeys alone. (It was especially inconceivable given that the law explicitly exempted Mexicans and Canadians from its protections.) But the arrival of tens of thousands of Central American kids this year has exposed just how badly Congress underestimated the urge to immigrate: A great mass of humanity will endure enormous risk at the least sign that they have America's blessing to flee here.

Now that these kids are no longer an abstraction, many of the conservatives who supported the Wilberforce Act would like to retract their votes. Once, they viewed child migrants as worthy of association with one of history's moral giants; now, some conservatives treat them as criminals who can't be ejected from our country harshly enough. But the unanticipated numbers of children availing themselves of the Wilberforce Act shouldn't undermine the initial logic for it. The bill's conservative authors understood that the United States has obligations to the world's most desperate cases—and that those obligations should play a decisive role in shaping our immigration policy.

On the surface, at least, the complex moral calculus of immigration has flummoxed Barack Obama. He has managed to find himself the villain of two wildly competing narratives. In the right-wing version, he's the lawless president—practicing a corrupt policy that buys Latino votes with his non-enforcement of immigration laws. On the left, he's guilty of precisely the opposite crime. He's the "Deporter in Chief," willing to heartlessly expel millions of immigrants in his naïve pursuit of a grand legislative bargain with Republicans. Neither of these narratives is especially fair. But their existence captures the difficulty of his task: designing a rationalized immigration system so that it becomes both more humane and more faithful to the rule of law.

At its core, the overriding obsession of recent U.S. immigration policy has been the sealing of the Mexican border. This is an old hobbyhorse that acquired greater urgency after 9/11, fueled by false rumors that our assailants had crept into the United States by land. In short order, spending on border enforcement tripled, to $18 billion in 2012. It would be silly to assume that this money has been spent wisely, especially given the charlatan contractors circling this pile of cash. But today our border increasingly resembles a forcefield, and migration from Mexico has plummeted. In 2006, the Government Accountability Office rated U.S. control of the southern border to be 69 percent effective; by 2011, that rate had risen to 84 percent.

Liberals tend to dismiss any fixation on the border—and somewhat understandably so. Conservatives invoke it as the primary immigration emergency when it is, in fact, a pretext for avoiding an unpalatable discussion of the fate of the eleven million undocumented people living in the United States. However border security isn't just a matter of law and order; it's also the foundation for a generous immigration policy. An anarchic border creates a foul political mood, which makes it harder to help the immigrants here and those aspiring to come.

And yet the border has an even greater importance than that. There's a strain of liberal political theory, most compellingly formulated by Michael Walzer, that holds that a community's sense of social solidarity and self-determination depends on its ability to deny membership to outsiders. This sounds like a fairly academic notion, but it's not.

Without a well-regulated border, we lose the capacity to make choices about whom we admit to our country. We end up simply taking those who manage to make their way in—which diminishes our financial and political capacity to accept others based on our economic need or their moral merit. But in the last decade, we've solved that problem. We have a secure border that affords us the ability to make choices—to prioritize the entry of the groups who most need our help, especially when we are directly responsible for their plight.

Central America has hemorrhaged migrants in recent decades. Its long civil wars—battles between U.S.-supported governments and Marxist insurgents—flared and abated and then flared again, with death squads preemptively squashing potential rebellions. Millions fled during these grinding conflicts. One in five Salvadorans came to reside in the United States. The numbers from Guatemala and Honduras were never quite so dramatic, though

> We have a secure border that affords us the ability to make choices—to prioritize the entry of the groups who most need our help, especially when we are directly responsible for their plight.

still fairly staggering. (There are more than one million Guatemalans living in the United States.) These departures—which were driven by the search for economic opportunity as well as the quest for safety—divided families and weakened the underlying structures of societies, creating the conditions for chaos.

After the cold war ended, the United States more or less fled the region, too. But the American appetite for cocaine remained. Honduras, with its unguarded coastlines, empty jungles, and convenient location, became a global capital of the drug business, with some 40 percent of U.S.-destined cocaine touching its soil on its journey northward. Gangs sprouted alongside this booming trade. Their growth was a tragicomic tale of the perils of unintended consequences. During the past two decades, the United States deported thousands of Los Angeles gang members back to their birth countries in the Northern Triangle, introducing hardened criminals and their tribal customs. These gangsters were often dumped with little warning and essentially no program for curbing their impending threat. Then there was the joint U.S.-Mexican war on drugs, which propelled gruesome Mexican criminal organizations into Central America in search of greater freedom to operate and new business opportunities.

The governments of Central America weren't prepared for this influx, to say the least. Gangs arrived just as these countries were making a ham-fisted transition to democracy—a transition that viewed the principle of law and order with skepticism. Correcting for the authoritarian abuses of the past, the judiciaries tended to think of offenders as victims of social injustice; prosecutors were viewed as implements of power-mad dictators. (According to official numbers, 98 percent of crimes in Guatemala aren't prosecuted.) And after all the civil wars and insurgencies faded into history, the security forces were scaled back, a particularly unfortunate stroke of bad timing. They are now simply outnumbered. Two years ago, the State Department estimated that there are some 85,000 gang members in Guatemala, Honduras, and El Salvador. In the face of this growth, the Honduran police force has shrunk to just 14,000—and a poorly paid force at that. Officers make $400 per month, supplemented by "war taxes" they have empowered themselves to assess.

It was inevitable that childhood would fall victim to such social decay. Since gangs recruit in schools, classroom attendance has collapsed. NGOs in the region report that thugs use rape to coerce girls as young as nine into their schemes. This is the expression of a society that has degraded the very value of life. In Honduras, death is concentrated in metropolitan abattoirs: The city of San Pedro de Sula is arguably the grimmest place on Earth, with 173 homicides per 100,000. By comparison, war-torn, refugee-ridden Congo has 30 per 100,000.

It's hardly surprising that the gangs would capture large chunks of the state in these countries. The vice president of Honduras's National Congress has estimated that 40 percent of the police force is tied to organized crime. Guatemala's security services were so thoroughly corrupted that the United Nations set up a special agency to combat criminal impunity—though three out of four murder cases still go unpunished. These are the classical preconditions for claims of asylum: When kids are targeted by gangs, they can't appeal to any authority for plausible sanctuary, because the authorities are implicated in their torment. Many of the children crossing the Rio Grande aren't trying to evade the border patrol but desperately seeking their protection.

One hundred and fifty years ago, the arrival of refugees from Ireland provoked a wave of draconian proposals for closing off access to the United States. The most eloquent rebuttal to these restrictions came from Herman Melville, who had himself recently crewed a ship from Liverpool brimming with immigrants. In his mostly forgotten novel *Redburn*, he waxed lyrical: "Let us waive that agitated national topic, as to whether such multitudes of foreign poor should be landed on our American shores; let us waive it, with the one only thought, that if they get here, they have God's right to come; though they bring all Ireland and her miseries with them. For the whole world is the patrimony of the whole world; there is no telling who does not own a stone in the Great Wall of China."

It's a beautiful passage, moving in its cosmopolitanism and big-heartedness. But Melville's expansiveness touches on the very anxiety that makes so many Americans wary of helping the migrant kids: the worry that opening doors for one group will inspire other groups to elbow their way in; that showing compassion for victims of violence in Guatemala will set an irreversible precedent that will require us to show the same compassion to victims of violence in Syria and the Central African Republic and Iraq and Congo. This isn't an unreasonable concern. U.S. immigration laws frequently end up ushering in far more new arrivals than their authors intended.

But ultimately, this anxiety is just an excuse for inaction. For starters, the proximity of Central America makes the scale of this crisis singular. So, even if our generosity to the border kids motivated other asylum seekers, the influx would be a manageable one. The odds of Syrian and Congolese children showing up at our airports in great numbers is exceedingly remote. They would need valid visas to even board flights to the United States. Besides, we've shown many times in the past that our immigration law can extend a hand to particular groups at particular times—Indochinese and Cuban refugees, to name two—without opening the border to all comers.

Over the decades, we've built a generous immigration system—and also provided it with rigid constraints, starting with a well-policed border. The fact there will always be another beleaguered group knocking on our door doesn't mean that we should turn away the unaccompanied kids who immediately need our help, especially when our society has contributed to their woes. Obligations can feel frighteningly endless, but that doesn't absolve us of their burdens.

The Most Entrepreneurial Group in America Wasn't Born in America

By Adam Bluestein
Inc. Magazine, February 2015

Derek Cha arrived in America as a 12-year-old with his parents and three siblings. They came for familiar reasons: "In 1977, South Korea was a poor country," Cha says. "My parents were looking for better opportunities and education for us." After the family settled in California, his mother worked as a seamstress; his father had jobs as a dishwasher and janitor. Cha delivered newspapers, helped his father with cleaning work after school, and got his first job at McDonald's at age 16.

Today, at 49, Cha is the owner of the 350-store chain of SweetFrog frozen-yogurt shops, which has more than $34 million in annual revenue. He employs about 800 part- and full-time workers in the 70-some locations he operates himself. (Like all the companies featured in this story, SweetFrog made the 2014 *Inc.* 500 list of America's fastest-growing companies.) Cha founded the Richmond, Virginia-based business in 2009, as the U.S. was slowly emerging from deep recession.

Risky? Yes. But increasingly, it is immigrant entrepreneurs like Cha who are most willing to take the risk of starting a business—and without the growth of immigrant-owned businesses like Cha's, the recession would have been much worse. From 1996 to 2011, the business startup rate of immigrants increased by more than 50 percent, while the native-born startup rate declined by 10 percent, to a 30-year low. Immigrants today are more than twice as likely to start a business as native-born citizens.

Despite accounting for only about 13 percent of the population, immigrants now start more than a quarter of new businesses in this country. Fast-growing ones, too—more than 20 percent of the 2014 Inc. 500 CEOs are immigrants. Immigrant-owned businesses pay an estimated $126 billion in wages per year, employing 1 in 10 Americans who work for private companies. In 2010, immigrant-owned businesses generated more than $775 billion in sales. If immigrant America were a stock, you'd be an idiot not to buy it.

Yet U.S. immigration policy has largely ignored the contribution of immigrant-launched businesses. Despite the bipartisan popularity of business-friendly proposals, including increasing the cap on H-1B work visas for skilled workers and creating a visa category for venture-backed entrepreneurs, the public debate frequently devolves into shouting matches over whether people should be deported and how quickly.

Even the biggest breakthrough in immigration policy in years—President Obama's announcement in November that he would take executive action—glossed over the role of immigrants as the nation's leading risk takers and job creators. Obama spoke of a "dynamic and entrepreneurial" economy, but left vague exactly what his action will do to help entrepreneurial immigrants prosper.

This omission no doubt reflects the limitations of what Obama can accomplish without congressional cooperation. And, of course, any changes he makes aren't necessarily permanent. They could be overturned by a new president in 2017—and Senator Ted Cruz of Texas and others have vowed to block provisions of the executive action from being implemented.

Driven by the politics of short election cycles, the U.S. is missing the larger economic cycle of immigration. Meanwhile, Canada has been advertising its new startup visa with a billboard on California's Highway 101, where every foreign-born engineer in Silicon Valley can see it: "H-1B Problems? Pivot to Canada." America has set up a legal thicket of "Keep Out" signs—which is both tragic and suicidal.

We should support immigration reform, and not only because it's in keeping with the American character of attracting world-class talent. As entrepreneurs know better than anyone, the American economy needs the dynamism and creativity of go-getters like Derek Cha. With the debate continuing to roil Washington, Inc. offers this modest prescription for immigration policies that preserve our national brand as the land of opportunity—and prosperity—for all.

Attract and retain more high-skilled immigrants

Michael Chertok and Adi Pinhas, co-founders of Superfish, a maker of cutting-edge visual search technology, started their company in a suburb of Tel Aviv with seed money from Israeli investors. But they came to the U.S. in 2008 to raise their first round of venture funding. "Back then, no one in Israel thought you could do a consumer tech company there," says Pinhas. "VCs in Silicon Valley got the technology, and were willing to wait for it to develop." Superfish—now headquartered in Palo Alto, California—has raised nearly $20 million in total funding and had revenue of $35 million in 2013. It employs 25 workers in the U.S. and an additional 60 in Israel.

"Being based in Palo Alto is huge," Pinhas says. "There is no need to convince anyone to do business with you. Even if you think you're visiting frequently and you read TechCrunch three times a day, it's not the same as being here working with your American team. The culture is different."

As much as high-tech entrepreneurs like Pinhas and Chertok need Silicon Valley, it needs them too. Indeed, without immigrants, there would be no Silicon Valley as we know it. In the '80s and '90s, the area attracted more foreign-born scientists and engineers than any other part of the country; by 2000, 53 percent of the Valley's science and engineering work force was foreign-born. Immigrant founders started 52 percent of new Silicon Valley companies between 1995 and 2005. And in 2012, immigrant-founded engineering and technology companies in the U.S.—heavily clustered in California—employed 560,000 workers and generated $63 billion in sales.

But a 2012 study underwritten by the Kauffman Foundation concluded that "immigrant-founded companies' dynamic period of expansion has come to an end." In Silicon Valley, the percentage of immigrant-founded companies has declined by 8.5 percent since 2005, the first such drop in recent history. Many attribute the decline to U.S. immigration policy. "It is getting increasingly difficult to hire high-tech talent here in the U.S., and increasingly easy abroad," says Emily Lam, of the Silicon Valley Leadership Group, an advocacy organization. "Companies are in a global competition for talent, and other countries are rolling out the red carpet for them while we are rolling out the red tape. The U.S. and Silicon Valley are still the places to be, but if Congress doesn't act soon, that won't last for very long."

> **Immigrant founders started 52 percent of all new Silicon Valley companies between 1995 and 2005.**

Surprisingly, there is overwhelming agreement about what the United States needs to do to turn things around. First, we need to make more H-1B "specialty occupation" visas available. A consistent shortage of these temporary work visas prevents U.S. tech companies from hiring the foreign-born scientific and engineering workers they need. The current annual cap for H-1B visas is set at 65,000, with an additional 20,000 reserved for foreign nationals graduating with a U.S. master's degree or higher. In 2014, there were 172,500 applications for H-1Bs, blowing past the quota within days of the first application-filing date.

If Congress had enacted the immigration reform bill that the Senate passed in 2013—or other bills that had made progress in the House—that would have raised the annual H-1B cap to 115,000 right away (and up to 180,000 over time). Obama couldn't raise the H-1B cap with his executive action; Congress has to do that. But he did expand and extend a program that allows foreign graduates with scientific and technical degrees from American universities to work in on-the-job training programs at U.S. companies. "This will be very beneficial to high-tech employers, who depend on foreign graduates," says Matthew Kolodziej, an immigration attorney in the New York City offices of Ogletree Deakins and a former legislative fellow at the nonprofit American Immigration Council.

More visas alone aren't the answer, though. An H-1B allows the holder to work in the U.S. for only up to six years—after that, he or she must leave or obtain a different kind of visa. "The real problem isn't H-1Bs—it's green cards," says serial entrepreneur Vivek Wadhwa, a Stanford Law School fellow and author of *The Immigrant Exodus*. "There are backlogs of tens of thousands of people in line who would start companies, but they're waiting for green cards." Unlike H-1B visas, green cards confer permanent resident status. Under the current system, high-skilled workers who have applied for green cards can wait decades for them to become available. The president's executive action would make changes that allow such workers to move and change jobs more easily while they are waiting.

The U.S. currently has a 140,000 annual quota on employment-based green cards. There are quotas for different skill categories, as well as per-country limits, which can push would-be immigrants from countries like India and China—who make up the majority of Silicon Valley's immigrant work force—onto decades-long waiting lists. The U.S. should drop the country limits and add 85,000 more employment-based green cards, as was proposed in a House bill.

Landing a green card usually requires a sponsoring employer; as the founder of a startup, you can't sponsor yourself. A proposed EB-6 "startup visa"—a component of the bill that passed in the Senate but stalled in the House—would offer a path to permanent citizenship tailored to entrepreneurs, allocating up to 10,000 visas annually to foreign-born founders whose companies raise at least $500,000 from qualified investors and create at least five full-time U.S. jobs. We should enact such a program—yesterday. The Kauffman Foundation estimates this startup visa would create as many as 1.6 million jobs in 10 years. Canada, the U.K., New Zealand, Ireland, and Singapore have already implemented similar visas.

In lieu of permanent legislation to codify the startup visa, Obama's executive action offered a sort of secret pathway for startup founders "who meet certain criteria for creating jobs, attracting investment, and generating revenue in the U.S." Few details were available at presstime, but the policy is a step in the right direction, say those briefed on it. "If entrepreneurs can show they contribute to job creation, the changes could allow them to enter the U.S. or make their entry legal retroactively by granting them 'parole' status," says Kolodziej, the immigration attorney. At presstime, it wasn't clear how long parole status would be granted, or what type of visa parolees could get after that time, but, says Kolodziej, "this is a very positive change, because current programs for entrepreneurs are based on treaties, and if the individuals do not come from a treaty country, their options are very limited."

By merits of Superfish's funding and job creation, Pinhas would clearly meet the requirements for a proposed startup visa. That would let him put down roots. Because his company had been operating for more than a year in Israel and doing business in the U.S., Pinhas was able to come here in 2013 on a nonimmigrant L-1 visa, which allows executives of established foreign companies to set up or work for a U.S. office. The three-year visa is renewable, but since approval isn't guaranteed, Pinhas says he is "planning accordingly." He and his wife are happy with the school their two sons attend, but, he says, "I wouldn't buy a house here yet—we might need to leave in a year."

Clear a path for less-skilled workers, too

Although highly educated founders of tech companies get a lot of attention, they're just one part of the story of immigrant entrepreneurship in America.

Currently, only a small fraction of immigrants have advanced degrees. And that's OK, because even without the benefit of a college education, immigrants tend to be far more entrepreneurial than native Americans. Only about a third of immigrant business owners have taken at least some college classes, versus 54 percent of native-born owners. And more than 37 percent of immigrant business owners haven't even finished high school, compared with 16 percent of native-born owners.

But despite the benefits of allowing more immigrants of all skill levels to live and work here legally, U.S. immigration policy makes it very difficult for them to do so. There are only about 5,000 employment-based green cards available each year for unskilled immigrant workers without professional degrees. And existing H-2A and H-2B visas for seasonal low-skilled workers are unpopular with employers because of complicated paperwork, and designed for temporary workers, rather than the longer-term workers increasingly needed in many parts of the economy. The U.S. should listen to the conservative American Enterprise Institute, whose 2013 study "Filling the Gap" argues in favor of the U.S. allowing more "low-skilled" immigrants to come here legally.

The arguments against low-skilled immigrants are familiar: They take American jobs, gobble up government handouts, and wreck communities. But research by the AEI, the Partnership for a New Economy, and others shows that the majority of low-skilled immigrants are a lot more like Derek Cha's family—working hard at jobs that Americans often don't want, and starting businesses without the benefit of lots of formal education. And many who have launched companies in the U.S. know the value of immigrants, both as founders and as employees.

Cha went to college for a year and a half before leaving to focus full time on running an art framing business with his father. "My father had always been in business in Korea, but he didn't speak English," Cha says. "But working 14-hour days, 7 days a week, we did well right off the bat." Their company expanded to more than 80 locations in multiple states, until the recession put them out of business after 20 years.

The sorts of jobs that Cha's father had before starting his own business—dishwashing and building maintenance—are now filled almost entirely by foreign-born workers. While the number of Americans with college degrees has continued to rise, in our service-driven economy, there are still lots of low-skilled jobs available. The dirtiest, most physically demanding, and most dangerous of these jobs—in fields such as construction, landscaping, and building maintenance, for example— are overwhelmingly filled by immigrants, who now account for more than half of all low-skilled workers in the U.S. These are jobs that native-born workers typically don't want.

A 2013 analysis of the Senate's immigration reform bill by the nonpartisan Congressional Budget Office estimates its passage would have resulted in nine million more people entering the U.S. work force in the next 20 years, with new immigrants participating at a higher rate, on average, than other U.S. residents. As a result, unemployment would tick up slightly for several years as labor markets adjusted. But after that, thanks to additional demand for goods and services, employment would be higher than projected under current regulations. Wages for all workers would be 0.1 percent lower, on average, after 10 years—but largely because new immigrants would earn lower average wages than other residents. And after 20 years, average U.S. wages would be 0.5 percent higher.

The broader economic payback is more impressive: Although implementing the legislation would cost $22 billion in the first 10 years—and between $20 billion and $25 billion in the next 10 years—it would reduce federal budget deficits by at least $700 billion in the next 10 to 20 years.

In addition to eliminating country quotas for employment-based visas, the U.S. should clear long backlogs in family-based visa applications, and create a W-visa category for less-skilled employees to work legally for up to three years (with a chance to renew and be sponsored for permanent residence). These are practical steps that would do more to curb illegal immigration than simply increasing border security, says Stuart Anderson, executive director at the nonprofit National Foundation for American Policy. "If we had a legal visa category that let people go back and forth, many wouldn't feel the need to put down roots and instead would work for a time and go back."

Immigrants want to work, says Cha. "I don't believe in handouts from the government," he says. "I'm a conservative at heart. But I believe that newer immigrants from poorer countries are hardworking and not afraid of doing jobs that people here don't want to do. If we can responsibly help them come here, it's a good thing for the country."

Support foreign-born entrepreneurs

Immigrant founders play a vital role as connectors to global markets—both abroad and here in the U.S. Immigrant businesses are 60 percent more likely to export than native-owned companies, and more than 2.5 times as likely to rely on exports for a large part of their sales, according to the Partnership for a New American Economy. Exports are responsible for about half of the country's economic growth in recent years.

Immigrant entrepreneurs are also uniquely qualified to create innovative business models that tap into the "hidden" needs of immigrant consumers in the U.S. Anurag Jain, a native of India and the co-founder of Prepay Nation in Berwyn, Pennsylvania, is a case in point.

By allowing immigrants to send small gifts of cell-phone minutes to relatives back home, Jain's company "solves two problems that most immigrants have," Jain says. "One is that immigrants want to help their families back home, but often they have minimum-wage jobs. And you really can't send money overseas without ridiculous fees." His business model allows immigrants to transfer as little as $2 worth of minutes at a time to family overseas, with no fee to the sender or recipient. (Foreign cellular network operators give Prepay a commission on sales.) Additionally, with Prepay, senders know where the money is going. "People want to take care of relatives' basic needs," Jain says, "but they don't necessarily want to pay for parties and alcohol." The company, founded in 2010, has revenue of more than $110 million.

"Being an immigrant myself obviously helps me understand the issues and the pain most immigrants go through," says Jain, who earned $50 a day when he came to the U.S. in 2001 with his wife, who was studying on a J-1 educational visa. (This type of visa allows spouses to work legally in the U.S.; spouses of H-1B visa holders, though, have been prevented from working, sidelining many educated immigrants who could be contributing to the economy. The president's executive action includes changes that would allow many H-1B spouses to work.)

Although many immigrant entrepreneurs choose to cater to a community they are familiar with, "I think success comes when you try to go out of your comfort zone," Jain says. "A majority of the mentors I got advice from are American citizens. If you're trying to do business, the more kinds of people you know, the better. If you just stick to your own community members, your perspective is going to be more limited."

Jain's mentorships came about accidentally—he rented space for his first business in a shared office where an attorney and another business owner were already working. "The three of us got together every few weeks to talk about problems in our businesses, and that helped a lot," says Jain. "They became good friends and brought me perspective I was missing." Among other things, they helped prevent business-etiquette gaffes. "In India, it's very common to give a favor in exchange for business. They told me that wasn't acceptable here."

Helping immigrant entrepreneurs become as successful as they can be is in the country's best interests. The U.S. should support a formal system of mentorship for immigrant business people. A program like the one proposed in both Senate and House versions of immigration reform bills would be a good start, awarding grants to nonprofits and state and local governments to run immigrant integration programs. The nonprofit group WelcomingAmerica.org is already running similar programs in such cities as St. Louis and Detroit, which are supporting immigrants as a way to spur stagnant local economies.

Legalize the undocumented

Ruby Polanco, the Honduras-born founder of Ruby Makeup Academy, based in Temple City, California, came to America like hundreds of thousands of other immigrants—she was brought here as a child. "The transition from Honduras was very scary," says Polanco, who was just 12 years old when she arrived in the U.S. almost three decades ago. With her mother and two brothers, Polanco lived in Los Angeles, in a 300-square-foot apartment with no kitchen. School, she says, was "very hard on kids who didn't speak English." And the convoluted process of obtaining green cards—particularly challenging for immigrants from Central America— added to the family's sense of insecurity. At 17, Polanco was a pregnant high school dropout, married to a man she'd divorce a year later.

Finally getting her green card, Polanco says, "changed my mentality. In my own crazy mind, I decided I wanted to make myself American, to make this country my country. After many years, I had the right to stay here." Polanco got a job as a cashier at McDonald's and eventually became a manager. After getting her GED, she attended community college, and later got a bachelor's degree in business management.

Since founding a school for makeup artists in 2006, Polanco now has four locations in the Los Angeles area, revenue of more than $2 million, and about 45 employees. Polanco has also become a visible entrepreneurial presence in L.A.'s Hispanic community. "You give a Hispanic woman $5 and she'll turn it into a million," she says, "but not a lot of people are investing money and time on these young women." Polanco hopes she can help other Hispanic women overcome an "illegal" mindset. "Even legal people here think very illegal," she says. "They think they can only do business in their corner."

Whether you call it "amnesty" or a "path to citizenship," doing something about the 11.7 million undocumented migrants who have settled in the U.S., two-thirds of them more than a decade ago, must be part of any serious immigration reform program. For too long, this issue has held back any and all immigration reform, with Republicans refusing to pass any bill that includes provisions for the undocumented, and Democrats refusing to pass any bill that does not. Keeping people like young Ruby Polanco and other ambitious immigrants in a drawn-out state of legal limbo serves no one. The president's executive action essentially kicks the can down the road, offering temporary relief from deportation and work permits for an estimated 3.7 million undocumented parents of U.S. citizens or legal permanent residents, and nearly 1.5 million people who entered the U.S. as children before 2010.

Like the rest of the president's executive action, this deal will expire unless the next president chooses to continue it—or in the unlikely event that the new Congress approves a path to citizenship like the one outlined in the Senate's immigration bill. That bill would have allowed undocumented adults who arrived in the U.S. before a certain date to live and work here legally—but without access to federal benefits like Medicaid, food stamps, or Obamacare health subsidies. After a period of at least 13 years—assuming they paid taxes, passed background checks, and stayed out of legal trouble—they could have qualified for citizenship. Those who were brought to the U.S. as children, like Polanco, would have been able to earn citizenship after five years.

Each year, about 65,000 undocumented students who have lived in the U.S. for five or more years graduate from American high schools. And then their lack of legal status keeps them out of higher education, the work force, and the military. Allowing these young people to live and work here without fear could increase federal revenue by $2.3 billion over 10 years, according to the Congressional Budget Office and the Joint Committee on Taxation.

Immigrant businesses are 60 percent more likely to export, a key factor to U.S. economic growth in recent years.

Stopgap measures, executive actions, and partisan standoffs don't cut it anymore as policy for a country that was literally built by immigrants. The business case for immigration reform is clear and compelling. It's long since time for politicians on both sides of the aisle to look at the facts—and beyond the unfounded fears—about immigration and start enacting pragmatic solutions. "For many years, the U.S. was the best place in the world to go start a company," says Jason Wiens, a policy director at the Kauffman Foundation. "If we don't provide ways for these people to stay here and create companies, we're going to lose out."

The Economics of Syrian Refugees

By John Cassidy
The New Yorker, November 18, 2015

In the wake of last Friday's attacks on Paris, much has been written about Syrian refugees, and the (remote) possibility that ISIS-affiliated jihadis might slip into the United States among the ten thousand displaced people (many of them children) that the Obama administration has committed to taking in during the next year. In contrast with discussions about immigration generally, there has been less comment about the economics of the issue. There are many arguments in favor of settling refugees here—not least what President Obama, responding to the announcement by some state governors that they would not accept Syrians fleeing their country's civil war, called "our values"—but from a financial perspective, too, there is little doubt that the U.S. has the capacity to absorb many more Syrian refugees, and that the long-term impact of such a policy would be positive.

Let's start with an obvious point: With up to seven million Syrians having been displaced by the civil war, many countries much smaller than the United States have already allowed in a lot more than ten thousand refugees. Since 2012 the European Union has received about 1.9 million requests for asylum, and even that number is dwarfed by the number of people who have sought refuge in countries adjacent to Syria. According to the United Nations, Turkey has taken in an estimated 2.2 million, Lebanon 1.1 million, and Jordan six hundred and thirty thousand.

Based purely upon these figures, you might think that the economies of these countries would be sagging under the burden, but they aren't. According to a new report from the Paris-based Organization for Economic Co-Operation and Development, the Turkish economy will expand by three per cent this year and by four per cent next year. Lebanon's economy is also growing, at a rate of about two per cent this year, which will expand to more than three per cent next year, the World Bank reckons. Despite an influx of refugees that now amounts to more than ten per cent of its population, Jordan, too, is bearing up. Its gross domestic product will rise by about three per cent this year, the International Monetary Fund says.

These figures make the point that, even in countries facing huge influxes of refugees, the impact on the economy as a whole is usually not very large. The biggest challenges in accommodating refugees are social and political, rather than economic. To be sure, there is a cost to screening, housing, and feeding the entrants, but even in Turkey, which has received more Syrian refugees than any other

---

country, this cost has proved manageable. In a blog post in September, Massimiliano Calì and Samia Sekkarie, two economists at the World Bank, noted, "The Turkish government has spent nearly 5.37 billion euros since the refugees first began arriving, entirely funded through its own fiscal resources. While this is undoubtedly a lot of money, there is no indication that this spending has jeopardized the country's fiscal sustainability." If you think about it, that's not surprising. Turkey's annual GDP is about eight hundred billion dollars. At about one and a half billion dollars a year, the cost of resettling the Syrian refugees has been less than 0.2 percent of the GDP.

In Lebanon, which is much smaller than Turkey, the cost of dealing with the refugee crisis has been greater relative to the GDP, but much of it has been met using money provided by international donors. Indeed, a recent study carried out under the auspices of the U.N. concluded that the refugee-aid packages actually boosted Lebanon's GDP by more than one per cent. (At the same time, though, the spillover from the carnage in Syria has hit tourism, one of Lebanon's biggest industries, hard. Overall, the U.N. study estimated, the crisis in Syria has lowered Lebanon's GDP by about 0.3 per cent.)

Another concern that has been voiced frequently about refugees, especially in Europe over the past few months, in response to the influx of refugees there, has been that refugees take jobs from native workers and reduce wages. The evidence from the Syrian experience suggests that this can happen, but that the effects aren't very

> **If the United States were to take in more Syrian refugees, the numbers would be tiny compared to what is happening in the Middle East and Europe.**

large. In many cases, refugees take jobs that natives don't want. They also set up businesses of their own and provide more customers for domestic enterprises.

Since so many of the refugees in Lebanon and Jordan are in temporary camps, the most relevant example for this pattern is Turkey. Earlier this year, the Center for Middle Eastern Strategic Studies, in Ankara, published a detailed study of what impact Syrian refugees are having on Turkey. The report did find that the influx is causing economic tensions in the south, where many Syrians are working illegally in the informal economy. The cost of home rentals has increased, making it harder to find affordable housing, and inflation has risen. "There is unfair competition between businesses that hire illegal workers and companies that do not employ illegal workers," the report said. "Locals believe that job opportunities have been taken away from them." However, when the authors of the report investigated these claims, they found that "Syrians are generally employed in areas that locals are not willing to work in. Thus, Syrians meet the demand in unskilled labor."

Not all the migrants are unskilled workers, however. Another study, by Soner Çağaptay, a fellow at the Washington Institute for Near East Policy, pointed out that many Syrian traders from places like Aleppo, which has been devastated by the civil war, have moved their operations across the border to cities in southern

Turkey, boosting business there. In general, Çağaptay wrote, "Turkish business, and the country's trademark export market, has registered remarkable success in dealing with the fallout of the Syrian crisis."

If the United States were to take in more Syrian refugees, the numbers would be tiny compared to what is happening in the Middle East and Europe. At the top end of the range, Hillary Clinton and Martin O'Malley have called for sixty-five thousand migrants to be admitted over the next five years. As O'Malley pointed out during last week's Democratic debate, "Accommodating sixty-five thousand refugees in our country . . . of three hundred and twenty million is akin to making room for six and a half more people in a baseball stadium with thirty-two thousand."

There is also a relatively recent precedent for the country admitting and successfully assimilating far more refugees than even sixty-five thousand. In 1975 and 1976, after the fall of the pro-Western regime in Saigon, about a hundred and fifty thousand Vietnamese were admitted to refugee centers in Arkansas, California, Florida, and Pennsylvania. During the late seventies and early eighties, as flotillas of desperate "boat people" set sail from Vietnam, the U.S. admitted hundreds of thousands more refugees. (By 1995, the total number was close to half a million.)

At the time, the policy of admitting large numbers of Vietnamese encountered a great deal of opposition. (In a 1975 poll, only thirty-six per cent of Americans were in favor of admitting them.) There were the usual self-contradictory worries that the refugees, few of whom spoke English, would take jobs and prove to be a permanent burden on the country. Several decades later, however, these concerns have proved largely unfounded.

Today, there are almost 1.9 million Vietnamese-Americans, more than half of whom live in California or Texas. Although the data shows that Vietnamese-Americans haven't done as well economically as some other Asian immigrants and their descendants, such as those of Korean and Chinese origin, they are generally earning a fair amount. Indeed, a statistical portrait put together by the Washington-based Center for American Progress shows that they're doing better than the typical American household. The median income among Vietnamese-American households is about fifty-nine thousand dollars, compared to a national average of about fifty-three thousand. The participation rate of Vietnamese-Americans in the labor force is a bit higher than the national average as well: 64.9 percent in 2014, compared to 64.3 percent for U.S. households as whole. And the unemployment rate among Vietnamese-Americans is lower than the national average.

There are still some problems: Vietnamese-Americans still tend to live in separate communities, a practice that is often associated with low rates of social mobility, and about half of them still have limited proficiency in English. Evidently, however, this hasn't stopped them from integrating into the U.S. economy and helping it to grow. They also generally reflect American economic ideals, a Pew Research study found: eighty-four percent of Vietnamese-Americans believe that most people can get ahead if they work hard, and almost half of them believe their children's standards of living will be "much better" than theirs.

Should the U.S. government decide to allow tens of thousands (or even hundreds of thousands) of Syrians to come here and stay, there isn't any obvious reason why they couldn't replicate the Vietnamese experience, or even surpass it. Unlike the early Vietnamese refugees, migrants from Syria would be coming to a country where, according to figures from the Census Bureau, about a hundred and fifty thousand of their compatriots have already made their homes. Certainly, the Syrian population in the U.S. is pretty heterogeneous in terms of ethnicity and religion. But its presence means that there are social and economic networks in place to help the new arrivals assimilate.

As many people have pointed out in recent days, Steve Jobs's biological father was a Syrian migrant who met his mother while teaching and studying at the University of Wisconsin. If we did the right thing and helped to alleviate the current humanitarian crisis, there would be no guarantee that we'd get another Jobs. But we could be pretty sure that, eventually, the Syrian refugees would repay the favor, and then some.

Bibliography

Abdullah, Halimah. "Immigrants or Refugees? A Difference With Political Consequences." *CNN*. Cable News Network, 17 Jul 2014. Web. 10 Feb 2016.

Aguiar, Angel and Terrie Walmsley. Economic Analysis of U.S. Immigration Reform." *Purdue University*. Purdue University, 2009. Pdf. 9 Feb 2016.

Anchondo, Leo. "Top 10 Myths About Immigration." *Immigration Policy*. American Immigration Council, 2010. Web. 6 Feb 2016.

Barro, Josh. "Just What Do You Mean by 'Anchor Baby'?" *New York Times*. 28 Aug 2015. Web. 16 Feb 2016.

Beeson, Ann, Helmcamp, Leslie, and Alejandra Cerna. "Immigrants Drive the Texas Economy: Economic Benefits of Immigrants to Texas." *CPPP*. Center for Public Policy Priorities, 17 Sep 2014. Web. 9 Feb 2016.

Berman, Russell. "The Conservative Case Against Enforcing Immigration Law." *The Atlantic*. Atlantic Monthly Group, 6 Mar 2015. Web. 9 Feb 2016.

"Beyond Red vs. Blue: The Political Typology." *Pew Research*. Pew Research Center, 26 Jun 2014. Web. 16 Feb. 2016.

Brito, Steve, Ana Corbacho, and Rene Osorio. "Remittances and the Impact on Crime in Mexico." *IADB*. Inter-American Development Bank, May 2014. Pdf. 9 Feb 2016.

Brown, Anna. "Key Takeaways on U.S. Immigration: Past, Present, and Future." *Pew Research*. Pew Research Center, 28 Sep 2015. Web. 6 Feb 2016.

Carcamo, Cindy. "Judge Orders Prompt Release of Immigrant Children from Detention." *Los Angeles Times*. Tribune Publishing, 22 Aug 2015. Web. 10 Feb 2016.

Cohn, D'vera. "How U.S. Immigration Laws and Rules Have Changed Through History." *Pew Research*. Pew Research Center, 30 Sept 2015. Web. 4 Feb 2016.

"Convention on the Rights of the Child." *OHCHR*. United Nations Office of the High Commissioner, 1995. Web. 6 Mar 2016.

"Chinese Exclusion Act (1882)." *Harvard University Open Collections Library*. Harvard University Library, 2016. Web. 5 Feb 2016.

Chow, Kat. "Immigrants Sending Money Back Home Face Fewer Options." *NPR*. National Public Radio, 10 Jul 2014. Web. 6 Feb 2016.

Davis, Bob. "The Thorny Economics of Illegal Immigration." *Wall Street Journal*. Dow Jones & Company, 9 Feb 2016. Web. 9 Feb 2016.

Diaz, Von. "How 5 DREAMers Are Rethinking Their Role in the Immigrant Rights Movement." *Huffington Post*. Huffington Post, 28 Apr 2014. Web. 9 Feb 2016.

Eichenwald, Kurt. "Illegal Immigration: Myths, Half-Truths and a Hole in Trump's Wall." *Newsweek*. Newsweek LLC, 14 Oct 2015. Web. 9 Feb 2016.

"El Paso Still Safe Though Next to a War Zone." *NBC News*. NBC News, 2009. Web. 12 Feb. 2016.

Ewing, Walter A., Daniel E. Martinez, and Ruben G. Rumbaut, "The Criminalization of Immigration in the United States." American Immigration Council, 2015. Pdf. 10 Feb 2016.

Foley, Elise, "Obama Responds To Anti-Immigrant Sentiment in Moving Speech to New Citizens." *Huffington Post*. TheHuffingtonPost.com, Inc. 15 Dec 2015. Web. 4 Feb 2016.

Ford, Matt. "A Ruling Against the Obama Administration on Immigration." *The Atlantic*. Atlantic Monthly Group, 10 Nov 2015. Web. 4 Feb 2016.

Frum, David. "The Problem With Downplaying Immigrant Crime." *The Atlantic*. Atlantic Monthly Group, 29 Jul 2015. Web. 7 Feb 2016.

Furman, Jason, "The Truth About Immigration and the Economy." *CNN*. Cable News Network, 9 Dec 2014. Web. 6 Feb 2016.

Gjelten, Tom. "The Immigration Act That Inadvertently Changed America." *The Atlantic*. Atlantic Monthly Group, 2 Oct 2015. Web. 6 Feb 2016.

Gomez, Alan and Susan Davis. "'Gang of Eight' Immigration Bill Clears Senate Hurdle." *USA Today*. Gannett Company, 11 Jun 2013. Web. 10 Feb 2016.

Gonyea, Don. "How the Labor Movement Did a 180 On Immigration." *NPR*. National Public Radio, 5 Feb 2013. Web. 9 Feb 2016.

Greenstone, Michael and Adam Looney. "Ten Economic Facts about Immigration." *Brookings*. Brookings Institution, Sep 2010. Pdf. 9 Feb 2016.

Gutting, Gary and Joseph Carens. "When Immigrants Lose Their Human Rights." *New York Times*. New York Times Company, 25 Nov 2014. Web. 9 Feb 2016.

"History of U.S. Immigration Laws." *FAIR*. Federation for American Immigration Reform, 2008. Web. 4 Feb 2016.

Jaffe, Eric. "More Immigration Means Higher Wages for All Workers." *Citylab*. Atlantic Monthly Group, 7 Jul 2015. Web. 8 Feb 2016.

John, Tara. "This is Why Border Fences Don't Work." *Time*. Time Inc., 22 Oct 2015. Web. 8 Feb 2016.

Johnson, Fawn. "How a New Class of Activists is Changing Immigration Politics." *The Atlantic*. Atlantic Monthly Group, 12 Jun 2014. Web. 9 Feb 2016.

Legrain, Phillippe, *Immigrants: Your Country Needs Them*. Princeton, NJ: Princeton University Press, 2006. 100–104.

Lehtinen, Vilja, "America Would Lose Its Soul: The Immigration Restriction Debate, 1920–1924." Master's Thesis, U of Helsiki, Sweden, 2002. Web. 10 Feb 2016.

Llosa, Alvaro Vargas. "7 Major Immigration Myths Debunked: Forbes." *Huffington Post*. Huffington Post, 1 June 2013. Web. 6 Feb 2016.

Lopez, Mark Hugo and Ana Gonzalez-Barrera. "If they Could, How Many Unauthorized Immigrants Would Become U.S. Citizens?" *Facttank*. Pew Research Center, 27 Jun 2013. Web. 8 Feb 2016.

Lopez, Mark Hugo and Ana Gonzalez-Barrera. "What is the Future of Spanish in the United States." *Pew Research*. Pew Research Foundation, 5 Sept 2013. Web. 10 Feb 2016.

Luzer, Daniel. "Dreamers Deferred." *Washington Monthly*. Washington Monthly, Jul/Aug 2013. Web. 10 Feb 2016.

Matthews, Dylan. "Five Things Economists Know About Immigration." *The Washington Post*. Nash Holdings, 29 Jan 2013. Web. 9 Feb 2016.

May, Caroline. "Obama: Syrians Seeking Refuge Like 'Jewish Refugees of World War II'." *Breitbart*. Breitbart, 15 Dec 2015. Web. 16 Feb. 2016.

Morrison, Patt. "Why Do People Cross the Border Illegally? It's Not What You Think." *Los Angeles Times*. Tribune Publishing, 25 Nov 2014. Web. 9 Feb 2016.

Nazario, Sonia. "The Children of the Drug Wars." *New York Times*. New York Times Company, 11 Jul 2014. Web. 10 Feb 2016.

Newport, Frank, "American Public Opinion and Immigration." *Gallup*. Gallup Organization, 20 Jul 2015. Web. 18 Feb 2016.

Ottaviano, Gianmarco, Giovanni Peri, and Greg C. Wright. "Immigration, Offshoring and American Jobs. *NBER*. National Bureau of Economic Research, Oct 2010. Pdf. 9 Feb 2016.

Padilla, et al. "The English-Only Movement: Myths, Reality, and Implications for Psychology." *APA*. American Psychological Association, 1991. Web. 10 Feb 2016.

Planas, Roque. "These Are The Real Reasons Behind Illegal Immigration." *Huffington Post*. TheHuffingtonPost.com, Inc., 25 Aug 2014. Web. 9 Feb 2016.

Robbins, Ted. "Wave of Illegal Immigrants Gains Speed After NAFTA." *NPR*. National Public Radio, 26 Dec 2013. Web. 6 Feb 2016.

Roberts, Sam. "How a Sonnet Made a Statue the 'Mother of Exiles'." *New York Times*. New York Times Company, 26 Oct 2011. Web. 16 Feb 2016.

Sakuma, Amanda. "The Failed Experiment of Immigrant Family Detention." *MSNBC*. NBC Universal, 3 Aug 2015. Web. 10 Feb 2016.

Santana, Maria. "5 Immigration Myths Debunked." *CNN Money*. Cable News Network, 20 Nov 2014. Web. 6 Feb 2016.

"Sexual Abuse in Immigrant Detention Facilities." *ACLU*. American Civil Liberties Union, 26 Nov 2014. Web. 9 Feb 2016.

Shane, Scott. "Homegrown Extremists Tied to Deadlier Toll Than Jihadists in U.S. Since 9/11." *New York Times*. New York Times Company, 24 Jun 2015. Web. 16 Feb 2016.

Stockton, Nick. "Turning Away Refugees Won't Fight Terrorism, And Might Make it Worse." *Wired*. Condé Nast, 17 Nov 2015. Web. 16 Feb 2016.

Swanson, Ana. "Remittances: An Economist's Remedy for Organized Crime in Mexico." *Forbes*. Forbes Inc., 30 Sept 2014. Web. 9 Feb 2016.

Taylor, Alan. "The American Beginning." *New Republic*. New Republic, 18 Jul 2013. Web. 12 Feb 2016.

Thompson, Ginger. "Where Education and Assimilation Collide." *New York Times*. New York Times Company, 14 Mar 2009. Web. 10 Feb 2016.

"Under-age and On the Move." *Economist.* The Economist Newspaper Limited, 28 Jun 2014. Web. 9 Feb 2016.

Urbina, Ian and Catherine Rentz. "Immigrants Held in Solitary Cells, Often for Weeks." *New York Times.* New York Times Company, 23 Mar 2013. Web. 9 Feb 2016.

Wang, Yanan. "Muslims are to Trump as the Chinese were to President Arthur in 1882." *The Washington Post.* 8 Dec 2015. Web. 16 Feb 2016.

Ye Hee Lee, Michelle. "Donald Trump's False Comments Connecting Mexican Immigrants and Crime." *The Washington Post.* Nash Holdings, 8 Jul 2015. Web. 6 Feb 2016.

Zong, Jie and Jeanne Batalova. "Frequently Requested Statistics on Immigratns and Immigration in the United States." *Migration Policy.* Migration Policy Institute, 26 Feb 2015. Web. 7 Feb 2016.

Websites

American Civil Liberties Union (ACLU)
www.aclu.org

Using litigation, advocacy, and public outreach, the ACLU protects the rights and liberties of immigrants. For more than twenty-five years, the ACLU has been at the forefront of almost every major legal struggle on behalf of immigrants' rights, focusing on challenging laws that deny immigrants access to the courts, impose indefinite and mandatory detention, and discriminate on the basis of nationality, and its website provides information about its various advocacy and publications, as well as a helpful "Know Your Rights" feature.

American Immigration Council
www.americanimmigrationcouncil.org

The American Immigration Council is a nonprofit, nonpartisan organization whose legal, education, policy, and exchange programs work to strengthen the United States by honoring its immigrant history and shaping how Americans think and act towards immigration. The website provides a wealth of information about the organization's work and lists legal cases relevant to various aspects of immigration law.

American Immigration Lawyers Association (AILA)
www.aila.org

The American Immigration Lawyers Association is a national organization established to promote justice, advocate for fair and reasonable immigration law and policy, advance the quality of immigration and nationality law and practice, and enhance the professional development of its members. Its website offers information about developments in immigration law, as well as legal resources and contact information by state.

Amnesty International
www.amnestyusa.org

Amnesty International investigates and exposes abuses, as well as educates and mobilizes the public about human rights issues worldwide. In a 2009 report, *Jailed without Justice*, Amnesty International uncovered the immigrant detention system in the United States as broken and unnecessarily costly. The organization calls for immigration reform to ensure immigrants are treated with full respect for their human rights and dignity, while also working to raise awareness and protect the rights of refugees, displaced persons, and asylum seekers both domestically and worldwide. The organization's website provides information about campaigns, research, and events.

Asian Americans Advancing Justice (AAJC)

www.advancingjustice-aajc.org

As a national advocate for Asian Americans, AAJC serves this community by promoting justice for all Americans through its work in public policy, litigation, public education, and the development of grassroots organizations. The organization also works to strengthen and expand federal immigration policies that promote family unification, integration, and naturalization, and its website provides information on its programs and annual reports and publications.

Central American Resource Center (CARECEN)

www.carecen-la.org

CARECEN is a nonprofit organization founded in 1983 by Salvadoran refugees determined to secure legal status for the thousands of Central Americans fleeing civil war. In its more than 30 years of existence, CARECEN, which is based in the Los Angeles area, has gone from a small grassroots group to the largest Central American organization in the country, providing low-cost immigration legal services, policy advocacy in immigration, education reform and workers' rights, and organizing know-how for parents, youth, and workers, with a website designed to help access information about its programs and services.

Cities for Citizenship

citiesforcitizenship.com

Cities for Citizenship is a major national initiative aimed at increasing citizenship among eligible permanent U.S. residents and encouraging cities across the country to invest in citizenship programs. Its website provides information about the organization's nationwide and localized, participating-city work and includes links to helpful resources, especially those focusing on citizenship and naturalization.

National Day Laborer Organizing Network (NDLON)

www.ndlon.org/en

NDLON works to mobilize and organize day laborers in order to protect and expand their civil, labor, and human rights, while also seeking to advance the rights of undocumented immigrants more broadly. NDLON advocates for safer, more humane environments for day laborers—both men and women—so they are able to earn a living, contribute to society, and integrate into the community. The organization's website provides information, in both English and Spanish, about its efforts and how to get involved.

US Immigration and Customs Enforcement (ICE)

www.ice.gov

US Immigration and Customs Enforcement (ICE) enforces federal laws governing border control, customs, trade, and immigration with the goal of promoting homeland security and public safety. In addition to detailing the work of this agency, the website provides links to official forms, such as the application for a stay of deportation or removal, as well as a detainee-locator search function.

Immigration Voice

immigrationvoice.com

Immigration Voice is a nonprofit organization working to alleviate the problems faced by legal, highly-skilled, future Americans in the United States. With a national advisory board consisting of key officials from previous government administrations, the former staff of current lawmakers, prominent attorneys, and constitutional experts, the organization acts as an interface between immigrants and the legislative and executive branches of the government. The website provides information about various facets of the organization's work, research, and advocacy.

Migration Policy Institute (MPI)

www.migrationpolicy.org

The Migration Policy Institute is a nonpartisan, nonprofit think tank in Washington, DC, dedicated to analysis of the movement of people worldwide. MPI and its website provide analysis, development, and evaluation of migration and refugee policies at local, national, and international levels. Its National Center on Immigrant Integration Policy provides policy research and design, leadership development, technical assistance, and training for government officials, community leaders, and others who seek to understand and respond to the challenges and opportunities that today's high rates of immigration create in local communities.

National Council of La Raza

www.nclr.org

Since 1968, the National Council of La Raza has been a nonpartisan voice for Latinos, a community it serves through research, policy analysis, and state and national advocacy efforts, as well as in programs at work in communities nationwide. In the areas of civic engagement, civil rights and immigration, education, workforce and the economy, health, and housing, the organization advocates for the economic, political, and social advancement for all Latinos. The website collects a wealth of information and resources on these various topics and promotes ways to get involved; it also links to the organization's many publications.

National Guestworker Alliance (NGA)

www.guestworkeralliance.org

The National Guestworker Alliance works to empower guestworkers to improve the conditions of their workplaces and to transform the terms of migration, so that workers can arrive to the United States on a path to first-class citizenship. Its website reports on recent developments in migrant workers' rights as well as ongoing campaigns with specific employers and organizations.

National Network for Immigrant and Refugee Rights

www.nnirr.org

The National Network for Immigrant and Refugee Rights (NNIRR) works to defend and expand the rights of all immigrants and refugees, regardless of immigration status. Since its founding in 1986, the organization has drawn membership from diverse immigrant communities and actively builds alliances with social and economic justice partners around the country. Its website collects articles on the topic of immigrant and refugee rights from various news sources and also provides information on its programs, a calendar of events, and information on how people can get involved.

Bureau of Population, Refugees, and Migration (PRM)

www.state.gov/j/prm

The State Department's Bureau of Population, Refugees, and Migration provides aid and sustainable solutions for refugees, victims of conflict, and stateless people around the world through repatriation, local integration, and resettlement in the United States. PRM also promotes the United States' population and migration policies, and its website explains its various policies, such as those regarding refugee admissions. The website also provides official government documents, alongside explanatory FAQ sheets.

Index

REFERENCE ONLY